The Futures of Racial Capitalism

The Futures of Racial Capitalism

Gargi Bhattacharyya

polity

Copyright © Gargi Bhattacharyya 2024

The right of Gargi Bhattacharyya to be identified as Author of this Work has been asserted in accordance with the UK Copyright, Designs and Patents Act 1988.

First published in 2024 by Polity Press

Polity Press
65 Bridge Street
Cambridge CB2 1UR, UK

Polity Press
111 River Street
Hoboken, NJ 07030, USA

All rights reserved. Except for the quotation of short passages for the purpose of criticism and review, no part of this publication may be reproduced, stored in a retrieval system or transmitted, in any form or by any means, electronic, mechanical, photocopying, recording or otherwise, without the prior permission of the publisher.

ISBN-13: 978-1-5095-4336-6
ISBN-13: 978-1-5095-4337-3 (pb)

A catalogue record for this book is available from the British Library.

Library of Congress Control Number: 2023932769

Typeset in 10.5 on 13pt Janson Text by
Cheshire Typesetting Ltd, Cuddington, Cheshire
Printed and bound in the UK by TJ International Limited

The publisher has used its best endeavours to ensure that the URLs for external websites referred to in this book are correct and active at the time of going to press. However, the publisher has no responsibility for the websites and can make no guarantee that a site will remain live or that the content is or will remain appropriate.

Every effort has been made to trace all copyright holders, but if any have been overlooked the publisher will be pleased to include any necessary credits in any subsequent reprint or edition.

For further information on Polity, visit our website:
politybooks.com

Contents

Acknowledgements	vi
Preface: Staying Human	viii
Introduction: If Not Theses, Then What?	1
1 What is at Stake?	8
2 Why Understanding Racial Capitalism also Returns to the Question of Social Reproduction	32
3 How to Think about Racial Capitalism in Times of Widespread Indebtedness	52
4 Borders – Small Adaptations in Familiar Techniques of Racial Capitalism	78
5 Prisons and the Carcerality of Transforming Racial Capitalism	105
6 Platform Capitalism as a Remaking of Racial Capitalism	121
Conclusion: Fun and Games	147
Afterword: Being Ridiculous	165
References	171
Index	208

Acknowledgements

Thank you to Karina Jákupsdóttir and to Jonathan Skerrett at Polity for their super-human patience and remarkable kindness through this process. I realize I have become the nightmare author who hides. I promise to work on it. What can I say? Events, as always.

My boundless thanks to the two anonymous reviewers of the manuscript. Without your gentleness and thoughtful comments this book would never have seen the light of day. A lesson to all the reviewer twos out there – snarkiness can stop people from ever finishing the piece, so why not be sweet if you can? We all need more ideas, not fewer, after all.

To the various colleagues and friends and comrades who shared space and chat and ideas over this period, please know that no work happens without that other stream of interchange. None of which makes you responsible in any way for what follows.

Special mentions for:

the RICE family, Sita Balani, Adam Elliott-Cooper, Dalia Gebrial, Luke De Noronha, Nadine El-Enany, Kerem Nisancioglu, Kojo Koram, you know you fill my heart with hope and giggles, and everything I ever write now is in secret conversation with all of you; the cockroach army of the University of East London, where the union is the real heart of any intellectual culture, especially Anna Caffrey, Clare Qualmann, Jill Daniels, Giorgia Dona, Aidan Kelly, Michael Cole, Lynne McCarthy, Claudia Brazzale;

Professor Corinne Squire, for her extreme tolerance for my going on and sharp insight into matters that trouble me, as well as her openness to being inveigled into new cunning plans and to keeping the door open to hope;

Professor Verity Brown who (almost) persuaded me that there is a place for leadership among academics and without whom I would have been spat out of the sector a long time ago;

Dean Curtis, who turned out to be quite a lot of fun despite being an accountant; I am your 'close friend' whatever you say, but you don't have to log it with HR because you are not the boss of me;

Wilf Sullivan, under-acknowledged uncle to black trade unionism in Britain; a lot of what we speak about it is floating around in this work, and I hope both of us have more time to make new things happen now.

All of my other families:

No More Exclusions and the untold pleasure of spending time with Zahra Bei;

chats about ideas, love and the place of intellectual work with Joe Kelleher, Sivamohan Valluvan, Alex Kelbert, Josh Virasami;

Pluto and Left Book Club for making a parallel intellectual space where I could do stuff despite my employer.

I know time is getting tighter for me and I have been trying to speed up and spit out the things I would like to say. Inevitably, this means a rough and readiness in presentation. And the endless tragedy of spoilt creation.

I am trying to come to peace with the understanding that all work is painfully flawed, no more than what could be achieved in whatever broken circumstances arose in that instant. But it is a hard lesson that has to be relearned each day. I wish this final version was closer to what I had imagined. I hope it is enough for some others to take the next steps.

Throughout, Swadhin and Abir have been incredulous that (a) I am writing another book about racial capitalism (b) I still have not finished it. I offer this imperfect creation to you. Tear it down and build something better.

Preface: Staying Human

The point of this work is to consider some of the central violences of our time and what might be learnt from utilizing racial capitalism as an analytic/descriptive frame of understanding.

As always, the only point of attempting such a thing is the hope that this is a way of thinking that can open the possibility of renewed connection and the building of something different and better. The point is not at all to say how racist everything is. It is, and there is no need to write more books to say this. If you need to be persuaded of the reach or extent or violence of racism, perhaps this is not the book for you.

It is also not a treatise on the state of the world. As things become ever more frightening, I am increasingly convinced of the need to write in a way that can ignite some new question or thought for others, because the challenges we face demand a relearning of collective thought as well as collective action.

The push to present a totalized account – where disagreement with any detail may lead to a long and possibly career-serving exchange but a further deferment of the question of what is to be done – is enticing but unwise. All writers, even academic writers, want to make beautiful objects. The fictional completeness of arguments is part of this display of artistry. But jarring times call for a different aesthetic. So, along with many far more accomplished others, I am trying to write in a way that calls to others to become complete. Because if there is to be a collective consciousness, then there must also be a practice of collective thought, a language where fragments call to each other and make sense together despite their disparate authorship.

All of which is a way of saying, again, that I don't have the answer. But I do know some things, and these things might be useful to you and help to make a different sense of the things that you know.

The two big things that I (think I) know are:

- we are witnessing an escalation and enlargement of practices of exclusion and containment. These practices are intertwined and are overwhelmingly racialized, although not always with the same languages of racialization.
- key components of what we have known as capitalist economics are undergoing transformation. This can be seen most clearly in the changing shape of business and in the apparent move away from the worker as primary location of value extraction.

All of this talk takes place against an unavoidable consciousness of limit and danger in the face of climate catastrophe. Each chapter tries to consider how adaptations are also a response to these dangers, in terms both of (attempting to) maintain existing position and in anticipation of the future impact on business. Most of the discussion to follow is not about fantastical varieties of green capitalism. Again, there are other books that cover this ground. Instead, my interest is in the work done by the 'racial' of 'racial capitalism' when we are confronted by climate emergency. If ever there was a dream of a postracial capitalism, that dream seems long ago. For us, the question is how the further mobilization of racialized divisions can operate to expel some populations from the terms of capitalist inclusion – more bluntly, saving the planet imagined as 'losing' some of us.

Since I started this work, these trends have become all too obvious. Claims which seemed outlandish only a short time ago are now so apparent that the point requires no argument.

We see, for example:

- explicit alliances between 'green' parties and nationalist parties (see Forchtner, 2019);
- new and/or enhanced tactics of state violence designed to expel the most vulnerable or least represented from the terms of national belonging and entitlement;
- explicit reference to the 'threat' posed by climate refugees, with few

available instruments to safeguard the lives or rights of those displaced by climate catastrophe (Ayazi and Elsheikh, 2019);

- explicit countering of climate emergency analyses with proposals to create the circumstances enabling survival for some, with a fantasy of withstanding climate change through the ruthless corralling of remaining resources (for an insight into the fractious discussion of green capitalism, see Engel, 2019; Malm, 2021).

In other, sometimes previous sometimes ongoing, processes of rendering other humans expendable, human beings are reduced to resources. Or, in situations of settler-colonialism, human beings are reduced to an expendable barrier to resources. Neither one is quite what is happening in the making disposable that characterizes climate crisis racial capitalism.

My guess is that the historically unprecedented growth of prisons and prison-like structures plus the also historically unprecedented construction of elaborate trans-state collaborative machineries designed to halt, siphon and trap populations in movement together signal a shift towards rendering some disposable in order to safeguard the survival of others. I do not mean here that such a plan is workable or based in any reasonable reading of the world.

We are seeing the rapid pulling together of a kind of 'save capitalism' version of ecological thought, in the process repurposing varieties of social reproduction as part of planetary salvation (for some). In the face of an increasingly anticapitalist green mobilization, most of all among the young, the widespread sense of emergency unsettles the certainties of capitalist realism. If the world really is ending, perhaps it is, at last, time to imagine the end of capitalism. The chapters that follow uncover some of the contortions that arise as capitalism attempts to adjust to the knowledge of urgent ecological limit.

Introduction:
If Not Theses, Then What?

I say often that the term 'racial capitalism' is a question, not an assertion or a doctrine but an opening for those able to take it. It is a question about how lives can be spoiled in so many distinctive and seemingly quite separate ways and yet all in the name of the same beast. It is a question about why it is that we seem so far apart from one another despite such parallel experiences of dispossession. It is a question about why the revolution is proving so hard to make, if we are truly all becoming the same kind of revolutionary agent despite ourselves.

Increasingly, I think the word 'puzzle' might be more apt than 'question'.

A question sounds like it might be solved at the level of the discursive, as if we have just not found the right rhetorical flourish to remake life as life.

A puzzle, on the other hand, presents an opportunity for play and for exploration. The pieces are all there somehow. The trick is only to look again to somehow leap into an understanding of how the puzzle can be unlocked.

And, as always, the biggest puzzle of all is how the rich and powerful continue to dominate. What is it about these complex structures of expropriation and exploitation, everyday wounds and not quite-getting-bys, that can continue despite the reliance on those who are getting hurt?

Part of the puzzle of racial capitalism is the reminder that the powerful have to work very hard and deploy extensive resources in order to maintain this violent and violating order. It is also a reminder that the other side do not have 'a plan' – they are also varied, in competition with each other and/or fixated on their own narrow interests. The troubling outcome that is racial capitalism arises from the jostling together of constantly adapting alliances of class interests, long histories of racialized violence and dispossession and the spinning out of ever-emerging processes of differentiation that disrupt our connections to one another. It is not an outcome of some racist masterplan, however much it might feel that way.

What follows lays out a series of puzzles of our time. Some clearly chart back through history. Others are shiny and new for now, presented as the next big thing right up until the point where they are not and some other shiny object or initiative has taken up our analytic attention. In each instance, I try to lay out what is puzzling and why we should care. I try, as far as possible, to avoid ethical critique – I assume all or most readers agree that the violence enacted on human and other bodies in the name of capitalism is wrong. I do not think, however, that the beast of capital is responsive to ethical critique. If we want to slay it, we have to understand how it works.

Introduction to project

The term 'racial capitalism' promises to totalize our knowledge and understanding, leaping over the untidy partial knowledges of dual systems or the parallel logics of intersectionality to unveil a new totalizing narrative. Admittedly, it is a totalizing narrative that encompasses difference and parallel logics within its terms, but it is nevertheless a narrative that seeks to encompass everything. Or, at least, this seems to be what people expect and want – a shorthand term that summarizes all human horror in a single phrase, with the implication that there is nothing more to learn. And perhaps there never will be.

In this work, I am trying, once again, to present an account of racial capitalism that persuades readers of the usefulness of this frame while also acknowledging the constant innovation that runs through the racial capitalism(s) of our time. Most of all, this work reminds us that capitalism is a tricky beast, the stuff of dreams, a colonizer of desire. To do this it moves in unexpected ways. An account of contemporary capitalism that mapped the pain and suffering, but without registering the strange pull on our sense of self, is too easy. We know all too well that capitalism destroys lives. The mystery is our continuing love affair with its promises despite this knowledge.

The overlapping crises of ecological collapse, economic limit and a resurgence of organized and popular violence targeting racialized groups has led to a renewed interest in debates surrounding racial capitalism. This has ranged from the return to excavating the racialized underpinnings of early capitalism, both in the Americas and elsewhere (Leroy and Jenkins, 2021), to a re-energized interest in state violence, including ecological violence, and the economic logics of state racisms (Pulido, 2017), to a re-engagement with analyses of crisis, economic, political, cultural and ecological (Danewid, 2020; Liebman et al., 2020).

This work seeks to extend this discussion to consider the implications of changing conceptualizations of contemporary capitalism for our account of racial capitalism. The discussion here builds on my 2018 book, *Rethinking Racial Capitalism*, moving on from this earlier discussion of reproductive and environmental crisis to consider the impact of highly discussed aspects of our changing capitalist world. In the process, the work seeks to address the urgent need to consider how capitalism is remaking itself in this time of ecological limit. These are very bad times indeed, and the question of how we might survive together is, necessarily, part of what we must try to understand in our critique of the violences of racial capitalism.

At the same time, and despite the understandable interest in its most violent and dehumanizing impacts, racial capitalism is not only coercive. My suggestion is that it is more useful to think of racial capitalism as a set of processes that distribute populations into racialized categorizations and racialized opportunities as part of the process of accumulation. In this way, processes or techniques of racial capitalism may hold allure or promise gratification or deliver subjecthood. This may be the case even for those who are racialized as subordinate. Although much of what follows focuses on the wounds caused through racial capitalism, I try throughout the discussion to leave room to remember the various investments and partial compensations that may exist alongside machineries of dispossession.

In order to understand this strange formation which seems able to anchor us in racialized statuses even as we are positioned and exploited differentially, we must engage with some key strands of contemporary thinking about emergent capitalism. The pages that follow rely heavily on the important work that helps us to comprehend the advent and direction of platform capitalism (Srnicek, 2016; Pasquale, 2016; Langley and Leyshon, 2017) and the broader conceptualization of data capitalism (Beer, 2019; Steinhoff, 2022; West, 2019). Admittedly, some of these conceptualizations seek to understand phenomena which are anything but new. However, the advent of systematic thinking about both the disciplinary formations of prisons (Gilmore, 2007; Wang, 2018) and borders (Walia, 2021; Gahman and Hjalmarson, 2019) and the shift in accumulation processes signalled by indebtedness (Lazzarato, 2012) and platform economics promises to unlock a new phase in our understanding of racial capitalism.

My earlier work (Bhattacharyya, 2018) laid out a framework through which to place the historical establishment of racial capitalism in a more recent setting of reproductive and ecological crisis. This sister work builds on this earlier discussion to consider in greater detail how we might understand racial capitalism as a set of practices and techniques embedded in shifting processes of accumulation and of state power.

Each of the central themes promises to illuminate a central question in debates about racial capitalism – that of how value might be extracted from populations through non-wage routes. As racial capitalism is a framework that seeks to understand the racialized division of populations as an element of capitalist development, a central element is the economic segregation that arises from exclusion from the formal waged economy, relegation to the periphery of the formal economy and, perhaps most importantly, the scraping of value from the realm of social reproduction but not through wage relations. The intensification of practices of imprisonment and bordering raises questions about the role of these structures of containment in enabling or safeguarding processes of accumulation. Discussions of platform economics and indebtedness point to the ascendance of non-wage methods of value extraction, to some extent echoing and extending modes of non-wagedness previously concentrated among the racially subordinated.

What racial capitalism?

It is Cedric Robinson's formulation of racial capitalism that animates the resurgent interest in this set of questions, shaped by the reference to Robinson's work within key documents and debates of the Movement for Black Lives and the global take-up of Black Lives Matter (Issar, 2021).

In *Black Marxism: The Making of the Black Radical Tradition* (1983), Robinson lays out a critique and extension of the terms of debate in Western Marxism in that moment. Robinson argues that the failure to register and engage with the Black radical tradition – that is, the history of thought, action and cultural production created across the

African diaspora in response to the world-shaping violence of enslavement and the trade in human beings – has hampered our collective ability to understand capitalism and our agency to make change. The three debate-changing correctives offered by Robinson are as follows.

- There is no one trajectory of capitalist development. Societies do not pass, necessarily, through a pre-defined sequence of stages in their economic and social relations. The particularity of history and context shapes the manner in which capitalism comes to be embedded in each location. This aspect of Robinson's argument echoes debates on the question of uneven and combined development, in that there is an insistence on registering the shaping role of local histories in the economic trajectory of each nation or space. However, the resurrection of interest in uneven and combined development has tended to imply, again, that this is the process through which all spaces and all populations are on a journey towards full integration into the capitalist world economy, with the strong suggestion that this is the road to a version of industrialization and proletarianization for all. In contrast, Robinson points to the experience of the African diaspora to argue that incorporation into global capitalism may take place through violence and transportation, leading to spaces which are forced to render value to capital but which are not on a journey towards industrialization. Without this insight, we cannot comprehend the anticapitalist agency of slave rebellions or anticolonial struggles.
- This is the second strand of Robinson's overarching argument: that capitalism does not make us all the same. In fact, far from rendering us all homogeneous and interchangeable in the marketplace, capitalism has extended and grown through a process of inhabiting and proliferating difference. The process of capitalist development is one of differentiation.
- The third element of Robinson's argument may be the most influential. The delineation of the Black radical tradition as a repository of revolutionary thought and a history of effective anticapitalist action is a retort to the abstracted theory of the endlessly interchangeable proletarian and a correction to the understanding of anticapitalist agency. The experience of the African diaspora has been one of violent expropriation, including of human lives themselves. Yet this subjugation of human life to the needs of capital was not understood as a process of proletarianization in mainstream Marxist discussion during the twentieth century. As a result, the political agency of those who fought

against enslavement and colonial occupation could not be understood as part of the anticapitalist struggle. Robinson argues, with justification, that this oversight limits our ability to imagine political change and to understand how people can become agents in shaping their own lives in the face of systemic violence.

There has been a massive and energetic 'rediscovery' of Robinson's work in recent years, largely shaped by the global Movement for Black Lives and the explicit references to Robinson's work in key documents shared across activist communities (Issar, 2021). Less discussed, although also in a process of reclamation, is the work of Neville Alexander (2003, 2013).

Alexander, a founding member of the South African National Liberation Front, was imprisoned for ten years on Robben Island as a result of his activity in the struggle against apartheid. He proposed an account of racial capitalism as conjunctural – with the interplay between the dynamics of race and class in South Africa arising from the particularities of that nation's troubled history and the distinct fascistic formation of the South African state. For Alexander, the core components of the apartheid system revealed a state founded on the three aspects of racialized dispossession, racialized exploitation and racialized job reservations (Clarno and Vally, 2022). Together this represented a distinctively South African model of accumulation through racial capitalism.

More recent re-engagement with the questions raised by racial capitalism centres the concept of expropriation. Nancy Fraser (2016) has summarized this as the addition of expropriation to the two 'exes' of exchange and exploitation. Classical economists have presented the world-shaping system of capitalism as a process of exchange, demanding an understanding of the workings of the economy figured as a system of abstract economic relations. This offered a capacity to understand the economy as a totalized process but not to uncover the social relations that underlie and are remade through economic life. Marx's critique is to reveal exploitation as the central motor of capitalism. Exchange cannot create value or enable accumulation – only exploitation and the stripping of surplus value from labour can do this. As a result of this groundbreaking insight, we are able to comprehend the agency of the proletariat in all of its world-historical potential. What we cannot comprehend is how the many others who suffer and have their lives and resources stolen become anticapitalist agents. This is the mass of humanity who are not waged workers for capital, including those whose lives have been lost to enslavement, colonialism and the theft of the resources of life. Fraser summarizes the critical insights of scholars of the Black radical tradition and Indigenous thought to add expropriation to the 'exes' that let us comprehend the workings of capital.

In our moment of multiple crises, there has been a proliferation of writing as people struggle to construct an analysis of racial capitalism that can help us to understand and overcome the violence and dispossession that is stealing our lives. Excellent examples of this work include Melamed (2015), Pulido (2017), Kundnani (2021), Danewid (2020), and Vasudevan and Smith (2020). In addition, a plethora of scholars have added the framing of racial capitalism to their analysis. I should be clear here that this work is not an attempt to outline my own definitive theory of racial capitalism. Neither is it an exercise in deciphering Cedric Robinson's true meaning and intention. And least of all is it an exercise in establishing my academic authority or in demolishing the argument or work of any other scholar. My project, both more modest but, I think, more urgent, is to see what we can understand of our shared predicament through the framework of racial capitalism. What follows is my best attempt to map where we are.

This work argues that the four frames of prisons, borders, platforms and indebtedness represent key disciplinary techniques in a moment where non-waged forms of value extraction become increasingly important, in the process remaking the terms of racial capitalism and displacing previous certainties about the centrality of waged work to proletarianization. These are practices of racial capitalism, not because some bodies bring racialized logics to the arena of the economic through pre-existing racialized status but because the positioning as a population vulnerable to non-waged forms of value extraction can be understood as a racializing process. The patterns of contemporary racial capitalism combine the legacies of longstanding racialized dispossessions and their continuing impact on the social status of some groups and the less predictable but ongoing shifts in racialized status arising from the crises and dispossessions of the present. If nothing else, I hope to persuade readers of the importance of keeping both challenges in our sights.

1

What is at Stake?

Let us begin by reminding ourselves what is at stake. Not the chance to win an argument. Not a corrective to offer the last word in some theorization of the social and economic universe. And certainly not a way of proving the impossibility of change. If what you take from the study of racial capitalism is that we cannot, will not and never will be as one in the pursuit of a better future, perhaps you have not been paying attention.

This means that, although there are plenty of places where the violence of racialized hierarchies are enforced within one space, there are also parallel 'economies' which both reflect and occlude racialized divisions. Think of the distinction between the stratified labour market (Ashiagbor, 2021) and the dispersal of our working and other lives through the informal economy (Webb et al., 2020) or the night-time economy (Shaw, 2010). More than an account of how we come to hate one another, racial capitalism helps us to understand that we may barely see one another, never quite meeting in the twilight zone between shifts or disguised by the shadows of the informal or criminal economy. Even when we appear to inhabit the same spaces, racial capitalism is a way of thinking about how we are invisible to one another (for a sobering account of the persistence of racialized segregation in workplaces and labour markets, see Jefferys, 2019).

I prefer to think that talk about racial capitalism has little to say about identity or the politics of identities. It is not a way of thinking that privileges any particular voice due to that person's experience. It requires, instead, some thought and at least a momentary pause on denunciation. It is not really a phrase to describe what one set of people does to another, although people can try to inhabit the structures of racial capitalism in an attempt to safeguard or further their group interests. Rather than a denunciation, I prefer to see the discussion of racial capitalism as an exploration of how elusive solidarity can be. Despite the horrors of so much human existence, somehow we remain unable to see one another, let alone arrange ourselves into a collective force.

I have written previously of the way in which I think of racial capitalism as a question – not so much a total theory as a nudge towards a more thoughtful way of thinking about the ways in which we have not yet been able to make ourselves or one another free (D. Bhattacharyya, 2018; G. Bhattacharyya, 2023). It is a little bit saddening therefore to see such a take-up of the terms of racial capitalism as a way of closing down discussion, conversation, exploration, imagination. Surely this is not the use that should be made of this potentially so open and generous a conception of the world. Admittedly the analysis of racial capitalism comes from the most ugly elements of human history. There is no way around that. However, the will to understand the workings of and the alternatives to racial capitalism are testimony to the continuing and deep desire among many humans to imagine some other way of living. And every time the phrase or the framing or the argumentation of debates about racial capitalism is used for another purpose, for the purpose of closing down the possibility of imagining other better, fuller lives for us all, it feels like a betrayal.

So, before we go any further, let us think a little bit about what the ethics of this inquiry into a changing racial capitalism might entail. I have said previously that my own work on racial capitalism wishes to *describe* a phenomenon that is quite hard to get your head around. I think there is something continually useful about the invitation to analyse the workings of a capitalism that places different segments of the world in different quarters of the economy in different logics and rhythms of the accumulative project. It is an invitation to document and to think again about what is documented, in an admission that the ability of capitalism to remake itself continues to be a mystery to us. Whereas the too quickly celebratory certainties of an officially already unified working class can elide attention to the manner in which people are not yet unified or, if unified, not yet able to act in concert, racial capitalism invites us to think about these particular dilemmas again.

Why, as my kids roll their eyes, would anyone try to write a second book on racial capitalism? I have some sympathy with the view of my children – which I take to be that (1) becoming associated with this season's buzzword gets in the way of thinking or thinking creatively, (2) it is a bit sad to try to do the same thing a second time, (3) the phrase 'racial capitalism' has become so widely and capaciously used it is becoming limited in its ability to convey anything.

At bottom, I think the concern is that centring discussion around the phrase 'racial capitalism' now feels as if you are suggesting there is nothing more to say and nothing more to learn. This is a way of seeing 'racial capitalism' as the answer, not the question. So we all start to be better at charting the interconnected violences and dispossessions of global racisms and capitalist expansion and the summary of all of this human suffering is . . . racial capitalism. Learn this phrase and it all seems to make sense.

I think one aspect of this too quick closing off arises from a sense that the history of racial capitalism has been an interconnected process of differentiating through fixing of status. Although 'fixing' here may be a metaphor that can range across spatial containment, ascription of status with or without legislative underpinning, splitting into segregated realms through residence, temporal arrangements and segmented labour markets, exclusion to the border or the camp or the wasteland or the necropolis or, more generally, to being or becoming surplus, it remains a metaphor (and way of thinking) that implies a completion of the action (for an account that centres the apparent fixity and fixing of race, see Bright et al., 2022). Perhaps a temporary completion, perhaps a repeated action that echoes the same history of dispossession down the ages. But, nevertheless, an implication of a kind of stasis.

By this I mean that thinking of racial capitalism as an answer can lead to a conceptual mapping of (more recent) human history as the emergence of a landscape or a machinery or a grid where the components of differential dispossession and disentitlement are established. We might retain the possibility that particular actors change place, but we are thinking in a way that assumes the range of places ('places') are there to populate.

This work begins from a different assumption – that we are living, again, through a moment where capital is remaking itself in unforeseen ways, and this unpredictability includes an unsettling and remaking of what we might consider as the components of racial capitalism. These might include, for the purposes of our discussion:

- an erosion and displacing of the wage as a central route to the means of life, both for those who may have been marked previously as 'standard workers' and/or 'worker-citizens' and for those previously considered to be subject to economic development leading to standard work;
- a significant shift in the organization of segmented economic space, both further collapsing together activities coded as production and those coded as consumption and radically remaking economic landscapes previously shaped by more stable modes of segregation and differentiation of racialized populations;
- an extension of bordering practices in ways that reveal cooperation between states and other actors to create a global system of capture, narrowed mobility, forced stasis and criminalization that goes beyond any one national machinery or narrative of foreignness (Arcarazo and Geddes, 2014);
- a trend of ever-increasing incarceration, with imprisonment and prison-like processes growing and extending across many regions.

This is not a completely 'new' racial capitalism. One lesson of racial capitalism talk might be that nothing is completely new, because sedimented histories of racialized and other dispossessions continue to shape the interactions and possibilities of the present. It is, however, an indication of a constantly adapting racial capitalism. The rest of this work seeks to persuade the reader of the benefits of remaining alert and open to these changes and their implications.

Accumulation by dispossession, primitive accumulation and other ways of thinking about proletarianization

This work is not a contribution to the far more specialized conversation about the details of accumulative processes in differing locations. That important debate lurks in the background of this and other more generalist works, but no knowledge of this particular technical language is required here (for some indications of key aspects, see Wallerstein, 1984; Amin, 2014).

For readers of this more tentative and impressionistic work, all that is needed is a passing reminder of why the question of how accumulation operates outside, alongside or beyond the productive economy has been so central to thinking about racial capitalism. I try here to lay out the steps of this interest in the most simple of terms – not to insult anyone's level of knowledge or understanding but to remind ourselves there is always someone who is meeting these suggestions for the first time.

David Harvey famously coins the phrase 'accumulation by dispossession' as part of a larger argument about the sequencing and character of primitive accumulation (Harvey, 2003). The phrase is a corrective to the underlying but barely spoken assumption that the practices described by Marx as 'primitive accumulation' – the varied processes of theft, violence, violation and taking by force that enable the agglomeration of private property as capital – should be understood as a historical phase (for an insight into the broader debate on this point, see Bonefeld, 2011, on primitive accumulation as the constitution of capitalist social relations). The implication here is that there is primitive accumulation in the pre-history of capitalism, but, once the violence is done and capital proper is born, another mechanism kicks into action. Whereas in primitive accumulation the violence may be out on display, capital proper can operate through the far more mysterious violences of exploitation and the commodity form.

As a result, we have been trained to think of the expansion of the realm of capital as a process that captures everyone into the wage relation and the networks of the commodity form eventually (for a non-didactic outline of the thinking behind this view, see Tilly, 1979). In a corrective to this, Harvey reminds us of the many forms of expropriation through violence that continue in every phase of capitalism's history, including in our own time. This encompasses violent land grabs (Hall, 2013), privatization of public services and assets (Mercille and Murphy, 2017) and the murderous violence of the 'new' extractivism (Veltmeyer and Petras, 2014). Instead of being misled by the term 'primitive', with its temporal and developmental associations, we should see the role of theft, murder and expropriation both in enabling what Harvey calls the spatial fix – the manner in which the periodic capitalist crisis of overproduction is addressed by finding/creating new markets, including through the use of force – and in forcing new populations into varieties of market relations without any necessary mediation through the wage form. We might (or might not) understand this as an expanded understanding of proletarianization as the violences of capital split people from the means of life.

Accumulation by dispossession and the remaking of global racial capitalism

Famously, David Harvey riffs off Luxembourg's account of the dual character of accumulation in his 2003 discussion of what he terms 'the new imperialism'. Harvey is writing in the moment of global protests against the US-led attacks on Iraq, in a moment when the resurgence of a highly militarized imperialist expansionism was forcing a reassessment of the celebratory theories of globalization that had characterized debate in the last years of the twentieth century.

In the aftermath of the demise of the Soviet Union, there is a period of overconfidence in the capitalist project. Looking back, there is something almost charming about this brief period of unbridled hopefulness, however tainted it was with market supremacism and a disregard for what were presented as the short-term disruptions of the forced transition away from planned economies (to get a sense of the heated debate on the left in this moment, see Halliday, 1990, and Thompson, 1990). While we know full well now that the rapid immiseration and stripping of publicly held assets arising from the dismantling of the Soviet bloc led to extreme hardship, including a rapid fall in life expectancy of an enormity rarely seen in human history (Field and Twigg, 2000), the period following the end of the Cold War served to narrow the range of economic thought and analysis receiving general attention.

The overarching impact of these transitions was to persuade much of the world that, largely, capitalism worked. Yes, there were some tweaks needed to ensure inclusion of all. Perhaps some cultural barriers for women and minorities that needed to be addressed. But, broadly, capitalism on a global scale was the least bad of available worlds, and the collapse of the communist experiment confirmed this. This was always also, in case we forget, taken as a confirmation of the superiority of both political and economic arrangements under the free market. There were the slightly wild-eyed accounts of McDonald's outlets as an indicator of democratic accountability (famously in the jokey reframing of theories of war by Thomas Friedman, 2000, which argued that no consumer-led liberal democracies had gone to war with each other) but also more serious discussions of the waste and kleptocracy risked in planned systems and both the efficiency and the people-centredness of various market experiments.

Perhaps most of all, these celebrations of the ultimate ascendancy of capitalism, defeating the communist rival, opened an optimism about an end to war (Clark, 2001). Or, at least, an averting of the risk of mutually assured destruction (for a review of these debates, see Sokolski, 2004). The psychic impact of the wars in Yugoslavia and the failure of the international community in preventing ethnic cleansing (Mirković, 1996; Mojzes, 2011) and the rapid return at the outset of the twenty-first century of the assertion of military might as the first and last arbiter of global ascendance unsettled all hopes of the so-called end of history. It also brought a scrabble across the political spectrum to remember the imperatives, logics and dangers of imperialism (Mann, 2004; Knauft, 2007). Harvey's account distilled these questions and guided readers, many of whom had come of age after the critiques of neocolonialism and with little political memory of the extreme violences of the Cold War, through key terms for an analysis of imperialism in our own time.

In particular, Harvey returned readers to a consideration of the spatial dynamics of capitalism. Transposing Marx (and Lenin) to an analysis of the role of the spatial fix in responses to capitalist crisis in the twentieth century, Harvey's life's work had already introduced a wider audience to an understanding of the role of space in the dynamic and remaking of capital (for a detailed overview and introduction, see Castree et al., 2023; for some of the greatest hits, see Harvey, 1982, 1989, 2002, 2007).

In *The New Imperialism*, Harvey lays out what he describes as 'the current condition of global capitalism' – repositioning an analysis of the 'new imperialism' in this context of a particular moment of capitalist restructuring. Harvey's focus is the realignment in global politics and economics that takes place around the 2003 US-led invasion of Iraq:

> Imperialistic practices, from the perspective of capitalistic logic, are typically about exploiting the uneven geographical conditions under which capital accumulation occurs and also taking advantage of what I call the 'asymmetries' that inevitably arise out of spatial exchange relations. The latter get expressed through unfair and unequal exchange, spatially articulated monopoly powers, extortionate practices attached to restricted capital flows, and the extraction of monopoly rents. The equality condition usually presumed in perfectly functioning markets is violated, and the inequalities that result take on a specific spatial and geographical expression. The wealth and well-being of particular territories are augmented at the expense of others. Uneven geographical conditions do not merely arise out of the uneven patterning of natural resource endowments and locational advantages, but, even more importantly, are produced by the uneven ways in which wealth and power themselves

become highly concentrated in certain places by virtue of asymmetrical exchange relations. (Harvey, 2003: 40)

Harvey makes this generative suggestion at a point where welfare capitalism was identifiably still functioning in some parts of the world and when public services remained an aspiration for many more (Taylor-Gooby, 2004). His discussion of accumulation by dispossession spans what we might now understand more readily as extractivism and the rearguard clawing back of social goods undertaken in the name of neoliberalism from the late twentieth century onwards (for an overview of debates around extractivism, see Gudynas, 2021; for an account of water privatization that places this challenge in the context of accumulation by dispossession, see Swyngedouw, 2005).

What is opened, then, by discussion of accumulation by dispossession is the possibility of capitalism remaking itself without necessarily remaking the revolutionary agency of the proletariat. People could be made desperate and brought close to death and without any choice but to sell their labour – that is, could suffer all of the violences of proletarianization – and yet could remain outside the wage relations that promised revolutionary agency. Accumulation by dispossession opened the very frightening possibility that capital could find a way to take our stuff and spit us out, and some of us could be rendered surplus, not gravediggers of capital in any immediately recognizable sense.

Accounts of racial capitalism also raise the question of those who are dispossessed yet may not be incorporated into the market for waged labour. This part of the discussion relies heavily on the very exciting and wide-ranging work examining varieties of labour and, increasingly, pointing to a far more variegated set of processes as creating the non-unified category of the proletariat (van der Linden, 2008; for earlier work on the incorporation of unwaged work into the global economy, see Collins and Gimenez, 1990). For the purposes of this work, a work that tries to think again about how the operation of racial capitalism might be adapted or remade by other recent shifts in economic life, understanding the dispossessions of capitalism as opportunistically squatting on top of a variety of histories of inequality and violence can help us both register the history of capitalism as a process enacted through varieties of differentiation and non-homogenizing of populations and equip us to comprehend a world where capitalism thrives without expanding the proportions or numbers of people who are waged workers (for a discussion of the apparent decline of standard employment, see Fudge, 2017).

We appear to be living through a time where human lives become more expendable (and they were never not expendable), the reach of capital seems deeper and more unavoidable, and the reproduction of capital appears, more than ever, to be at odds with the reproduction of life. However, to build a picture of the world as it is, not only as we wish it to be, we must extend our gaze from exploitation to also include dispossession – and to move beyond the wage to also include housewifization.

A world of housewives

The historical development of the division of labour in general, and the sexual division of labour in particular, was/is not an evolutionary and peaceful process, based on the ever-progressing development of productive forces (mainly technology) and specialization, but a violent one by which first certain categories of men, later certain peoples, were able mainly by virtue of arms and warfare to establish an exploitative relationship between themselves and women, and other peoples and classes. (Mies, 1986: ch. 3)

By unpacking housewifization as a process, Mies helps us unlearn the assumption of naturalized gender roles and renders visible both the often unregistered work of social reproduction and the active remaking of the business of 'social reproduction' as an outcome of (capitalist) development.

Housewifization is the assemblage of processes that work to naturalize and invisibilize some forms of work, housing these forms of work as 'domestic', and in the process instituting a parallel framework by which such work can be exploited at one remove. To be clear, Mies presents housewifization as a process that can attribute the category of 'domestic labour' to all kinds of work. The use of the term 'housewife' is itself a kind of poking fun at naturalized accounts of domestic work, revealing that, of course, 'domestic work' can encompass pretty much any form of work undertaken by humans. It is the category of housewife – with all of its connotations of where work is done and by whom, as well as the explicit exclusion from wagedness – that pushes us to understand that capital can and does make use of this division of labour, both the division in tasks and the division in status and symbolism.

For our purposes, what is important to note is both that the tasks allocated to the housewifized continue to offer up value for capital and that the tasks categorized as housewifized can change in all directions. This is not a story of a formal economy of waged work that becomes increasingly central, in the process expanding and absorbing more and more workers. Perhaps the 'formal economy' does expand at some times and in some places, but never in a manner that eradicates the realm of housewifization. Mies goes on to outline the invention of domesticity as an offshoot of capitalism, with the nuclear family taking root first of all as the prime location of bourgeois conspicuous consumption. However, and despite the importance and interest of this argument, the larger point for our understanding of racial capitalism is Mies's account of the domestic as a site of the remaking of capital. What distinguishes the work of Mies here is her insight into the capaciously defined domestic and its ability to house a range of non-waged activities that could and can be recuperated into the circulation of value.

What is described is a mechanism by which the activity of social reproduction enters the market not as a supplement to the productive economy, or through the reproduction of the waged worker, but as its own activity with value expropriated and circulated without reference to a wage. Both indebtedness and the platform economy revolve around a version of this scraping of value from human lives without passing through the wage relation. The rest of this book tries to explore the puzzles thrown up by this shift in the world towards accumulation processes that are not reliant on labour exploitation or which combine the exploitation of waged labour with additional parallel forms of value scraping. Because these are the puzzles through which racial capitalism as we know it is remade.

Housewifization, extractivism and thinking about the edges or the 'outside' of capitalism

Harvey and Mies help us to think about how varieties of violence build expropriation into the remaking of capital, including through reaching into the realm of social reproduction. To bring these insights together with a broader understanding of dispossession as a core process of the establishment and defence of property relations, we need to attend to the insights of Indigenous thought and the analyses of settler-colonialism (Coulthard, 2014; Dunbar Ortiz, 2014; Smith, 2021; for an inspiring and insightful introduction to debates around settler-colonialism, see Englert, 2022; for an account of the varied views of the use of 'settler-colonialism' among First Nation scholars, see Konishi, 2019).

The critique of settler-colonialism as an underpinning of the birth and the continuation of capitalism helps us to think more clearly about modes of extractivism that operate by rendering us as interlopers on the Earth, in debt to private property through the very attempt to stay alive. Once we start to think of enclosure as capitalist capture of all that life requires, or 'capitalism's mobilization of diverse configurations and significations of space to deprive people of what they create in common' (Sevilla-Buitrago, 2015: 1000), our current predicament makes more sense.

We learn to better comprehend such processes of collective expropriation and their centrality to the framing of property and property relations through the sharing from scholars of colonialism and indigeneity (for some examples, see Bennett, 2005; Di Giminiani, 2018; Trujillo, 2020). In his mind-expanding account of the thievery underlying the system of private property, Nichols summarizes the formative place of processes of violent dispossession in the ongoing making and remaking of property relations.

> Dispossession . . . 'transforms nonproprietary relations into proprietary ones while, at the same time, systematically transferring control and title of this (newly formed) property. In this way, dispossession merges commodification (or, perhaps more accurately, 'propertization') and theft into one moment. (Nichols, 2020: 8)

The second element, as formulated by Nichols, is the manner in which the dispossessed are posited as 'owners', but only, as Nichols puts it, '*retroactively*' (ibid.).

If we wish to think more about the capture of human and other populations into circuits of capital but without recourse to the wage, we might think again of the extensive insights arising from the discussion of extractivism. This debate might be understood as arising from the mobilization and analysis of Indigenous communities across the world, with extractivism providing a language through which to comprehend the varieties of expropriation undertaken through colonial domination. Extractivism requires monopoly or near-monopoly control over a natural resource, a state machinery focused on extracting value without accountability, access to the infrastructural network required to extract, store and transport to ensure maximum value stripping, the concentration of profits in private hands, and the degradation of the environment with social costs arising from extractivist processes being borne by the public.

This has been summarized as 'production without reproduction' (Ye et al., 2020) and 'self-reinforcing practices, mentalities, and power differentials underwriting and rationalizing socio-ecologically destructive modes of organizing life through subjugation, violence, depletion, and non-reciprocity' (Chagnon et al., 2022: 760).

The stretch to comprehend the manner in which financialization has hollowed out everyday life in so many places, including extracting further value from those who appear to have been exited forcefully from the formal economy, has led to a revisiting of the terms of extractivism. In particular, the debate about neo-extractivism (Svampa, 2019; Brand et al., 2016; Acosta, 2013) responds to the emergence of state forms that requisition the wealth arising from natural resources, in the process restructuring the state to become a present-day echo of an earlier neo-colonial state:

> the idea of a neo-extractivism that would place the region at the forefront of a renewed form of dependence and primarization of the economy. The novelty, compared to other historical periods, comes from the state's ability to use and direct a certain part of the extraordinary rent from natural resources. (Gago and Mezzara, 2017: 576)

Much of this discussion has focused, with good reason, on sites of direct extraction. Our understanding of the acceleratingly destructive misuse of cheap nature as capital seeks to survive climate catastrophe has been expanded by the attentive work of scholars of mining, of deforestation and of land-grabbing. However, Gago and Mezzada push us to move beyond an account of extractivism that focuses only on 'the literal sites of extractive activities', because

> In this mode of analysis, where concepts such as dispossession become central, the category of exploitation itself is obscured, and the production of value by those populations, which finance itself already calculates as nonmarginal, is ignored. In this regard, we must add that our project of expanding the concept of extraction is methodologically and politically connected with a long history of struggles and theoretical elaborations that have broadened the concept of exploitation itself. (Ibid.: 577)

We might categorize the struggles and elaborations of the terms of racial capitalism as a strand in this long history. Overall, we learn to see a capital that ranges widely, incorporating human and other populations into its ambit through techniques of dispossession without any detour through wagedness. There is work of various sorts, but the expansion of capital's reach occurs through a different and more diffuse conglomeration of processes.

This expanded account of extractivism, placed squarely within the terms of highly technologized societies where finance has entered everyday life, invites us to think more expansively of the terms of capitalist reproduction. Gago and Mezzadra formulate this in the following terms:

> If extraction is a constitutive feature of the current operations of capital, it is necessary to pose the question of how capital itself relates with what in traditional terms could be called labor but that—as seen in the examples of the digital and the financial—increasingly takes the form of a complex and highly heterogeneous social cooperation. (Gago and Mezzadra, 2017: 579)

There are two important insights here for our interests. One is the reappraisal of the relation between capital and labour, with the implication that we must extend our sights both to include and stretch the wage relation and to understand additional non-waged processes as part of the labour–capital relation. Second is the introduction of the concept of highly heterogeneous social cooperation as the model through which to understand how human life is interpellated to become part of the machine remaking capital. To return to our interests, we might replace the term 'highly heterogeneous' with 'highly differentiated', perhaps with a renewed curiosity about the benefits of such heterogeneity/differentiation to the project of transforming all human society into a site of extraction.

Disrupting solidarity

I have taken to saying that racial capitalism should be understood as the process through which capital at once extracts value across locations and organizes us in ways that disrupt the possibility of solidarity. I think the formulation is useful, not least because it nudges towards ways of mobilizing with and through an understanding of the processes of racial capitalism. However, it is a little too easy to point to the disruption of solidarity as the necessary focus. What is elided is an understanding of how the process of differentiating populations through broadly economic means is itself a technique of value extraction.

It sounds obvious but bears repeating. Capital does not arrange itself to anticipate and/or minimize the resistance of the working class. Perhaps momentarily there are class stand-offs where this happens, almost always within one nation or region. I am not discounting the very extensive resources that both states and freelance elites have devoted to stamping out any whiff of an alternative narrative. Of course the history and present of class struggle reveals these highly orchestrated clampdowns again and again. My point is not that repression in the name of safeguarding profit does not occur. It clearly and bloodily does.

My point is that capital does not act as one subject, certainly not globally, and that global capital is not analogous to a state. In any case, the insight of racial capitalism talk is more than only the claim that capital seeks to divide the working class. The more interesting claim is that the differentiation of populations is itself an element of how profit occurs.

Previously I have argued vociferously against transforming Capital into a unified subject pursuing either racism or repression as a unidirectional interest. Capitalism is dehumanizing and deadly incidentally in the pursuit of profit – the transformation of human and all life into no more than resources for the reproduction of capital.

However, perhaps with the benefits of hindsight, we might think of capitalist trajectories as incorporating processes that disrupt solidarity and social connection and which, sometimes, mobilize racist and other divisions. This is something apart from the overt violence of strike-breaking, armed intimidation and murder or 'white' wage rates. Instead, we might think of this as the manner in which capital assesses investment opportunities and risks, in the process incorporating adjustments developed as the political and social ramifications of capitalist expansion have travelled through all human societies – adjustments that register, anticipate and navigate possible resistances and possible opportunities arising from differentiation and division.

I think I have been guilty of underplaying the radical contingency of each particular instance of the remaking of racial capitalism. There are the broad brush strokes of the story and there is a value to sharing our understanding of the broad strokes, in the understanding that the overarching narrative only assists us in orientating ourselves in the specificity of any instance. However, here I want also to remember that capital adapts to the events of history and the altering risks and opportunities created through our human responses and the unexpected remaking of economic possibility through events.

The debate about racial capitalism seeks to take our understanding of racism away from the terms of aversion and interpersonal friction, yet it remains difficult to talk about racism in any form without imputing a kind of moral failure at some point in the process (and, of course, aversive and interpersonal racism has serious impacts, including on the health of racially minoritized groups: Larson et al., 2007; Cobbinah and Lewis, 2018; Nazroo et al., 2020). The analysis of Capital includes plenty of outrage and considerable detail of the degradation to which human lives have been reduced, but the thing that makes the analysis is not the outrage, it is the ability to pinpoint the mechanism that motors such dehumanization. For those of us who wish to imagine a world beyond the degradations of capital, it might be as well to try to remember this and to attempt to raise our heads from that which disgusts and enrages us. In our world on fire, where the remaking of capital increasingly fails to coincide with the remaking of life, how might we understand the intensification of the degradation of life? And, in understanding this, might we imagine what is needed for our collective survival?

Of course these questions have already been thought about in a great deal of detail. Perhaps not always as an element of racial capitalism. And very often without any attention to the issue of race and racialized divisions at all. But we do know quite a lot about how work and working lives shift away from massification and large-scale production and the kind of concentration of human existence that occurred in the industrialization of the nineteenth century (for discussions of post-Fordism, see Amin, 2011; for some thoughts on disorganized capitalism, see Harris, 2019). There is an established body of research that tries to help us to understand the dispersal of work as itself a technique of exploitation, including to understand the parallel processes of relocalization, where work is relocated to new peripheral zones but remains subject to interdependency between workers, and also with local services, and dispersal, where tasks are distributed via online platforms across indefinite geographies (Lehdonvirta, 2016). Linked to this, we have become far less certain about the manner in which classes are remade (despite the bad temper this discussion has elicited, the questions relating to the class identity and agency of the precariat remain urgent for our time: Standing, 2011).

In my view, the lack of certainty is a political benefit to us. A kind of closed mindedness and dogmatism around the nature, the reach, the location, and perhaps even the character of the class subject has prevented a more fruitful open and expansive discussion of how the promised power of the class agent might be unleashed. If racial capitalism is a question rather than a dogma or another totalized account of the world, the question is, what is it that keeps us apart from one another when our lives are all brutalized through the same system, perhaps through the same or similar enemies? On reflection, I think that many of those who express irritation if not outright anger at the very term 'racial capitalism' hear this as a kind of liberal sop, as if those who discuss racial capitalism imagine a capitalism that might be livable, perhaps even pleasurable, if only it were not racial. For this audience, we might repeat – the analysis of racial capitalism is an anticapitalist endeavour. The point is still to slay the beast. There is just further debate about the nature of the beast and the weapons most likely to lead to an effective victory.

The two broad areas of change under discussion here are shifts in the role and activity of the capitalist state and shifts in practices of value extraction. In differing ways, each area of change raises questions about established processes of racialized division and subordination. While state activity in the areas of bordering and carcerality appears to signal a more insistently racial state (for more on this model of racist state violence, see Goldberg, 2008), with increasing use of state resources to fund the punitive machinery of sorting/containing/expelling subordinated groups, the reconfiguration of the state more broadly seems to abandon some previous racialized disciplines. Most markedly, the interdependence of racialized hierarchization and welfarist logics, an interdependence that has drawn increasing critique in recent times (Neubeck and Cazenave, 2001; Perocco, 2022), begs the question of what happens to that extensive machinery of racialized entitlement, semi-entitlement and disentitlement that operated through welfarist systems. The dismantlement of so many aspects of the social wage in turn erodes much of the material and symbolic benefits of racialized belonging (Garner, 2011).

There is a need to chart the connections between the experiences of racism that make people unwell, depress their earnings and ability to gather assets, and erode the quality of their lives and the experiences of racism that push them to the edge of survival or lead to death. This is an ongoing tension in any attempt to map 'racial capitalism'. There is no easy equivalence between discrimination and extreme dispossession. However, equally, it is not helpful if the use of the framework of 'racial capitalism' works to minimize or trivialize experiences of racism within the metropolis or its satellites. The promise of racial capitalism as a way of thinking is the possibility of understanding the interconnections between the racism that casts some parts of humanity into the void while simultaneously creating painful hierarchies of being within spaces of (relative) affluence.

For now, it is enough to note:

- 'Capital' may function according to a familiar logic, but 'capitalists' pursue this logic through varying and located means;
- innovations in the organization of capital may unsettle or destabilize established patterns of racialized entitlement and disentitlement;
- 'racial capitalism' is not a term that implies that all capitalists are racist in the same way, only that racialized or race-like divisions are likely to be mobilized for the purposes of accumulation.

In times of intense capitalist crisis, the reconfiguration of the capitalist class throws up new questions about the framing of race, racism and access to the means of life. This does not, unfortunately, mean that the racisms of capitalism are disappearing (they might be, but there is little sign of that at present). However, it does mean that racisms, including the most deadly racisms, may become unpredictable. At least one aspect of this unpredictability stems from the ability of capitalist innovations to hail marginalized groups, even mobilizing the experience of marginalization and dispossession as an aspect of colonizing life-worlds.

Whodunnit?

Whatever the pleasures and distractions of the personal story, racial capitalism is a whodunnit, not a romance or a tragedy. The point is neither to mourn (bad luck) nor to celebrate (resilient survival). Mourning and celebration have their place, but this is not it. What a story about racial capitalism should tell is who did it, and how, and why. Most of all, it should be a tale about who can undo it. We seek to identify the perpetrator not because we can instigate any machinery of retribution. Vengeance, however righteously deserved, is not on offer here. When we look for the perpetrator, it is because the perpetrator reveals the saviour, the structures that enable the violence promise to mark out the path to ending the violence. It is a whodunnit in order to tell who might yet still come to undo it.

So it is mysterious but also hopeful. And it rests on the dumb fuckery of believing that things can be known and that capitalism is a machine that can be comprehended, not a spectre to scare small children, and that, in our comprehension, we also unlock the possibility to unmake it.

As always, there is a danger of slipping into the conspiratorial. In this further incarnation of racial capitalism as a horror movie, here the near corpse of a global ruling class bloated on the spoils of previous generations of dispossession is injected with new life.

The vim in this injection – the fizz, the current, the secret ingredient guaranteed to zhuzh up a pallid form of domination – is, of course, raciality. As we will go on to consider, this is not a raciality of fixed and unchanging categories. Oh no, nothing so predictable for us. Instead, this is the raciality of convenience or of desperation, the raciality that can bridge old and new racisms. A raciality that conjures up new identities for the most luckless of our time – and then makes those identities feel as old as time and just as unchanging.

Raciality is the mode of class tactics to maintain unearned privilege and to claim the power to categorize and organize populations again. This is not an account of an explicit politics – at least, not in most cases. The emergence of a renewed far-right politic register across the world has amplified the expression of overt racism (Traverso, 2019). We have learned to expect insincere defences of the right to free speech and hard to sustain distinctions between hateful speech and its consequences and that which can be identified as hate speech (Titley, 2020). However, the formations of racial capitalism tend, I think, to be more coded than this. Certainly, racial capitalism can work its subjugating magic without recourse to racial hatred. As we struggle to rearticulate visions of justice in the face of a diffuse yet highly organized nationalist and/or racist right, it seems important to highlight this point again. Some of what we wish otherwise does not require any overt machinery of hate-making at all. Hatred may not come into the picture. And yet this raciality without any necessary hatred might still kill you.

In a context of struggles within the dominant class, techniques of racial capitalism can emerge as aspects of the repertoires of particular sections of the dominant class (including those in decline) *or* as an indicator of new formations and tactics of domination that are emerging. So although this is not a whodunnit with one perpetrator who can be captured and held accountable, it is a whodunnit that seeks to distinguish components of the crime and to discern the differing roles among perpetrators.

What the discussion of racial capitalism can offer, therefore, is a route to think of proletarianization as occurring divergently. Instead of a unitary (imagined) trajectory, this is an account of proletarianization that registers the very different paths and outcomes of dispossession as an outcome of capital formation and accumulation. However, it remains a discussion of proletarianization. Racial capitalism is not a way of thinking that seeks to conjure up a plethora of new class identities or agents.

This means, of course, that things might change for the subordinated as well. The process of mutation means precisely that things may not remain as they were and, for our purposes, may become less predictable. Despite itself, the mutations of racial capitalism might open new and different opportunities for some of those who have been racially subordinated. Although none of us enter the terrain of the racial unmarked and these histories of racialized marking clearly have a continuing impact, the rapid remaking of local economies unsettles these categories. In some cases the status of racialized subordination might serve to enable entry into some new arenas of work, regardless of the low status of such roles.

'It can . . . be argued that migrant labour serves an infrastructural role for these platforms – one that is as vitally important to their business model's viability as the steady influx of investment capital' (van Doorn et al., 2020: 2). Van Doorn and his colleagues summarize the employment approach of platforms as 'selective formalization' – entry and onboarding are more open, offering a particular benefit to migrant workers and others often excluded from formal labour markets, but at the same time formalization of processes pushes risk onto the worker and absolves the employer from responsibility while also instituting extensive systems of surveillance and monitoring via client feedback and electronic tracking. These insights arise from research conducted with gig economy workers across six cities – Amsterdam, Bangalore, Berlin, Cape Town, Johannesburg and New York – each with their own legislative and migratory context. Yet despite the diversity of locations, all sites showed a reliance on migrant workers among the platform work that ran the city, and migrant workers regarded the opportunity to work via platform as a means of bypassing the formal and informal exclusions of the market in standard work.

This is not to say that entry ensures empowerment. The varieties of work undertaken in the gig economy show this. However, as arenas of work shift around, we might see uncertainty around previously well-established racialized barriers to entering work. We might see uncertainty about what is and what is not work at all. And, in that process, some other interlinking aspects of recognition, inclusion, voice – they might also seem a little less predictable. Although racism does not disappear – far from it – in a world in flux it can be much harder to discern what the wages of racialized privilege look like.

The puzzles of our time

The challenge, then, is both to register the continuing impact of sedimented dispossession and to remain alert to the emergence of new modes of expropriation and rendering surplus. Racial capitalism as a framework offers some clues about how to see both ends of this challenge. Due to the diligence of so many scholars, we can understand more clearly now how accumulated violences of racialized dispossession underpin the emergence of capitalism as a variegated but global entity (for some examples, see Leroy and Jenkins, 2021; Pulido, 2017; Dorries et al., 2022; Danewid, 2020; Issar, 2021). At the same time, the framework of racial capitalism opens our collective understanding to techniques of differentiated entitlement and the manner in which emerging or shifting processes of dispossession or exploitation or expropriation can meld together histories and innovations of racism and racialized positioning. Without becoming too sentimental, we should all understand that these are the kinds of knowledge that can let us fight and let us win.

So, and without wishing to overclaim the importance of academic writing in our collective quest for survival, this work tries to think again about racial capitalism in order to see the changing beast(s) that we face. How do we all become repositioned in and through the innovations of capitalism? And what might that do to racialized dispossession? I hope what follows is sufficiently open and suggestive to be of use to those trying to build unexpected solidarities across the range of projects for collective survival. I have done my best to signpost readers to relevant reading in each theme. However, equally, I hope the summaries here are sufficiently clear for those dreaming of a better world whether or not they reside (temporarily) in the academy. As always, I am trying hard to avoid the less than useful academic habit of pretending to have the last word. Most of what follows is incomplete, most of all an indication of what troubles me and which should trouble others, in my view. So I am still pushing the idea that racial capitalism is a question but also trying to refine my understanding of what the question might include at a particular moment.

The question of who is rendered surplus and how

In our time, and in recent times, plenty of energy has been devoted to trying to grasp the movements and dynamic of the global economy. If anything, this has been among the most central questions of the last thirty years, a question which for some time travelled under the guise of globalization (for a reminder of these preoccupations, see Panitch, 1994; Kiely and Marfleet, 1998; Hirst and Thompson, 2011). Perhaps now we lack an overarching term for what has happened to our turbulent transnational connections to one another. Awareness of the sometimes excessive claims of globalization theory has made it harder to summarize our moment and history of complex interconnected dispossession. How does the global economy function in a way that still keeps us separate, casting some regions into carnage and disaster while creating strange hybrid societies in other places of excessive wealth and extreme deprivation – with highly segregated populations inhabiting parallel economies which span the super-rich and the barely eating poor? The throwing together of the winners and losers of the global economy might be one element of the shifting world we are trying to understand. The throwing up of the most precariously positioned populations into every nook and cranny of changing urban landscapes or underprotected bonded labour or new forms of microwork dispersed across increasingly uncertain landscapes of wasteland and encampment reveals something of the destiny of those vulnerable to being rendered surplus in our time.

In the discussion that follows, the process of being made vulnerable to being rendered surplus is tracked through the arenas of bordering and penality and through the changing landscapes of indebtedness and the platform economy. The coming together of old and new violences plus adjustments in the day-to-day reproduction of capital lead to a remaking of racial capitalism on familiar and yet not identical terms. Something shifts, even as so much of the dead weight of history continues to press down so heavily. In particular, we might note the shift to viewing large sections of the world as expendable in the face of climate crisis, while extending economic processes fuelled via platforms that promise to include everyone, wherever and however they are located. We seem to be entering a moment where the mouthpieces of global capital are happy to announce the obsolescence of a large section of humanity (and other life-forms) while also celebrating the opportunity for all who survive to enter the global economy as a variety of microworker (for a discussion of the relationship of climate catastrophe to genocide, as trigger, backdrop or enabler, see Zimmerer, 2017). Perhaps we have seen before this simultaneous push towards large-scale carnage by neglect alongside a call to universal inclusion through the market (for a reminder of the increased hunger as an outcome of structural adjustment programmes, see Escudero, 1994; Hickel, 2016). I don't want to fall into the trap of suggesting that we are witnessing something quite new and that it is only its newness that merits our attention. My point is only that we should seek to understand the statements of increasingly justifiable expendability and increasingly widespread economic inclusion as clues to how and where we should enact solidarity for collective survival.

Doubt again

Previously I have written that no non-racial capitalism has been experienced yet in the world. Perhaps there can be a capitalism that is not racial(ized), but this is not what we have learned and witnessed from the history of capitalism so far.

What I have not said so openly is my uncertainty about whether a non-racial capitalism might emerge, could be emerging. My view has been that the mobilizing of differentiation as a means of enabling parallel processes of value scraping from populations is part of how capitalism remakes itself. The differentiation may not be called 'race' – and has not always been, at least not in all places – but the ability to squat in histories and presents of differential status and, through this, to institute spaces of wagedness and also other spaces of not-quite-wagedness or less-wagedness or value stripping outside the wage – that seems to be part of how capital can colonize a whole range of human lives. The lesson of racial capitalism is not that something called 'race' is always there, pre-dating capitalism and shaping its possibilities. Instead, the analysis of racial capitalism teaches us that capital is remade not by making the world anew – or, at least, not completely anew. Capital remakes itself through squatting in the divisions and categorizations and opportunities of sedimented histories of dispossession. The landscapes of past battles, including the battles of class struggle, alongside the divisions of belief and cultural practice and accumulated status and imagined former status, underlie each phase of capitalism, informing and enabling its remaking through differentiation.

Central to the observation of racial capitalism is this suggestion that incorporation into commodity circuits need not include incorporation into a flattened proletariat, let alone a proletariat where our work and our worth become increasingly the same as all others in the class. Whereas once we may have taken this insight and revisited trajectories of industrialization, desperately seeking signs for where and how a globally unified industrial working class might emerge, now perhaps we should reflect on how a system fuelled by stealing the very stuff of life from us all (albeit through different means) positions us differentially in the face of climate catastrophe.

The difference that we are living through – and it is taking place at breakneck speed – is the adaptation within the calculations of the global elite to accommodate climate catastrophe. We have moved all too quickly from denial (there is no real threat, and climate change is a much more marginal issue than the green lobby acknowledges) to expressions of concern to imagining a future for capitalism beyond ecological collapse. It is impossible to imagine business opportunities or economic resilience beyond ecological collapse without a tacit acceptance that some very considerable numbers of humans and non-human neighbours will not survive (for an instructive account of the dangers of some approaches to green tech, see Paulose, 2022). Global debates about climate refugees (Biermann and Boas, 2010) and the battle to gain recognition for the crime of ecocide (Short, 2016) both reflect this danger and address the reconfiguration of racial capitalism embedded in all fantasies of survival for some. We know already, all too well, that attempts to retain capitalist business as usual for some sections of the world's population relies on rendering many others surplus, in the process consigning them to violence, hardship and early death.

However, if we think of the logic of racial capitalism as something that always works and works in favour of the already dominant, we are in danger of transforming the business of analysis into a pacifying process. There is no point mobilizing to change something that can always remake itself and which is impervious to our attempts to unmake it.

A more useful (and more attentive) account of racial capitalism might seek to reveal the fragility of every remaking and the shonkiness of the accommodations reached. It might even point to the places where things cannot be remade and some other arrangement must be reached.

The histories of class struggle that make up the long saga of human existence are not only about resistance. We return, for good reasons, to the question of who can resist and how. But the other half of the story, of the loss of power and the fall from grace, has excited less imagination. Of course, the point for us is not to imagine the psychic costs of obsolescence for former members of the ruling class. That is an interesting project and merits attention, but not for our immediate purposes. For us, in our shared attempt to comprehend the changing landscape of racial capitalism and the possibilities to resist and dismantle these processes of violence, what is of interest is the circumstances that displace some from a position of dominance.

Why bother trying to think about capitalism at all?

Although it cannot be said too often, it is worth saying again: the critique of racial capitalism is insistently anticapitalist. This is not a recouping of capitalism under some other guise. It is not veiled liberalism. It is not saying, 'Aha, let us not think about capitalism as the main enemy because we need to deal with the racism among anticapitalists first.' Instead, to focus on the formation and reproduction of racial capitalism is to say, if we really wish to see and comprehend and face this monster, perhaps all we need to do is raise our heads a little and look around, look who else is harmed, and try to understand what our connections to those others might be. The call to attend to racial capitalism is a challenge and a question, not only in terms of analysis but also for organizing. It is also a kind of call to arms which refuses too easy answers to the question of solidarity. How we are in meaningful and material solidarity with one another in manners that can safeguard our collective survival and build a new world, while understanding that saying it or wishing it does not make it so, that is the life-or-death question at the heart of the study of racial capitalism. Because solidarity is not an assertion or a chorus, it is a puzzle. A puzzle that must be tackled anew, perhaps in every generation, perhaps constantly throughout all our attempts to imagine and build a better world.

2

Why Understanding Racial Capitalism also Returns to the Question of Social Reproduction

The story of this book, a story about the changing monster of racial capitalism in our time, cannot be told without a consideration of the role of social reproduction. Although social reproduction has become such a broad-ranging debate that it is difficult to know where to start, it is impossible to raise the questions of racial capitalism, questions about access to the means of life under capitalism for those excluded, partially excluded or only occasionally included in the waged labour market, without a consideration of the role of social reproduction (for some examples of the expansion of debate in relation to social reproduction, see Mezzadri, 2019; Bhattacharyya, 2017; Ferguson, 2019). And alongside this longstanding focus on the implications of variable access to wagedness, newer questions arise as we appear to enter economic arrangements where wagedness takes place alongside a range of other processes of value scraping.

The question of how life is remade under capitalism, alongside but sometimes in contradistinction to the remaking of capital, has been opened up again as a central question for any anticapitalist project. This is distinct from the attempts in an earlier moment to insert the practices of social reproduction into an account of economic life that imagined us all to be born into the role of fully-fledged and self-maintaining worker-citizen without any contribution from the vagaries of care and unpaid work (to understand both the moment of this necessary correction and the move into a broader conceptualization of the role of domestic labour, see Molyneux, 1979). Instead, in this moment where waged work is changing beyond recognition and non-waged realms of the economy appear to stretch and expand until work becomes only one more component in a bundle of economic activity that intrudes into every corner of life, what we understand to be 'social reproduction' becomes a changing question.

What might such a shift do to the terms of racial capitalism?

Racial capitalism makes sense as an explanatory framework for a world where value must be squeezed out of populations, *either* through wagedness *or* by scraping value from non-waged realms, including the realm of social reproduction. If the relations between wagedness and non-wagedness are in a process of transformation or mutation, then this framing of the questions of racial capitalism needs to be revisited.

Of course, none of this is to suggest that wagedness disappears, and few theorizations of rebranded capitalism argue this. What is being considered is not the end of waged work. Instead, these are ways of thinking which seek to understand a world where much of the organizing of human life for the production and extraction of value does not fit easily into our previous accounts of employment. In their annual survey of global employment trends, the ILO identified in 2018 a continuing decent work deficit alongside substantial proportions of workers engaged in vulnerable employment. With the impact of Covid, many all over the world have been thrown out of regular employment, with the greatest detriment suffered by poorer nations, lower-paid workers and the informal sector (ILO, 2018, 2022). 'The worker' still exists and, often, still has a pretty bad time of things. However, the centrality of 'the workers' to processes of accumulation has become, at the very least, somewhat less apparent. Capitalist intensification does not now, if it ever did, signal a proletarianization where local populations are transformed into interchangeable workers interpellated through the wage relation. Some may be, but for many others proletarianization is experienced in other ways, including a displacement from previous routes to the means of life and a resulting vulnerability to a variety of exploitative practices, none of which quite represent an entry into waged work.

With the displacement of wagedness, racial capitalism must be remade slightly differently. If we understand one aspect of the racialized differentiation of populations as occasioned by differential relations to wagedness, semi-wagedness and non-wagedness, the changing status of waged work demands a reconsideration of this framing. Semi-wagedness and non-wagedness cannot easily carry the weight of racialized demarcation, because these modes of organizing populations have seeped into spaces of relative privilege. Not, we should note quickly, in the manner of third-worlding the North or any other similar nationalist or racist lament. We are very far from witnessing a flattening down of the Global North to the living standards imposed on the world's poor. However, the emergence of modes of value extraction that bypass the wage relation and yet are not linked to previous techniques of population differentiation creates a new mystery of racial capitalism. If there is no easily identifiable ideal economic subject, how does the sorting and racialized differentiation of populations continue across the arenas of economic life?

The shift we are living through takes this further, displacing the status of waged work as exemplary model of value extraction in favour of other more dispersed methods of scraping value from the business of human life. Notably, this tendency is apparent in the metropolis and the Global North and, arguably, has entered those regions previously demarcated as home to the labour aristocracy in the global division of labour (for an excellent account of the implications of extending precarity in the Global North, including a belated disruption of nostalgia for the labour organizing of high Keynesianism, see Lazar and Sanchez, 2019). Whereas much of the world has never quite entered the model where 'the economy' can be centred around the waged worker as norm and standard of what economic citizenship is, the disruption and remaking of those zones that once imagined themselves as 'developed' or 'industrialized' pushes us to think again about what it might mean to be racially subordinated in economic terms.

Returning to the place of social reproduction, including the manner in which practices of social reproduction are positioned in and through racialized hierarchies while also representing techniques for navigating and surviving landscapes of racist violence and dispossession, offers an insight into how the raciality of racial capitalism works in a moment of economic transition, not least because it allows us to return to the question of what we understand as the economy.

Economics has been depicted all too often as another order of the world, one that impinges on our ability to live, but over which we have no control at all. A key benefit of thinking about social reproduction is the way it brings economics right back into the everyday. Instead of thinking of economics as somewhere apart, in a world of bankers and high finance, we start to think of economics as the very business of life (for examples of feminist economics exploring the translation of social reproduction into terms comprehensible through economic measurement, see Braunstein et al., 2020). Everything we do to keep on. All of the taking care, cooking, cleaning, birthing and everything else that remakes our bodies today and every day. That is also the stuff of economic life. One part of the analysis of racial capitalism is to identify how this other realm is also central to our division from one another and our dispersal across space. Without thinking about the business of keeping life alive, we will not understand how differential status emerges. And neither will we understand what it is about economic activity that makes human life, as opposed, as we are encouraged so often to think, to how human life can remake the economy.

The insight that emerges with the analysis of racial capitalism is that the realm of social reproduction is also grabbed back into the mainstream economy. And not only that: it is scraped back in ways that cement our differential status (for further discussion of this suggestion, see Bhattacharyya, 2018). This is not only at the level of the household. Feminist critiques of economics and accounts of social reproduction have taught us to understand the many varied ways in which the work of (mainly) women has been erased and made invisible. This is how we come to learn to undervalue the work of care and the remaking of life (this argument and the analytic language on which it relies is made most famously by Federici, 1975, 2020). This is also how we come to understand the productive economy as beyond these other transactions or practices. So far, so familiar. Work is the stuff that makes money and that demands money, that creates wealth. That makes stuff, perhaps, or at least the stuff that will make someone or other rich. Everything else is just housework. Or perhaps it is just leisure, or play, or at least something else, but it is not the realm of productive work. This supposed distinction between productive and non-productive work lies deep within the heart of racial capitalism. Of course, there is much work that is expropriated, or forced through violence, and certainly not waged in the sense that the wage relation suggests. All of that work still takes meaning within a logic of the productive and the non-productive. What remains hidden is the extent to which being relegated to the realm of the non-productive makes invisible a range of human activity and, for our purposes, a realm of the economy. Unlike an earlier debate about domestic labour, characterized by a critique that seeks to uncover the supplementary yet essential contribution of domestic work to the work and value extracted from the household by the employer (for a formative example, see Vogel, 2013), racial capitalism as a framework of analysis encourages us to conceptualize social reproduction a little more broadly. Instead of regarding the household – with household here closely associated with a particular set of affective and familial relations – as the unit and vehicle of social reproduction, the lens of racial capitalism invites us to consider a broader network of relationships and practices as contributing to the social reproduction of individuals in smaller and larger groups.

Previously I had understood the realm of reproductive labour as a kind of elastic space which gave variable supplementarity to the realm of the productive. This included, of course, the textbook model of the work that reproduces the wage labourer each day and as a class, but it also went far beyond that to include all of the unacknowledged and often unseen labours and activities and collective endeavours that keep life afloat, in the process making it possible for capital to skim off surplus labour from some particular tasks through the contract of the wage (see Delphy, 2016, for a still illuminating account). To stretch our understanding, we might think of reproductive labour as the larger ocean of economic activity, in which all other more quantifiable forms of economics swim. At the same time, we might think of reproductive labour as always in a symbiosis with the realm of nature, perhaps sometimes indistinguishable from the so-called realm of nature. Such an understanding opens the possibility of recognizing a non-capitalist infrastructure, sustaining life and spanning species, combining human endeavour and natural resources to live lives in the way that makes life itself possible. Thinking in this way helps us to see a little bit more clearly where the various thefts of capital take place and why, and also, importantly, to understand the ways in which other non-capitalist and pre-capitalist practices that continue alongside capitalist modes of life are necessary for the moment of value scraping to take place.

We might think of an interconnected sequence of thought that can begin at a number of points but which demands that we move back and forth across segments. Most noisily, the concept of the productive economy takes centre stage (and this is already in play in classical political economy, the stuff that Marx has in his eyeline) and is revealed to be reliant on a transfer of value from worker to owner of the means of production – so this is one subsidy or one form of 'theft'. In order to understand what has been stolen, we are guided not only to understand the moment of exploitation where work is exchanged for a wage but also to think further about what must be undertaken before and around the wage relation for the moment of exploitation to operate. This, then, becomes the more established account of reproductive labour. What must be done to remake the worker and the class of workers, on the whole understood as housework and baby-making, and another form of subsidy/theft.

The framing of racial capitalism represents another segment that casts these first two stories in a very different light. Thinking about racial capitalism calls into question the boundaries and reach of the 'economy', unsettling the claims of the 'productive economy' and instead pointing to the complex interdependence between processes of expropriation and processes of exploitation.

The question of racial capitalism already encourages us to think of social reproduction as a complex network that moves far beyond individual households, or even communities, and which includes cooperation between human and non-human, between the natural world and the social world, and which brings together a range of material, emotional, cultural and social resources to remake life as we know it (although not explicitly engaged in debates about racial capitalism, it is useful to see Haraway, 2016; Moore, 2016; Chen, 2012). Racial capitalism helps us to see this complex machinery because some of the terms of racial subordination have been precisely focused on the disallowing of the household or the familial or of propriety in all the forms implied by the productive household-cum-family (for an account of the continuation of genocidal logics in settler-colonial settings, see McKenzie et al., 2016; for a discussion of the continuing disruption of Black families, see Jean and Feagin, 1998). Racial capitalism points us to all the ways in which those deemed outside of these respectable practices also find themselves in different shadowlands of the economy, including the informal economy (Chen and Carré, 2020), the shadow and illicit economy (Talani et al., 2013), sex work and adjacent economic activity (Sanders, 2008), and the gig economy and precarious work of all kinds (De Stefano et al., 2022). At the same time, living in the economy's shadowlands, for whatever reason, itself circles back round to cast doubt on the affective relations conducted by those people. How life can be remade outside of the terms of heteronormativity and privatized domesticity is a central strand in the discussion of racial capitalism. It is a discussion that merits far more discussion but might include questions of Afro-fabulation (Nyong'o, 2018), a transnational exploration of proletarian nights (Rancière, 2012), and an expansive engagement with the call to abolish the family as a means to retrieving care, mutuality and love (Weeks, 2021; Lewis, 2022).

Housewifization and racial capitalism

When Maria Mies outlines her theory of housewifization, as we saw in the previous chapter, she is pointing us back to an understanding of how processes of social reproduction become sources of surplus value without any necessary mediation through wagedness.

In our moment where we see considerable remaking of the condition of wagedness, with various erosions of the status of workers and attempts to deny the employment relation (see Woodcock and Graham, 2019), the question of how non-wagedness also becomes a source of surplus value merits some attention. Housewifization shows us how a range of non-waged activity can be captured by the market and enter the money economy. Mies herself gives an example of how microcredit can lead to households relinquishing part of their non-waged livelihood (in her example, the raising of goats for milk) in order to service the debt. In effect, aspects of social reproduction are commandeered to extract cash repayments. Housewifization as a concept encourages us to think in more elastic ways about how our lives are given over to the imperatives of capital, particularly if we are not interpellated as 'workers'. As my interest is in trying to understand how the movement towards indebtedness and platforms operates to decentre and occlude wagedness, these broader conceptualizations of expropriation and extractivism help to explain how capital continues to steal our life-force.

Debt and social reproduction

Debt ties us into a future contract of repayment – interest is the price paid for delaying the transaction. In the process, rather than offering money earned through *previous* labour or other endeavour, we pledge the economic fruits of future endeavour in order to gain access to cash, goods or services in the present.

In a time when wagedness increasingly is combined with indebtedness as a strategy for living/surviving, what is the place of social reproduction in these multiple bargains (see Roberts, 2016)?

To pay a debt is also a pledge to stay alive – postpone repayment for long enough and the borrower will always 'win'. Varieties of liability linked to affective ties are designed to deter us from this final default (for some insight into the manner in which debt burdens translate over space and time, see Datta and Aznar, 2019; for one account of how debt squats within affective ties to create collective subjects of financial precarity, see Green and Estes, 2019).

When we pledge to repay a debt in the future, we also pledge the continuation of the social reproduction that remakes our life. Our ability to enter any contract of debt requires this assurance. More even than our formal economic prospects, the infrastructure to sustain life is a necessary requirement to becoming indebted. Because, of course, the price of debt can be extracted by one or other process of housewifization. As long as the terms of debt can be enforced, the resources of life can be taken as payment (for a heart-breaking account of the systems creating debtor's prisons in the United States, see Alexander et al., 2010).

How does this remake racial capitalism and the differential expropriation of value from the realm of social reproduction? I have tried to argue previously that the economic subordination of racialized groups – through barriers to economic participation, including in the labour market, through arbitrary depression of wages, through formal and informal enclosure in a manner that temporalizes and/or spatializes subordinated status – means that the racially subordinated are likely to bring a greater supplement to the formal economy through practices of social reproduction (Bhattacharyya, 2018). This occurs because the structures of racial capitalism position them at the edges of the waged economy and outside of the terms of creditworthiness (for an account of financial abandonment, see Leyshon and Thrift, 1995; for a broader account of financial exclusion, see Carbó et al., 2005).

To understand how we imagine modes of survival as racial capitalism remakes itself, we need to be attentive to how practices of social reproduction also are remade to fit changing landscapes of crisis (as an example of the psychic costs of crisis and the finding that white men with less than college education are the group most likely to report despair among the US population, see Graham and Pinto, 2021). If the experience of being racially subordinated or marginalized has led to a greater reliance on the realm of social reproduction, then an increasing squeeze on public services and social goods again increases the pressures to create practices of social reproduction that can sustain life despite the withdrawal of resources (for a discussion of the broader crisis of social reproduction, including the suggestion that high-income societies are destined to become care economies, see Hester and Srnicek, 2017). It is important here not to romanticize. The impact of exclusion or marginalization from the formal economy is painful, often terrifying, sometimes deadly. Even the most innovative approaches to the business of social reproduction cannot conjure food and water from the air. The move away from the relations of waged work towards precarity, informality and task-based payments represents a move to extend theft by capital. We may or may not have tricks and hustles enabling survival (Thieme, 2018), but the further informalization of work is an aspect of the fall in wage share and is designed to steal more from our labour and lives (for an overview of falling wage share as a global phenomenon, see Bengtsson and Ryner, 2015).

Rather than nostalgia for the heteronormative family wage of military Keynesianism, these challenges demand a refocusing of our energies away from techniques to remake the standard worker – both because affective arrangements have changed and because work rarely enters our lives in this arrangement now. There are two notable elements in this adaptation of the positioning of social reproduction: the changing demands of capital, now perhaps seeking the remaking of a capitalist subject who is a hybrid worker/consumer and the as yet unmediated gap between how a changing capital orchestrates the world and how human life can be sustained in such a world.

As I write, I understand that capital is and has always been fuelled by a death drive that threatens all human life and also itself (Han, 2021). However, I also think that the battles against and within capitalism have been to achieve a foothold for the maintenance of life and that momentary accommodations such as limiting child labour represent the tussle between class power and the incursions of capital. As capital changes itself, we too must adapt our modes of survival and our techniques of encountering and battling its violences.

Some of this is mundane. Shifting from a rhetoric of the family wage to a demand for an assured hourly wage reflects the changing shape of working days and nights and the need to frame wage claims in a manner that refuses the arbitrary segregation of worker from worker within the same workplace (for an invaluable reflection on the process and impact of the '$15 and a union' campaign across US workplaces, see Minchin, 2022). However, equally and less heroically, we also adapt and stretch our practices of social reproduction to maximize our chances of sustaining life. We might think of this as the extension of practices of hustling into the realm of social reproduction, or, perhaps more properly, a greater pressure on practices of social reproduction to mediate between the price of proletarian labour and other activity via the market and the costs of maintaining life.

Transition in the organization of waged work is occurring unevenly (of course) and therefore is already enmeshed in longer histories of racialized expropriation, exclusion and exploitation. Those entering the new worlds of work are already shaped by the routes of economic inclusion or non-inclusion of the previous phase. As a result we see some odd configurations – with a rapid collapse of some forms of until recently 'stable' work alongside the equally rapid expansion of varieties of precarious work organized to occlude or deny the terms of employer–employee relationship (for a very useful overview of changing working arrangements in the aftermath of the 2008 crash, including the increase in part-time and insecure work, see Bell and Blanchflower, 2010). The complaint across the overdeveloped world about the plight of the 'white' (or sometimes racially privileged through other terms) working class arises, in part, from this contraction of forms of work associated with this group and enjoying varieties of protection and benefit, including a broader social recognition tied to full access to social goods (Mondon and Winter, 2019).

At the same time, racially subordinated groups (who had already been expelled from higher quality work in previous phases of crisis, or who never reached the levels of inclusion and social protection necessary to access such stable work) are over-represented in some of the growing segments of the labour market (for a discussion of the propensity of precarious work among racially minoritized groups in the UK and the mental health impacts of this, see Bowyer and Henderson, 2020). Although this is underprotected work, it is work. As racial capitalism undergoes this particular phase of mutation, it might appear for a moment as if those who had relied on the relative privilege of their racialized status to access and maintain stable and more protected forms of paid work are now becoming disadvantaged in the labour market. We can look at accounts of the decline of work in some previously well-regulated sectors to understand how economic restructuring can be portrayed as a crisis of racialized privilege (High, 2020). The other side of this is the disproportionate numbers of racially subordinated people in new and/or growing forms of precarious and underprotected work (to understand the centrality of migrant labour to the functioning of the gig economy, see Altenried, 2021).

Both groups, those falling out of previously more protected forms of work and those over-represented in growing but underprotected forms of work, are positioned to enter indebtedness. However, the terms on which they enter debt differ. While those being spat out of declining employment sectors may borrow on the basis of past earnings, including assets such as their homes, those without a recent history of better paid and more secure work must borrow on the basis of future earnings or other income. For those carrying the weight of sedimented histories of racialized dispossession, becoming indebted requires a wager on the capacity of future social reproduction to sustain life and enable repayment of the debt. A portion of that which is undertaken to access the means to life is sacrificed towards the debt – in effect asset stripping our futures, including our future affective relations.

Platform capitalism and social reproduction

Platform capitalism signals the dismantling, perhaps the final dismantling, of one phase of economic organization. This is the world beyond the speculations about post-Fordism and post-post-Fordism (for a readable review of this debate, see MacDonald, 1991). While we might now consider these earlier attempts to describe the move from one dominant framework of economic organization into another as a kind of intellectual premonition, almost grasping a future that had not yet quite arrived, the extent of the transformation and dispersal of the 'corporation' has taken us all by surprise. Please do not adopt a cynical knowingness here. However well-established the operation of platform corporations has become, it is as well for us to acknowledge how great a shift this has been from the manner in which both anticapitalists and business schools had conceived of corporations and their actions until very recently (for an account of the transformation of corporate form by platforms, see Frenken and Fuenfschilling, 2021).

Platform capitalism disperses the processes of profit-making across time and space, infiltrating the places previously nominated as 'home', or 'leisure', or 'community' and transforming each into another site from which surplus value can be scraped (I use this unwieldy term in order to keep in mind that we remain uncertain about the mechanisms through which surplus value is transferred to corporate hands in these locations, or, at least, cannot reduce this transfer to one discrete process). Tressie McMillan Cottom explains this process of what she terms 'predatory inclusion':

> To both expand and exclude, the platform-mediated era of capitalism that grew from Internet technologies specializes in *predatory inclusion*. Predatory inclusion is the logic, organization, and technique of including

marginalized consumer-citizens into ostensibly democratizing mobility schemes on extractive terms. (McMillan Cottom, 2020: 443)

The process described points us to the simultaneous illusion of being included alongside the extension of extractivist processes. As popular and scholarly analyses of financialization have taught us, extractivism rails across societies, transforming all manner of social activity into sources of extractible value. What is added by the operation of platforms is, firstly, the appeal to our subjugated and subjectified selves with articulation and inclusion via platform *feeling* like recognition and inclusion when precious little else does and, secondly, processes to capture and render legible increasing aspects of our lives and behaviour, in the process extending the reach of what can be imagined to be a resource for capital.

Social reproduction as a target of organized violence

Although we are living through a moment of extreme threat to gender non-conforming, trans and queer communities, the state–business collaboration to shape and constrain sexual and affective lives in the interests of capital has undergone some significant shifts in recent years (for a very careful and insightful piece mapping the components of global campaigns against 'gender ideology', see Corredor, 2019). Perhaps across much of the world there is a lag in state measures, where legal and other official frameworks have been designed to promote and protect particular versions of the heteronormative household as a building block of both market and nation (for an account of the discrimination faced by LGBTQ+ people across the world, see Lee and Ostergard, 2017). However, the arrangement of work and work-like activity now far more rarely implies or demands this form of living arrangement (and this is not a new point; see Fraser, 1994). States may continue to champion ideas of the family and heterosexual marriage, including through active policing of gender identities and sexual activity, but the (apparently) easy interdependence of family–state–economy promised by Fordism feels out of time now (for an excellent account of the shifting policy and employment context away from the family as implied by Fordism, see Cooper, 2012). Instead, the working day has stretched beyond any limit, while work itself has become increasingly dispersed, eating into all other times and spaces of life.

Capital no longer hails us as the family unit imagined as the bedrock of economic development in both post-Second World War reconstruction and/or the remaking of the decolonized nation. Instead, we see varieties of work that erode the space and time for family life, increasingly push adults to outsource care of dependants to others, a blurring of the working day that includes an extension of the employment relation into all hours of the day and night for some, and a wilful erosion of the distinction between paid work and life for many others (Lehdonvirta, 2018). For large parts of the world, there seems to be a return to modes of economic activity that preceded the mass factory, with smaller-scale workshop-cum-household production processes where, once again, babies crawl among the debris of the production process (Selwyn, 2019, suggests we might understand these as global poverty chains). Similarly, a range of digital workers must relinquish any separation between home and work life, including accommodating themselves and their loved ones to the temporal demands of transnational working (Gurumurthy et al., 2021). Piecework, which never went away, is extended across sectors – and, once again, the struggle to maintain life pulls whole households into the efforts to complete whatever batch or bundle or order is in play (the World Bank presents the exponential growth of online homeworking as an opportunity for women to work while juggling childcare and avoiding male-dominated workplaces; Kuek et al., 2015). In the process, gains that might have felt assured, of schooling at the beginning of life and rest at the end, are under threat again.

I do not mean to suggest that we are witnessing a turning back of time. Historical shifts are never so easily predictable, and, even if we see a return of some older evils, they are configured differently across a different landscape. However, I do think we are living through a moment when capital is experimenting with adapted approaches to regulating the realm of social reproduction. For those carrying the burdens of expropriation/exclusion/exploitation by racial capitalism, the terms of economic survival may leave little space for more established practices of social reproduction. Although these terms are a marker of how tight times are, there is a little space for innovation in affective and living arrangements. In an echo of the shifts that enabled an earlier generation to create urban gay communities, the disorganization of economic spaces via platforms also wedges open greater possibilities for trying out different forms of relationships and ways of being (Klesse, 2014; Richards et al., 2017).

However, at the same time, the stepping back from intervening in the day-to-day practices of social reproduction, not least by contracting public services, is accompanied by a hyping up of 'emergency policing' approaches to regulating social reproduction. New possibilities open up, but, simultaneously, there is a renewed viciousness in the vilification of gender beyond the binary and sexuality beyond the heteronormative.

What positions social reproduction?

It helps us to think more clearly about the space of social reproduction if we begin by visualizing all human endeavour as an aspect of social reproduction – the business of life has been to stay alive, as individuals, as groups and as a species. The social arrangements around work whereby the labour of some is requisitioned by others open the possibility that some human activity can fall outside the realm of social reproduction. This is thinkable only because this activity is taken to further the social reproduction of some other individual/household/group.

Instead of considering the manner in which social reproduction is arranged around work, it might be better to think of how 'productive work' is inserted into the landscape of social reproduction. How are some bodies freed for some hours to pursue work outside and beyond that necessary to maintain life?

The benefits to the employer of splitting the location of work away from the home and into the mass workplace are well known. This is the stuff of textbooks. Mass workplace brings mass production brings standardization brings an orderly workforce brings profit far beyond what could be achieved before this massification. So, despite the disregard for the home-space or domestic aspirations of the worker, industrialization opens an increasingly clear distinction between the home and the workplace (McDowell and Massey, 1984).

Alongside this spatial demarcation of the place that is not the place of work, there is a tussle over the time that must be given to work and, by implication, the time that must be regarded as not work. These are the battles over the working day, battles which rest on the understanding that there must be time that falls outside the working day, whatever the dehumanizing practices deployed to squeeze as much as possible from the worker.

What matters, for our purposes, is what difference racialization makes to the demarcation of the space and time of social reproduction and of the non-reproductive work.

We are now living through a time in which we can less and less maintain the happy fiction of the standard worker employed full time on an open-ended contract in receipt of a wage that can sustain their life and also the life of their dependants, able to work regular hours in a known and stable location, to predict the course of their working life, and to support each significant life stage, from youth to parenthood to old age, through their working endeavours. As we see that particular fantasy crumble before us, perhaps we must ask ourselves what then happens to the assumptions about reproductive work that surrounded that particular fiction of what employment could and should be. Most obviously, we have moved far beyond ideas of the family wage incorporating the dependent partner or of the worker who sustains an entire familial household. At the same time, of course, we can see that there are very many types of households and far more expanded households than those imagined in an earlier moment of dual systems analysis (for a discussion of how multigenerational households lessen the impact of poverty, see Lofquist, 2013; for an account of transnational families arranging care across borders, see Bryceson, 2019). At the same time, there are so many – too many – households in which there is a disparity between the numbers working externally and the numbers of mouths to be fed (to get a sense of patterns of in-work poverty across Europe, including a breakdown of where household poverty arises due to several people being supported by one income, see Schwarz, 2021).

Changes in the service landscape have accompanied the loss of bargaining power that is represented by the move away from the family wage. This includes a huge increase in the range and type of personal services and cheap services linked to everyday survival across urban and semi-urban spaces. If we look at businesses connected to food preparation, for example, we can see the extreme and relatively sudden shift towards outsourcing this particular element of day-to-day reproductive labour (for an account of international use of food delivery services, see Keeble et al., 2020). To understand this most starkly, we can look to the conditions of untethered migrant workers all over the world who buy in varieties of canteen service just to be able to eat (for a notably celebratory account of state-run canteens for poor urban workers in India, see Nirmala and Seethamma, 2018). In the process, the wage is no longer conceived as including an element for someone in the household to shop, to chop, to cook, to serve, to wash up. There is no longer a need to imagine workers' accommodation as including a kitchen and a space in which to eat or a demand to consider regulating the working day in a way that allows that whole other set of labours to be carried out somewhere by someone. The low-paid work of the cities of the Global South already operated through this hand-to-mouth version of wagedness, free of the small gains of regulation we might associate with the Fordist/welfarist moment (Davis, 2008; Bandyopadhyay, 2009; Tarulevicz, 2018). What shifts is the extension of this rhythm of life/work into more sectors and more locations, until all sorts of people live their lives pushing portable calories into their mouths between varieties of gigs, squeezing down the time taken to maintain their own bodies because making a living cannot accommodate any slack (for an account of the squeezed existence of women drivers for Didi Chuxing, the Chinese ride-hailing platform, see Kwan, 2022; for an account of women's experience in urban industrial work in India as unsustainable and depleting, leading to a 'return' to the informal sector, see Mezzadri and Majumder, 2022).

Some years ago, when Westerners heard of the factory–canteen–dormitory cultures of a rising Asia, there was some horror because the dream of waged work enabling the privacy of the domestic was blown apart (a much discussed broader account of factory living in China, which gathered some of this dismay, is Chan et al., 2020). We could see that this was not a labour that would allow us an affective life even in the shortest bursts of domesticity. Not a labour where working hard would ensure leisure at the end of the day. Not really a labour that pretended any longer to give a path to becoming more human. Instead, all of those pleasurable human activities that remake life, not only the fuelling but the relationships and the rituals that accompany such fuelling, had been stripped back to the bare minimum. If calories could be injected down the production line, it felt as if that would be embraced as part of an efficiency gain (for a heart-breaking account of the factory–dormitory total workplace model and its consequences for the lives of workers, see Ngai and Chan, 2012).

Now, although most parts of the world have not seen any return to the massified production of, say, phone companies, we still see working lives where the space of daily leisure, and particularly that space of daily leisure that seeps into the requirements of daily reproduction, has been squeezed to the point of invisibility (writing on such phenomena tends to be grouped under ideas of the crisis of social reproduction, or sometimes the crisis of care; see, for example, Federici and Jones, 2020; Zechner and Hansen, 2015; Brown et al., 2013). Being able now to have a meal with your family is presented as a luxury to be stolen back from the normal rhythm of working life.

It is worth reminding ourselves, myself included, that the reproduction of capital is a really multi-headed beast. Yes, there is the dull kind of slow rebuilding of institutional power. I imagine that kind of reproduction a bit like an old-fashioned shipyard, where the blocks are already well defined and interchangeable, and that the process of reproduction is to make sure they get from ship to harbour to port side, but not much is done, apart from moving through time and space the same components of capitalist production. Perhaps what is more interesting is that we know that this kind of big institutional reproduction is always accompanied by all kinds of other much more unpredictable patterns of the reproduction of capital. There is certainly a much more hurried, worried, high intensity fissuring, jittering kind of remaking of capital's promise, often associated with the higher ends of technological development, perhaps also tied to the very edge of consumer culture. This is a way of thinking about the remaking of capital which is more than progressive, earth shattering and also kind of unsustainable. Impossible to be in yet impossible to leave. Heavily intoxicating in all directions at once. Perhaps attempting to teach you what you want but also absolutely giving it, or at least a fragment, to you in ways you really have not dreamt of before. It's a conundrum, and it seems worth remembering that Marx is warning that the fetish takes up all the space of capitalist consciousness.

This is not a warning to say we used to be fooled, but now we are free. It is a warning to say that you might never completely break the spell of the capitalist fetish. So at least know that it is there. We might take the frenetic yet seductive jittering around as part of a kind of reconstructed, or changing and shifting fetishism of the commodities of our time. Yet alongside all of this I wonder if there is also a kind of reproduction, sometimes capitalist, sometimes adjacent to capitalism, that takes on more organic patterns and that sees itself as part of a symbiotic relationship with many others, perhaps even with the land or the water or the air, certainly with some other living things (for more on non-capitalocentric accounts of social reproduction, see McKinnon et al., 2018). This animal element might be regarded as a reminder of human interdependence with other life-forms, and the processes of social reproduction that arise through such networks of interdependence operate to transform their contribution to the remaking of life into another supplement to capital (for discussion of the supplement that nature offers to capital, see Moore, 2015; Patel and Moore, 2017). We might think, then, of social reproduction as spanning the remaking of the labour force in direct and predictable day-to-day ways, the remaking of humanness in the broader and varied interactions that make up sociality, and the remaking of life in the complex but largely unacknowledged interdependence between life-forms (for influential examples of work in this area, see Moore, 2015; Haraway, 2016).

The reproduction of capital intersects with these three broad realms of social reproduction, clearly sitting on top of these processes that remake life. At the same time, the reproduction of capital spans the mechanical replacement of productive forces and the constant reinsertion of capitalist innovation into everyday life. While the former can be dully predictable, indicating the replenishment of machinery and storage and transportation, the latter represents some of the most alluring aspects of the colonization of the life-world. The reinsertion of capitalist innovation into everyday life brings together the reproduction of productive forces with the reconstruction of consumer markets and the transformation of capitalist subjects in a constant circuit of renewing capitalist desire (Stiegler, 2011). It is the aspect of innovation that ties our dreams and hopes to the remaking of capital, as we learn to express our possible futures through the techniques of progress shoehorned into our consciousness of self and of our connections to others. This is more than the marketing that encourages us to collapse our sense of self into the attainment of highlighted commodities. Instead it is a more textured disciplining of life, rendering us far more than workers for the machine, until the terms of our entertainment and rest, as well as our aspirations and hopes, become indistinguishable from the energies needed to remake this jittery, unpredictable but magical set of projected outcomes.

In this sense, racial capitalism also remakes itself in and through our desires, and perhaps this also includes the folding of racialized status and meaning into our sense of self and our articulation of pleasure.

Without the privilege of family

Racialized dispossession has operated to deny the right to family life to many – through the violence of enslavement or of displacement, or as an outcome of ethnic cleansing. A central impetus informing these violences has been the assertion that such people were less than people, incapable or undeserving of the affective relations of family (Gutman and Sims, 1978). It is this racialized logic that renders disruption into ordering. There is no breaking of what is already unmade. Instead the process of brutalization is championed as a kind of making by force, a making of a brutalized (near)humanness where no humanity was before (Naimark, 2002).

The habits of racial thinking can encourage us to normalize racial fictions even when seeking to comprehend the workings of racism. So let us raise and then park one well-meaning misunderstanding from this habit: the racially subordinated do not have a superior capacity for love, for mutual sustenance or for creating practices of survival out of nothing. It just feels that way. And it feels that way because of the constraints and violences of racialized dispossession.

We cannot begin our attempt to understand the differential racialized positioning of social reproduction work by asserting, or by quietly assuming, the substantial distinctness of affective forms among the racially subordinated. It is tempting, I grant you, but it is a slippery and highly misleading slope to fall down.

Racial subordination does not arise in response to something about the subordinated group – race has no meaning that precedes the moment of subordination. Even the things we might love most about ourselves and our own, the techniques of survival and joy and resistance, cannot be understood as an underlying racialized essence. Somehow we have to stretch our ability to think ourselves in a way that allows us to see our most precious practices as arising in dialogue with our torment. Admittedly, it is not a static relationship. There is no one-way once-and-for-all determination. But, equally, there is no pristine pre-history which grants attributes that then enter the fallen world.

What can we surmise then? Some things are documented fairly well. We know that some forms of racialized dispossession have, over time, shaped the affective forms of community survival. Here we might think of the complex support structures of the favela or of the slum, perhaps increasingly also of the camp (Perlman, 2010; Darychuk and Jackson, 2015). At the same time, we understand that histories of racialized violence have shaped the psychic repertoire of the subordinated and perhaps also of the privileged. Here I am thinking of the attempts to reconsider the mythologies of subject formation through the experience of the colonized. This includes the insightful but troubling work of Memmi ([1957] 2013), schooling us in the terrible interdependence of colonizer and colonized, endlessly in danger of becoming frozen in this dyad that strips all parties of their humanity. It spans the plethora of work unpacking the legacies of enslavement, including the repeated demonization and othering of Black family life and the mythologization of the superhuman capacities of Black women (for some influential entry points into this literature, see Roberts, 1999; Spillers, 2003; Hartman, 2016). We might place all of this against the backdrop of Fanon's desperately painful analysis of the psychic consequences of colonial violence and the whole bloody transfer of the lessons of psychoanalysis to the pathologies of colonial (and postcolonial?) life (Fanon, [1952] 2001). Racial capitalism also shapes our capacity for and recognition of love, in uneven and unpredictable ways, but always with the danger that violence might warp our humanity.

3

How to Think about Racial Capitalism in Times of Widespread Indebtedness

Indebtedness as everyday life

The decentring of the wage as the (imagined) central technique to access the means of life, with all of the accompanying assumptions and structures that present employment as the baseline of inclusion, citizenship and survival, signals something important about our moment.

It is useful to remind ourselves that:

- there is some consensus about the fall in the real value of wages for all apart from the most highly paid, and this fall has been going on for some time (for an account of the US labour market since 1979, see Donovan and Bradley, 2019; for a discussion of Australia, which also examines the global incidence of wage stagnation, see Stewart et al., 2018);
- levels of personal debt have increased rapidly in many of the spaces where reliable data exists (for a discussion of burgeoning personal debt in European nations, see Ferretti and Vandone, 2019; for a broader discussion of the risks of the debt economy for human well-being, see Montgomerie, 2018);
- despite one strand of literature on personal debt adopting a judgemental tone and deriding the indebted for their participation in the

consumer economy, it is likely that debt has formed one aspect of the response to falling real wages for many (for a discussion of falls in real wage rates, see Blanchflower et al., 2017); in addition, indebtedness has operated alongside precarity and varieties of exclusion, offering a route to meeting immediate needs, however dangerous the costs of this route might be (for an account of predatory lending in the US, see Soederberg, 2018);

- the changes in the landscape of employment, including changes enabled or accelerated by platforms, push increasing numbers towards varieties of multiple employment, side hustles, alongside a concerted pulling away from the employment relation by employers. This fragmentation of working lives, an additional move occurring alongside the fall in the real value of wages, creates the context in which rapidly increasing personal debt takes place.

This chapter is influenced by work arguing for an expanded understanding of extractivism and a recognition of the role of such extractivist practices in creating the non-homogenizing landscape of capitalism in every era (most famously, Gago and Mezzadra, 2017, and Mezzadra and Neilson, 2019). However, there is also something to note about the non-waged survival practices available and utilized in our moment. Among these, debt has become a far more widespread and substantial element of day-to-day household spending across the world. Two highly influential and very innovative accounts can help us to think about this conjuncture. One is that presented by Jackie Wang in the heart-breaking *Carceral Capitalism* (2018), the other the differently enraging insight of Lucí Cavallero and Verónica Gago in *A Feminist Reading of Debt* (2021). From very different starting points, both works guide the reader to understand the role of indebtedness as a technique of social discipline and differential dispossession and, through this, as a weapon of class violence.

Wang's ground-breaking work lays out the manner in which techniques of what she terms predatory accumulation are employed to transform the distribution of social goods and the regulation of social space into punitive measures, operationalized to extract a variety of fines from the poorest as a form of extractivist practice. In Wang's discussion, the focus is on the business of local government, an endeavour which lost central government support in Reagan's America and through this period becomes reliant on a system of collecting fines which targets the poorest. We can see echoes of this shift towards fine-based local government funding in other parts of the world, although rarely with the highly coordinated pathways into a broader carceral system that we see in the United States. However, I wonder, and Wang implies this also, whether this moment of propping up an appearance of local state infrastructure is also an in-between phase before the remaking of local infrastructure through other (perhaps even more punitive and more uneven) means.

Cavallero and Gago present us with something like this scenario, outlining the impacts of debt austerity on a whole society and, against this, the urgent need to chart a feminist path towards survival. As they explain at the outset of their discussion, 'We cannot understand debt in its contemporary form only by looking at public debt (debt taken out by the state), while ignoring indebtedness in everyday life.' The authors make this point to affirm their contention that (1) social movements must incorporate an understanding and accounting for debt in their political activity and (2) understanding debt uncovers its role in sexist violence. Together these points lead to what they term 'a movement of the politicization and collectivization of the issue of finance.'

The combined insights of Wang and Cavallero and Gago reframe how we might think about a society of indebtedness. From them we learn:

- societies remade through the imposition of the supposed disciplines of financialization bring the realm of social reproduction directly to the market. Financial instruments create the indebted household, where the debt is serviced by the combined efforts of the household, spanning formal and informal work and varieties of 'non-work';
- indebtedness and carcerality go hand in hand. The position of the indebted, the position of being always guilty before capital, implies a carceral state. As debtors are always defaulters-in-waiting, the indebted society requires carceral regulation;
- debt can and does lead to desperation. Reliance on unpayable debts in order to access the means of life (an unhappy experience now common across many locations) may no longer lead to suitably disciplined economic subjects. Disillusionment and exhaustion arising from indebted lives can bring an altered consciousness of the promise and limitation of life under capitalism.

When Lazzarato (2012) presents the account of indebted man, the implied logic within the theory is of a world where those who were once waged workers increasingly become debtors. So the move is from ways of living centred around the wage towards ways of living centred around debt. In the account of indebted man, this is a society-wide trend

– perhaps a tendency felt most starkly by those who previously enjoyed the status of exemplary worker-citizens. In case we forget the longer histories of racialized differentiation and dispossession through debt, we should remember there is another literature aligned to the account of racial capitalism through which we learn of the role of debt in maintaining racially subordinated communities in many places and times (for an instructive introduction to debates about the punitive experience of debt for Black communities in the US, see Seamster, 2019; for a discussion of the place of indebtedness in systems of racialized extractivism, see Byrd et al., 2018). Whether occurring through differential wages, underprotection of some in the labour and financial market, or other racialized subordination by way of official action or inaction, this differentiation has been supported and enabled often by racialized classification or other parallel forms of systemic hierarchization.

Once we start to think of these processes of differentiation through uneven protection in the arenas of work and finance, not as an addition to an economy based around production and wage labour but, instead, as the central motor of capital accumulation, which is of course what Lazzarato (2012) argues, we must think again about the landscape of racial capitalism. What is being described is a world where waged work continues to exist but, increasingly, is not the only or the main source through which life is maintained. Indebtedness describes the manner in which a waning wage economy, or perhaps the beginning of a post-wage economy in a world which is already insistently monetized, continues to tie populations into the market. As long as we have no option but to take on greater and greater debt in the quest to maintain life, and as long as that indebtedness ensures that not only our lives today but also our lives tomorrow are already sold to the needs of capital, then business pretty much as usual can carry on. It is, of course, a model that posits populations as consumers more than as producers, but it does ensure that the circuit of commodification continues.

For me, reading Lazzarato's account of indebted (hu)man reframed many things – not only assisting in my grappling to understand the operations of the austerity state but also guiding me through some of my confusion at the transformation of the imagined capitalist subject as work transmuted into a different and more fleeting disciplining of life. Sometimes a book comes along at just the right time to recalibrate your head, and reading Lazzarato was that for me. I don't want to spend time here adding to the (very extensive) genre of Lazzarato studies or to pretend that I offer a corrective to some or other absence in the theorization (for some entry points, see Adkins, 2017; Charbonneau and Hansen, 2014; Terranova, 2013). The highly suggestive and broadly painted account of indebted man is not focused on the differentiating techniques of racialization, and does not pretend to be; later works by Lazzarato centre questions of race and the war machine fuelling the destruction of the world (Alliez and Lazzarato, 2016) and of the fascistic within and through global capitalism (Lazzarato, 2021). It is not a global theory of debt and, again, does not pretend to be. It is, however, a way of thinking that can open up our approach to considering debt as at once an economic and a social discipline.

There are some other elements of indebtedness that have been less developed in the discussion certainly, that other history of indebtedness exemplified by populations who are forcibly excluded from labour markets and often from their land and their previous means of life, in the process coming to rely on varieties of debt to survive (Sassen, 2013a; for a heart-breaking account of the life-wrecking impact of impoverishment, irregular migration and indebtedness, see Stoll, 2010). For these groups, it is not the case that there was once a time of moderately regulated Keynesian-inflected social democracy with wage labour and, from that, there has been a fall into neoliberal fragmentation of labour markets, dissolution of work and necessary indebtedness. While we can see something like that narrative applying in some parts of the world in some kinds of location, particularly in some kinds of urbanized space, at the same time other spaces may become increasingly indebted without ever having been incorporated into the circuits of wagedness.

Racial capitalism if everyone is a debtor?

The debtor–creditor relationship – the subject of this book – intensifies mechanisms of exploitation and domination at every level of society, for within it no distinction exists between workers and the unemployed, consumers and producers, working and non-working populations, retirees and welfare recipients. Everyone is a 'debtor,' accountable to and guilty before capital. (Lazzarato, 2012: 7)

From the very outset, Lazzarato presents an account that unsettles the baseline categories that have informed left triumphalism for 150 years. To suggest that we have entered an era where the 'mechanism of exploitation' continues with no distinction between the productive worker, previously the rugged hero of pretty much all revolutionary fantasies and also the pin-up of choice of business innovators, and others is quite a jolt. How will we know where the struggle is? Or who can lead it and win? If even part of what Lazzarato suggests is accurate, we all need to think again about the nature of the class agent and about how we can chart our connections to one another. Without the reassuring centring of the productive worker, questions of class consciousness are blown wide open again.

Of course, Lazzarato is not the first to suggest a more diffusely constructed proletariat. The broader discussion of both racial capitalism and the construction of the working class offers us a literature crammed with examples of the complexity and diversity included within the terms of the productive worker. This includes, for example (and further reading):

- van der Linden's extensive work to document the variety within the ways of working imposed by capitalism and the suggestive, if contested, concept of the subaltern worker (van der Linden, 2008);
- the debate about the hiring out of enslaved Africans in the plantation economies of the Americas, linked to varieties of wage-earning and to direct roles in market-orientated economic activity (Martin, 2004);
- the suggestion of partial proletarianization or peripheral proletarianization as a more apt descriptor for some regions (Amin and van der Linden, 2008);
- the very longstanding but still transforming debate about the relationship between peasantry and proletariat, including both the acknowledgement of multiple forms of work and an examination of the role of the peasantry in creating the conditions that make waged work possible for others (for a discussion of the struggle of peasants to resist and regulate expropriation, see Bernstein, 1977);
- how varieties of informal work, including so-called 'self-employment', can be understood as forms of proletarianization (on the informal proletariat, see Davis, 2006).

However, in all of these varieties of proletarianization, there is an exchange of labour directly or indirectly for payment. The payment that accrues is for tasks completed, so wagedness and also varieties of near wagedness or alternatives to wagedness all imply this retrospective payment. Indebtedness changes this so that, in the contract of the debt, we pledge our futures. We should avoid being overdramatic here. Humanity has worked around varieties of bondedness since antiquity, and the future, too, can be segmented and quantified and its promise closely regulated (for an important account of the place of forced labour in the emergence of the global economy, see De Vito et al., 2020). The point is not that debt is an open-ended contract. The point to understand is that indebtedness disciplines human life to meet the needs of capital in quite different ways to the discipline of the wage. How we are constituted as subjects of capital(ism) alters. Even if we consider indebtedness as only a growing but not dominant component of the remaking of capital, the rapid increase in personal debt in some regions, alongside a likely unrecorded recourse to informal forms of debt in other parts of the world, demands our attention (see Kose et al., 2021, for a historical account of waves of debt, although the optimism of this account is hampered, sadly, by a pre-2022 belief that low interest rates will continue).

Previously I have thought of the differentiations of racial capitalism as occurring through differential positioning in relation to (an idea of) standard work. Central to this ordering has been the place of wagedness as the prime economic status in some communities and not in others. The extension of indebtedness reveals a greater uncertainty about the security, sufficiency and reach of wagedness (for an account of the combined pressures of the 'New Economy' and the resulting further immiseration of low-income households, see Edgell et al., 2012). People still work for wages, of course. But the balance sheet of daily life requires debt, and, as the debt becomes a larger and more persistent portion, the arrangements of economic life tilt from the disciplines of wage-earning alone to include the somewhat other demands of debt management (for an overview of the scale of household debt across the world and the risk to economic stability, see Hays, 2018). We become different creatures as we come to order our lives around debt rather than, or as well as, earnings. Lazzarato has described this as a shift into being always already guilty, with indebtedness: 'the indebted man [is] at once responsible and guilty for his particular fate' (Lazzarato, 2012: 8).

This is another aspect of Lazzarato's account that unsettles. The entity he describes, the indebted person, embodies both a shift in the economic and a shift in the capitalist subject. In fact, in much of his telling, Lazzarato moves between the impact of structural change in the economy and cultural change (or something like it). The account of indebtedness resurrects terms that had been banished from talk about economic practices such as guilt and blame.

Structures of indebtedness reveal what perhaps we have known all along, that economic contracts are shaped to be punitive. This, too, has been an insight from analyses of racial capitalism. The sedimented histories of dispossession that make up racialized economic landscapes demonstrate the punishment enacted through so many instances of economic contract. This is one element of 'whiteness' as property, as racialized power absolves the bearer from adhering to contracts, economic or other, with those deemed lesser (Harris, 1993). It is precisely the pretence that such contracts are entered freely with equal resources and agency that enables the violence of economics. What is theft is disguised as a matter of contract. The events of recent years have expanded this view, making many others look again at the terms of economic contracts as often a form of thinly veiled violence or extortion (see, for example, the energetic discussion around debt refusal by Debt Collective, 2020; and Snider, 2018, on the crimes of capitalism in the gig economy).

Despite an extended period of celebration on the part of champions of the market, a period that included many excessive boasts about the democratic and even the human rights credentials of market-orientated societies, capitalist economics is increasingly revealed to be a rigged game. The ascendance of heterodox economics and the demand by students for an economics that can address our moment of crisis both indicate a shift in the perception and credibility of the discipline since 2008 (Feraboli and Morelli, 2018). Alongside this failure, the entrenchment of indebtedness is accompanied by the extension of carcerality. Together these processes (re-)create a capitalist landscape in which the most common experience is an expectation of punishment or of coerced obedience (Wacquant, 2009). The recent histories of racial capitalism reveal this experience of coercion in the name of economic and social inclusion to have been imposed as another differentiating technique. The constraining and highly punitive disciplines of an economic landscape where the experience of being racially subordinated limits access to work and a stable income while also curtailing, all too often, access to mainstream financial services created an experience of being vulnerable to punishment while both earning a(n insufficient) wage and servicing a(n extortionately framed) debt (for an account of the punishing impact of navigating life via the 'fringe economy' of amalgamated predatory practices targeting the poor, see Karger, 2005). The double disadvantage of discrimination in the labour market and underprotection in the realm of borrowing has marked one kind of marginalized status, recognizable across a range of locations and consistent with the naturalization associated with racialized subordination (for an account of predatory lending to the so-called middle class in the United States and the far greater detriment to Latinx and African-American communities, see Warren, 2004).

To understand what is happening in our moment, we need to pause to consider the shift from debt experienced as a low-risk route to enhancing consumer spending, with little impact on the day-to-day stability of households, to debt experienced as a constant drain on resources needed to meet the expenses of living today. My contention is that indebtedness is becoming more punitive for more people, but in a manner that maintains the racialized disciplining of populations as a mode of protecting class interests.

Indebtedness and the non-waged sphere

What the media calls 'speculation' represents a machine for capturing and preying on surplus value in conditions created by modern-day capitalist accumulation, conditions in which it is impossible to distinguish rent from profit. The process converting control over capital production and property, which began in Marx's time, is now complete. (Lazzarato, 2012: 21)

This is central to the account of indebtedness. Whereas previously critiques of capitalist exploitation focused their energies on the wage relation, Lazzarato presents a framework to comprehend the agility of value capture. We might hold back from calling this exploitation but recognize the close affinity between exploitation through the wage and expropriation through debt. This excavating of value from the non-waged sphere brings ideas of indebtedness into direct dialogue with accounts of racial capitalism. In an earlier phase of racial capitalism the distinction between populations able to enter and those excluded or semi-excluded from wage economies played a key role in demarcating racialized divisions. Degrees of access to wagedness served as one racializing technique, and one which, of course, worked to sew waged populations into the wider constraints of the wage relation. We might consider the concept of the standard waged worker here as a kind of fictional ideal through which degrees of inclusion, protection and choice are marked. Perhaps almost no one occupied the imagined fullness of identification implied by standard waged work, but it is a concept that functions, nevertheless, as a marker of what tidy and proper economic inclusion and citizenship should be. It has been the ideal type from which all other variants of economic status and activity take their meaning.

For us, the question becomes: if wagedness is displaced from this central role in the actual and symbolic organizing of economic meaning and life, how then might we understand the processes allocating variegated status via differentiated economic activity? If our ideal type loses its lustre, what then?

An unresolved puzzle from my previous work is the tension between thinking of racial capitalism as a way of mobilizing racialized divisions, with these serving as a means of enhancing value scraping and accumulation, and thinking of racial capitalism as a method of trialling and extending increasingly dehumanizing modes of value extraction. In the first way of thinking, the maintenance of racialized hierarchies assists processes of accumulation for some and is an intrinsic aspect of a broader machinery of exploitation/expropriation/exclusion. In the second, racialized hierarchies operate as a transition towards entrenching techniques of hyper-exploitation and/or dispossession across multiple populations. The first account suggests that differentiation operates as a method of reconciling some key tensions within capitalist expansion and also of enabling continuing value extraction through multiple methods. The second implies, if never quite states, that we all become interchangeable eventually but that the practices of dehumanizing value extraction enabled through histories of racism become the standard of what can be done to populations.

I fear that I have argued both angles, within the same work and across my writing career. If pushed, I think it is hard to decide that it is one or the other. Both continue alongside each other – but they represent very different logics.

The questions this raises include the following.

1 Does differentiation through racial capitalism operate by distributing populations into differing arenas of economic activity? Or by distributing populations into hierarchies of value/vulnerability within arenas of economic activity?
2 Does the expansion of processes of dispossession dismantle or lessen the racialness of racial capitalism? Or do other processes of differentiation among those suffering dispossession continue to renew racial capitalism but in shifting forms?
3 Can the deployment of techniques of racial capitalism at once extend increasingly dehumanizing processes of value scraping and also initiate new forms of exclusion?

The formulation of the indebted subject intensifies these questions. A number of aspects of indebtedness have acted, previously, as markers of racialized subordination in the economic sphere or have been associated with such subordinated or marginalized status. The point to note about indebtedness is that it does not, of course, flatten the economic landscape. There might be an extension of indebtedness across a range of occupations and locations. Perhaps not being able to make ends meet has become a kind of normality, but it has not done so in anything like the same way for all groups of people. Much of the literature about financial and economic resilience points to this – the state of indebtedness for many, and for many marked by a longer history of racialized dispossession, is a state of constant danger (for a discussion of the experience of racially minoritized people facing bankruptcy in the UK, see Ekanem, 2013; for a painful but instructive account of responses to school-lunch debt as an indication of state violence, see Atkinson, 2021). For some people, to be unable to service their debt is to fall completely out of any day-to-day security.

We might think of our time as a transition phase where the balance between wagedness and indebtedness is in negotiation. Equally, we might understand that the uncomfortably familiar landscape of differentiated racial capitalism is just about passing – with all that it has meant in terms of differences in wealth and assets and protection through official forms and the ability to make and uphold contracts and the recognition of full citizenship in a way that enables reasonably consistent accessing of social goods. What is happening is not that these nebulous social goods have extended to all. Instead we see these aspects of subordination and exclusion extended, unsettling previous reliance on differential privilege (a privilege often experienced primarily as the ability to avoid the racist punishment meted out to others). In this period of unsettlement, previous histories of dispossession continue to cast a shadow over the present, but, simultaneously, new catastrophes can strike, casting the previously secure into near abjection. Indebtedness does not remake the landscape of need or vulnerability in predictable ways, pushing all living standards down a few points or adding a set proportion of additional debt to every household budget. Instead, in its decentring of previous settlements around wagedness or the fantasy of the citizen-worker, indebtedness can both further limit the choices of the barely getting by and hollow out the race–class privileges on which the respectability and moderate comfort of some others previously relied. We might think of this as yet another example of how we come to live differently shitty lives.

When we take all of those factors into account, we can understand that the landscape of indebtedness, even in a situation where wages are uncertain and insufficient for many across racialized categorization, is one where those with longer histories of racialized dispossession are likely to be made far more dangerously vulnerable by the situation of being in debt. This is a landscape that remakes itself by exacerbating the disadvantage of those already less protected, not least through forcing recourse to the most dangerous routes to indebtedness and once again opening those already vulnerable to the dangers of the necropolis and the criminal economy.

Precarity, vagabondage and debt

The deepening reach of indebtedness reflects increasing precarity across the labour market. This does not mean that such precarity did not exist previously. We have many documents to indicate the tenuous grip on the means of life for many waged workers across different periods and locations. Waged labour has always also meant this kind of hand to mouth existence for too many (for an account of precarious work in Egypt and India under British rule, see Bent, 2017; for a broader discussion of the need to reframe debates about precarity in ways that encompass work in the Global South, see Scully, 2016). However, what seems to have shifted is something in the balance of power between employers and workers, so that what we have come to regard as standard work, with all of its minimal but necessary safeguards, is retreating away from the realm of possibility for many (for an account of the decline in standard employment in formerly industrialized economies, see Stone, 2013). In its place, we see a whole range of short-term variably contracted tasks, lifetimes spent on the edge of stable work, forms of employment designed to disguise or refuse the employment relation, and an overall move to a world where those who must work must also spend significant amounts of time scavenging for work (for a ground-breaking discussion of the emergence and impact of microwork, see Jones, 2021; for a ten-country overview of the microwork workforce, see Posch et al., 2018).

In this landscape, debt has a very different importance. Without indebtedness, the everyday resources of life cannot be accessed (for a careful and illuminating account of the impact of access to market borrowing in tying poor communities in India into debt bondage through wage advances, see Guérin and Venkatasubramanian, 2022). People don't eat. School clothes are not bought. Heating bills are not paid. The everyday grind of getting to and from work cannot take place. So, although indebtedness does not replace the wage, we seem to have entered an era in which wagedness implies the supplement of indebtedness (for a discussion of the 'fringe economy', the set of predatory financial services that exploit the urgent need for cash among low-income Americans, see Karger, 2005; for an account of the racialized impact of the family budget gap in the United States, see Joshi et al., 2022). This may not be for everyone, but for increasing numbers and in many places (for an important challenge to the narrative of survival indebtedness, outlining the correlation between strong collective bargaining and good public services and sufficient confidence to take on mortgage debt in OECD countries, see Johnston et al., 2021; to understand how medical debt but not other forms of unsecured debt can increase food insecurity for low-income families in the United States, see Brewer, 2020). Perhaps unsurprisingly, the indebtedness of the broader population has come to be regarded as a risk to the economy despite the logics of financialization (for an indication of concerns that increasing levels of household debt can lead to a hampering of macro-economic goals, see Alter et al., 2018).

The shift we are seeing in the nature of work is not occasioned solely by the rise of the platform corporation, but there is something indicative about the business arrangements of the platforms that helps us to understand how work has become so dispersed, so unregulated and apparently so resistant to the forms of worker organization that have been developed over the last few centuries (for an explanation of how platform work can elide existing structures of regulation and an argument for revised and updated regulation, see Pulignano, 2019). It is the platform economy that makes it possible to disperse so many tasks differently within the marketplace. The platform makes it more possible for employers to imagine work without workers, perhaps to fantasize a wholescale remaking of the economy that abolishes the worker altogether, while distributing increasingly unregulated and poorly remunerated work tasks via digital means to increasingly desperate populations. While we might wish to argue that there is a high degree of (employer) fantasy in this account, it remains the case that many of the regulatory gains of the global labour movement are under threat or have been eroded already (De Stefano et al., 2021). In their discussion of the geographical questions raised by structural disemployment, Pierce, Lawhon and McCreary argue for a need to rethink our framing of the battle to retrieve human dignity and access to life from the ravages of capital:

> political contestations need to grapple not primarily with the exploitation of labour but rather the division between those with access to employ-

ment and those without. The increased and likely increasing numbers of unemployed, under-employed, and informally employed people require that we develop political and economic subjectivities beyond those of labouring bodies and towards a decoupling of the allocation of material resources from the moral valorization of labouring. (Pierce et al., 2019: 96)

We are entering an era where some labour continues to be essential, although denied recognition of this role, and the infrastructure that previously enabled worker organization has been disrupted and dispersed. Unsurprisingly, the question of worker agency in this differently dispersed working environment has garnered extensive attention (for examples, see Jones, 2021; Vandaele, 2018).

Two other strands of this work, bordering and prisons, point to overtly violent structures administered in the main by states. These are also explicitly racist structures that have played a central role in the making and remaking of the racial state and which contain within their logics unambiguously racialized systems of punishment, exclusion and categorization (to return to some of the most instructive writing on these points, see Goldberg, 2008). To this extent, borders and prisons represent a far older and all too familiar machinery of racialized violence. However, I do wonder if there is something about the changing economic landscape suggested by indebtedness and platforms that calls up something new or extended from the realms of bordering and imprisonment. Perhaps the throwing open of work in the process, if not abandoning at least making blurry previous certainties around status, job, demarcation and sense of security and work, leads to a reinvigoration of disciplinary measures (some writing about working-class identities and economic change reflects on this, such as Linkon, 2018). The tasks of spatial sorting, of segregation, of differentiation that might previously have occurred in part through the combination of an uneven labour market (Jonas, 1996), entrenched discrimination (Wrench et al., 2016; Roediger, 1991), state collusion and the underprotection of some communities (Goldberg, 1992, 2008) now, perhaps, are reallocated to a return of the overly punitive across the piece.

There is something reminiscent of the emergence of laws against the vagabond here (Cresswell, 2016). If 'workers no longer recognized as workers' are forced to claim the ambivalent status of non-worker – out roaming free, scavenging for work as they can, but equally untethered from some of the other social and spatial and state-administered groundings of previous labour market arrangements – perhaps the ramping up of such punitive measures as the border and the prison reflects the parallel dispersal of employer and state-administered disciplinary machineries.

As we have come to an expanded account of extractivism, through the combined insights of Indigenous scholars and scholars of financialization, of colonial extraction, and of the various names we call the monsters that emerge from neoliberalism, capital increasingly positions human populations as tenants in a world we do not own. Yet far from acknowledging the impossibility of enclosing the Earth as a private asset, we find human populations facing versions of proletarianization that separate us from the means of life but do not offer reabsorption into the economies of mass production. As a result, we are transformed into multiple renters – with the capture of all necessary resources of life by capital. Previously, accounts of the role of rent have pointed to the rentier as a figure operating in parallel and parasitically to the capitalist. The rentier lacks the innovative impulse of the capitalist, transforms nothing and fails to put capital in circulation. Yet we understand that capital can include rent-seeking arrangements in its repertoire, not least as a method of incorporating more of the energies of human life into a source of value that can be claimed for accumulation.

Previously, we might have considered the continuing influence of the rentier class as operating as a disciplinary mechanism linked to the disciplines of wagedness. Something shifts, however, in contexts where populations have no option but to pay rent (not only for housing or land, but sometimes also for access to essential resources such as energy or water, or, increasingly, to be legible to authority).

Indebtedness as a new moment of capitalism

A central element, and the shift of the patterns of racial capitalism in our time, has been the reworking of the role of the wage in everyday life. Increasingly, we see a squeeze on the living standards of working people all over the world in ways that indicate the non-centrality of waged work in the experience of proletarianization. As a result, we find ourselves living through a moment when there is an increasing interest in how capitalism is transforming. As others have noted, this has led to a whole range of qualifying phrases, all designed to indicate that the capitalism we are living is unlike the capitalisms of the past (for some well-known examples, see Zuboff, 2019, on surveillance capitalism; Srnicek, 2016, on platform capitalism; Fraser, 2022, on cannibal capitalism). This work is inevitably part of that tendency. It is very hard to think about contemporary capitalism without seeking to mark the difference of our time. Perhaps that is the tragedy of every generation – the belief that your own time represents something peculiar and particular and unique and that your understanding of that uniqueness reveals that yours is the generation to make the break.

Despite this danger, I want to say something about why I consider it useful to think of a mutation of racial capitalism taking place in our time. I believe the assumption has been that everything outside of the productive formal economy must be understood in relation to this space of the real economy where real things happen. That is the logic of capitalism that we have become used to analysing. We can see things which are not quite formal economics, but only in relation to an idea that the real economy resides somewhere. In addition, this discussion has a kind of spatialized metaphor embedded in it. The productive economy is surrounded by that which is not the productive economy. It is buoyed up by the work of social reproduction. It runs alongside varieties of accumulation by dispossession and extractivism. I say all this knowing full well that my own work has replicated this logic.

Previously, I have thought of racial capitalism as a lens through which to understand what goes on in the reproduction of capitalism alongside the formal spaces of production. I have accepted that there is a kind of centrality to the production economy, that this thing that is spoken about so often in discussions of capitalism actually takes up the main and central space and that all other human activity comes to take meaning in relation to this thing, which is both the core of capitalist activity and the core activity required to reproduce capitalism. As the astute reader must have realized, I am much less sure about this particular metaphor now. Instead, it seems to me that there is no longer an assured centrality to what we think of as the productive economy. Alongside other activities, instead, we might think of a global economic landscape in which many fragments are operating or tied together by the logic of accumulation.

What we have learned is not only that capital does not proceed in one register across all spaces but also that this variety of registers and techniques is in fact part of the process through which capitalism as a whole is remade. In our time this starts to become a much more urgent issue to understand. We are no longer trying to ask politely for issues of non-wagedness to be accommodated within the analyses of Great White fathers. This is not an account of how we have been excluded and must be included. It is not a claim for representation at all. Instead, we should understand that it is impossible to see how we are wounded by the movements of capital in our time if we cannot also understand the processes of differentiation and parallel development that have divided us into populations who are positioned to be quite unlike one another. The reason why this insight has become so much more urgent for us is that the fantasy of the ever-expanding industrial wage economy seems to have evaporated. It is a model of economic growth and success that maps poorly onto the history of economic change in the recent decades of the globe.

A point to remember here is the sense in which there is a space that is ordered, seen and legislated for, however imperfectly, and the space beyond. There was a period, quite understandably, in which the space of exception came to animate our collective imagination (Agamben, 2005). I think that moment was very much focused on ideas of the limits of legality and of sovereignty as the exercise of legality. Now I wonder if there is something about economic reproduction in a moment of climate catastrophe which places the space of abjection somewhat differently. The demarcation of who is in or out, who lives or dies, perhaps no longer fits easily with our understanding of political decision-making, however broadly we define political agency. Instead we start to see a different combination of forces which make the state of exception something like logistical or operational. Certainly something narrated in quite different ways from the terms of the war on terror and those who cannot have rights. I say this in passing because the suggestion that some people, some things, some animals, some ways of life, will inevitably fall off the edge of civilization and out of consideration seems to have become embedded both in our analytic approaches and in nearly every institutional response at either national or international level.

Although it is far from the focus of this work, there may be something instructive about looking at the particular machineries that have given rise to this dismantling of the aspiration to universalism, across political rights, economic inclusion and the terms of belonging to the human race at all. Whereas previously the exclusions from that universalist language were in bad faith, even though we know now that bad faith was constitutive of those formations, it seems to me that we are living in a different moment of concerted rolling back of terms previously regarded as valuable because of their potential for universal reach. Citizenship may be one such, but I think the terms of climate catastrophe are throwing up others. What we are living through is a global economic formation, rapidly restructured through the period of globalization, deeply financialized in ways that have remade what states can be and how they can function and, alongside this, a kind of decentring of what we previously recognized to be waged work.

So the new masters of the global economy increasingly seem to survey the Earth and its populations as a variegated landscape from which value can be extracted through a variety of means, some segmented, some overlapping. Every population can offer something potentially, albeit on differential terms, yet no group needs to be absorbed into the civilizing process of Fordist arrangements. That particular set of arrangements designed to remake a particular kind of wage labourer seems to be over. Instead we are seeing the emergence and consolidation of interconnected disciplinary processes of economic life which together position and control variegated populations in ways that continue to render us up most effectively for processes of value scraping while still squeezing some additional benefit from ensuring that we do not become the same.

As the combination of very rapid and somewhat unpredictable economic restructuring alongside climate catastrophe and the collapse of some kinds of political institutions takes place, across human lives we can see a widespread disruption to previously established ways of life. By ways of life here, I really mean no more than the ways in which human beings have arranged themselves to be able to survive and also have some fun and a sense of at least temporary security. For large parts of the world these elements have not been available for some time, and for some of the more affluent parts of the world the sense of temporary ease that could be achieved through accommodating oneself to the disciplines of wage labour no longer seems available. As a result, we might revisit concepts of deproletarianization and reproletarianization, processes where the factors that created one kind of working identity and community are collapsing while at the same time something akin to a previous account of primitive accumulation is occurring in many spaces, including the most unexpected. The stripping away of any protection or entitlement in ways that seem to champion the needs of capital beyond any other consideration unwrite some centuries of labour agitation. Even the thin regulation of law seems to be escaping us, now that corporations themselves claim rights on a par to the human.

Shitty work

The additional impact of racialized subordination in the labour market is to force some segments of the population to do work considered too dirty, dangerous, low paying or too all-round horrible for others to take it up. The continuation of caste-based discrimination in urban workforces, including through the folding of caste stigma into structures of precarity, offers an unhappy but instructive example of this process (Mendonca et al., 2022; Ganguly, 2018). The concept of dirty work – work believed to involve contact with physical or ethical 'dirt', such as refuse processing, caring for frail and elderly people or sex work – also illuminates this issue (Simpson et al., 2012; Simpson and Simpson, 2018). But shitty work is more than this: it encompasses both low-status work and dirty and dangerous work and also the varieties of work designated too dull or fleeting or lowly to merit effective regulation. Shit-work is absolutely central to how we might think of racial capitalism. It is impossible to extend the terms of what decent work could be and still retain the differentiation that underlies the harshness of racial capitalism. Some workers have to feel relieved or superior despite all evidence to the contrary. And shitty work fulfils that aspect.

There are well-documented racialized elements to these demarcations. Work that is associated with the racially subordinated can become shitty work, the kind of work no self-respecting member of the racially privileged group would choose to do (for an account of the long historical association between racially minoritized women and forms of subordinated care work, see Glenn, 1992), but more often some forms of work become the default place that subordinated workers can go.

There is nothing surprising about seeing an erosion of working conditions across the board alongside a reinvigoration of racialized differentiation between kinds of work or even kinds of task (for an account of increasing in-work poverty across Europe, see Schwarz, 2021). We can see that the extension of a variety of precarity across the labour market does not in fact erode differentiation. There is an extension of the characteristics of shitty work to far greater numbers, but this is not the same as reducing all potential workers or task fulfillers to the same status. This is, in part, the argument of Vallas and Schor (2020) when they point to the variegation in digital work. As far as is discernible, the fictions of race continue to divide and locate populations in ways that shape their access to work even in this most depleted form (for an early account of microwork in seven African nations which cautiously points to the trend towards renewed extractivism, see Mothobi et al., 2017). Some of this is a continuation of previous work patterns.

Work in areas such as IT, admin and other office-based tasks seems to continue to reflect the racialized divisions of the time just passed. Yet, even with the erosion of conditions, there is still a veneer of respectability about this kind of work. People think they understand what it means and what it entails and what it says about them. And even in this debased form that produces a series of tasks none of which leads on to further learning or, more importantly, an actual proper contract, it seems that those operating in this section of the labour market continue to view these forms of what we might call white-collar work through the lens of respectability, not solely through an analysis of the contractual terms (Freeman, 2010). At the same time, other kinds of work which have been highly stigmatized, even when regulated better in terms of conditions and pay, continue to reflect the racialized divisions of the labour market. Cleaning and caring are the prime examples here, with extensive data from different locations revealing the extent to which more affluent parts of the world (meaning here the metropolises of both North and South) could not fulfil the day-to-day requirements of social reproduction for the most vulnerable without the underpaid and under-recognized labour of the racially subordinated or, often, the recent migrant and, in either case, those largely barred from other sections of the labour market (to understand the centrality of those who clean in a time of climate catastrophe and continuing colonial violence, see Vergès, 2019, 2021).

Differential status in the workplace has in part been anchored by the attribution of racialized status. Much of the academic work in this field looks backwards to spaces in which racialized categorization is anchored and, more than anchored, strictly and violently policed through legislation (for some examples, see Tomaskovic-Devey, 1993; Kmec, 2003; for an illuminating discussion of the role of sedimented histories of residential segregation in shaping the racialized outcomes of America's foreclosure crisis, see Rugh and Massey, 2010). These are instances of the overtly racial state where racial categorization becomes the lens through which access to other kinds of social recognition, status goods, and employment, all are refracted (Goldberg, 2001). In this space of the racial state, the racialized differentiation of labour markets has played a central role in establishing and perpetuating what we learn to think of as the wages of whiteness – or, more properly, the wages of racialized supremacy (Roediger, 1991).

The boundaries of belonging and status ensure that different kinds of work are made open only to certain categories of people. Of course, also too predictably, this means that shitty work is allocated almost exclusively to those deemed lesser (Ashforth and Kreiner, 1999). Racialization within the labour market, with the additional anchoring of state or legislative intervention, ensures that only those of subordinated racialized status are likely to do such shitty work and, in turn, that shitty work becomes associated with these groups (Simpson and Simpson, 2018). For most of the time in which labour has organized, this has meant additional barriers to achieving formal organization because of the ways in which racially subordinated status has also disrupted the other components of collective action, including importantly the ability to take collective action without deadly repercussions (for a discussion of the global cleaning industry that suggests the decline of workplace organization arises from a combination of the dismantling of Fordism and the stigmatization and dispersal of workers in 'dirty' industries, see Aguiar and Herod, 2006). At the same time, the impact of associations with shitty work has also played into a kind of respectability politics across the labour movement in many spaces. Sadly, the dignity of labour has often not been a concept that extends to all forms of labour, and the manner in which some forms of work have been racialized and also gendered has limited the inclusion of such tasks within battles about the quality, dignity and safety of work (Jefferys, 2007; Virdee and Grint, 1994).

These earlier periods of labour market demarcation show us the ways in which the active intervention of the racial state serves to disrupt and confound possibilities of cross-racial class solidarity. For us, it is probably more important to consider what happens to the wages of whiteness when these anchoring infrastructures of racialization are no longer so readily available (for an account of the fragility of 'white identification' in sites of neocolonial/neoliberal violence such as Puerto Rico, see Godreau and Bonilla, 2021). My hunch is that the landscape of labour mobilization and racialization is in flux. This does not mean that we are moving towards the longed for transracial/postracial solidarities of utopia. Maybe, maybe not. What is more important to think about is how, in particular moments of battle over the terms of work or the terms of life, techniques and disciplines of racialized differentiation can and cannot disrupt more unusual class solidarities.

My suspicion is we have been living through a time in which the characterization of work has extended the non-standard far beyond the so-called lower echelons of the labour market and far beyond an easy demarcation of racialized status. Yes, it is still the case that shitty work is concentrated in particular subordinated communities. At the same time, access to slightly better regulated and better paid work is far more limited in such communities (Fisher and Nandi, 2015; Thiede and Monnat, 2016). However, an extension of precarity across the whole economy changes the association with racialized subordination of such shitty work forms (despite the rapid global spread of 'non-standard' employment, I note Ritu Vij's important warning that it is the liberal subject of the Global North who has been made 'precarious' and that the description of precaritization risks eliding the long historical experience of insecurity across the Global South; Vij, 2019). What once we may have seen as the psychic wages of whiteness are beginning to lose their anchor in popular consciousness because that kind of work and status is just not available for many people any more (Green and Livanos, 2015, 2017). This means that we are witnessing a whole series of labour struggles around shitty work led by those most deeply precaritized, most likely to be racially subordinated, perhaps marked as other, different and lesser in multiple ways, and the experience of precaritization that is flowing across the labour market allows such struggles to be framed as potentially universal (Però, 2020; Transnational Social Strike Platform, 2019). The degradation of work opens the possibility to unsettle racialized differentiation in the labour market.

If not massification, then what?

Previously, there has been an assumption of massification in most theorizations of the proletariat. It is the massive bringing together of the working class in giant temples of production, smashing up previous social relations and remaking all of our links to one another, that creates the revolutionary class agent. This is an agency based on proximity, shared interests, shared consciousness. All of those elements implicitly rely on an idea of *something like* the factory, or at least the massified labour process of the factory, to occur. And certainly, for much of the twentieth century, work across sectors moved towards economies of scale. However, for some decades now this has not been the direction of travel in how work is remade. In fact, the seemingly endless attempts to categorize which phase of capitalism we are in often returns to this issue of how work is arranged because how work is arranged is a clue about how profit is extracted, which lets us know, albeit indirectly, something about the dominant methods of accumulation in our time.

So it might be helpful to think about massification, and what other than massification we are living through now. Platform capitalism of course, on the one hand, is a much more ambitious and far-reaching mode of massifying the labour force. However, this specification is no longer reliant on a bringing together of workers, or having the same kind of regulation of working life. Instead, platforms enable a kind of dispersal of workers around tasks. There are some key elements to remember here. One element of the battle over working conditions under platform capitalism occurs at the boundary around waged work and social reproduction. Platform capitalism seems to us in this moment where, admittedly, we are fairly early in the journey to seek to remake the worker as not a worker at all. To seek, as far as possible, to offload the responsibilities of the employer and to act as if the employer is in fact no more than another contracting party who happens to have access to key information for that economic task, information that can be farmed out or shared or administered to a range of other independent contractors, previously known as workers. In the process, it is implied, all parties can make a profit, because all parties are entrepreneurs or independent contractors. Why it matters to the employer to deny the employment relation is that this denial cuts to the heart of the small gains that organized labour has achieved over the last hundred years or so. Every small limit on what employers can ask of their workforce is eroded completely if there is no employment relation. In some ways, there is a kind of audacity in the move to say, 'I don't know why you're looking to me for your employment rights. I have nothing to do with your employment.'

These arrangements also blur the boundaries of the working day and the working space by collapsing down the moment of 'not employment' to each task undertaken. The variety of practices used by Amazon, by Uber, by Lyft or by Deliveroo seek to push all elements of not only social reproduction but also the underpinning of so-called productive work into the realm of the social reproduction of the worker (Means and Seiner, 2015). We have been used to a system in which the employer provides the context and the time necessary for that task to take place. This might look like a workplace with an understanding by all parties of when the working day begins and ends, battles around working time notwithstanding, or when different shifts begin and end. It might include a place where workers may go to undertake those tasks, the tasks which are paid work, unlike other things in their lives. Within that place, there may be an acceptance that the employer will provide equipment necessary to undertake the task; the materials necessary to produce whatever may or may not be being produced; and the administrative infrastructure to allocate tasks and to mediate the relations between workers in the chain of production or whatever. While in the chain of production, there may have been sufficient facilities for workers to fulfil their bodily functions during the working day, not only toilets, but also some space to rest, an opportunity to eat and drink, sufficient heat and light, as necessary for the task. Previously we might have expected business considerations to lead to at least some minimal maintenance of the building to ensure the safety of the workforce and of the valuable investment and production of the employer.

Of course, every element of that list has been a point of struggle since before industrialized work began, and the outcomes of those struggles have been very uneven. I do not mean to suggest that there was a previous moment of civil industrialized work which we must now mourn. Instead, I want to suggest that these elements of the time and space of work, of the material infrastructure of work, the health and safety measures around work, are precisely the aspects that reveal the variegated terrain of racial capitalism. The uneven application or reach of regulatory law is itself an indication of the map of racialized division, or at least of variable entitlement. What is challenging for us now is the level of the onslaught on the regulation of working spaces. To be clear, what I am describing is the manner in which platform capitalism is also, at least at the initial moments, an attack on the wages of whiteness. All of those small differentials between truly shitty and slightly less shitty work have been the stuff of mythologies of a labour aristocracy and, for our purposes, for the fraction of the working class who can be incorporated into the national story. Take that away, and what does whiteness mean?

What changes in our time

Whereas the supported indebtedness of Fordist expansion took place alongside a massification of production and an accompanying concentration of residence, the indebtedness of our moment is more dispersed and dispersing (for a summary of the crisis of Fordism as a global crisis and paradigm shift in the global economy, see Lipietz, 1985). In the shift away from production as the prime organizing activity of economic space, towards a greater role for the complex and interdependent networks of logistics (defined so broadly that perhaps all life can be included here), the disciplinary impacts of indebtedness also alter, at least somewhat.

Central to this different dispersal of indebted populations is the manner in which debt is recorded and enforced. Indebtedness requires entry to the most punitive modes of data sharing – what is owed by whom joining the other elements of our data footprint and the anticipatory economy that thrives on predicting where the opportunity for profit will arise (for a discussion of the moral hazards arising with the datafication of lending, see Aggarwal, 2022). As was learned so painfully through the 2008 crash, patterns of debt, including debt arising from lending calculated to be unpayable, also offer opportunities for future profit (on the rise of the subprime lending industry, see Cutts and Van Order, 2005). Racialized differentiation can be folded into forms of speculation reliant on predicting who may be a poor debtor – with poor debtors here transformed into a different and often lucrative opportunity for predatory lenders. As these are forms of indebtedness structured to force some populations into varieties of debt bondage or other highly constrained situations, we might consider the extension of indebtedness on punitive terms as a form of carceral practice through economic means (on systemic racism in the US housing market which creates the landscape for predatory lending, see Dickerson, 2020; on the disproportionate impact of the subprime crisis on minoritized communities, see Powell and Rogers, 2013).

In a terrible echo of an earlier era of vagabondage, the cutting free from one way of maintaining life also throws up, again, intertwined modes of punitive class violence, with class violence indicating here the complex machinery of punishment, exploitation and limit, as described in another context by Widick (1989). Perhaps we are living through an adaptation in the disciplines of proletarianization, with populations dispersed as a result of uncertain access to work, extreme degradation of resources as some sectors transition out of existence, and an overall sense of understandable panic in the face of climate emergency. In this moment of turbulence, capital perhaps must work to ensure the disciplines of proletarianization persist – if not through wagedness necessarily, at least through a variety of means that tie the remaking of human life to the remaking of capital.

Instead of imaging racial capitalism as the replenishment of longstanding racialized divisions within an economic map where the massified productive economy is surrounded by less enfranchised wastelands, we might picture how indebtedness seeps into carcerality – with every encounter with authority including an assessment of the 'guilt' and/or 'potential' of the indebted.

The paucity of standard work, alongside crises in other routes to access the means of life, brings different populations to indebtedness. This encompasses rural populations no longer able to sustain life through previous agricultural practices and/or pushed off land (Sajjad and Chauhan, 2012; Hall, 2013); migrant workers both when transitioning between locations and sectors and during the everyday hustle of life when the only economy is informal (LeBaron, 2014; Hoang, 2020); those clinging to standard work, but with so great a decline in the real value of wages that debt must make up the shortfall (Roberts and Soederberg, 2014); those seeking to survive in spaces of crisis, with this spanning economic collapse, climate emergency, war and repression (Gallagher and Hartley, 2017); those caring for aging or sick or disabled dependants without access to meaningful social goods; those trying to retain their former normalcy in a collapsing metropolis; and those seeking to fashion a life-raft or an escape route.

The extension of indebtedness to create conditions to monetize all instances of human desperation, of course, also leads to a reaffirmation of patterns of racialized dispossession. Sedimented histories of dispossession shape the location and leverage of today. Levels of desperation reflect the cumulative impact of such dispossession, both in the frailty of bodies and infrastructures of life and in the barriers to accessing security or assistance. In the context of long-established landscapes of racial capitalism, the transformation into modes of economic life where jobs transmute into tasks, where employers disguise themselves while assembling massive platforms, and where we seem to see an expansion of the absolute immiseration of proletarianization but without any recuperation into (identifiable) structures of massification and wagedness, indebtedness threatens bondedness. For some, this is a bond that must be carried into their future life, limiting what and where the debtor can be or go. For others, the bond is carried by the household, so if the escape to the metropolis fails (whether by leaky boat or deportation machine), the household becomes held in the dangerous bond of indebtedness (O'Connell-Davidson, 2013). For too many, the desperation to access the means of life ties them into varieties of dubious contract where, against all logic, they are deemed to have sold themselves or to have accrued debt from enjoying the privilege of working (Barrientos, 2013). The nets of bordering and carcerality tie the new wretched of the earth into these impossible contracts – rendering them always already illegitimate, never deserving of protection (Shelley, 2007).

4

Borders – Small Adaptations in Familiar Techniques of Racial Capitalism

There is a long history of regarding the placing, containment and move-ment of populations at the behest of capital as indicative of the need to control and discipline labour power (Kleinman, 2003; Castles, 2011). Humans, in this telling, become reduced to labour power and potential labour power, and it is only this aspect of human life that informs the disciplinary organization of populations by or for capital. As a way of thinking, this approach has yielded some useful insights, and the discussion of this chapter relies heavily on such literature. However, in our attempt to see the puzzle of a changing racial capitalism, we also think again of how we might understand bordering as a technique of population placing that contributes to the remaking of capital beyond the control and disciplining of labour markets.

What is new about bordering?

The familiarity of bordering as a technique of racialized state violence can suggest that the detail of bordering practices remains constant. Perhaps we battle about this or that aspect, winning a little more dignity here, losing the right to be treated as human there, but the overall logic of the border has become embedded in the logic of political common-sense. Few now question whether 'migration' is an issue requiring political intervention and response.

This chapter argues that, within this well-established familiarity, we also see some adaptations in the political arrangements around bordering. My interest is in the mutation of bordering that arises in a time of transnational cooperation in bordering practices. We may be familiar with softer precursors such as Schengen and its collaborative discipline of shared bordering across the European Union and, at the same time, remind ourselves that Schengen disguised the emergence of Fortress Europe (to be reminded of the workings of this double movement, see Kofman and Sales, 1992; Bia, 2004). However, the coupling of bordering with sovereignty – a coupling asserted increasingly loudly – can obscure the extent to which bordering is a matter of interstate negotiation, with all the imbalances and compromises that entails.

The increasing emergence of interstate arrangements of bordering unsettles some of the previous common-sense around immigration control. In their account of the emergence of greater interstate agreements regarding immigration, Hansen, Koehler and Money (2011) formulate five hypotheses: a functional need for cooperation; a convergence of policy goals; a system of incentives and/or sanctions to secure adherence from all parties; without a system of incentives/sanctions, any cooperation will be informal and 'non-binding'; and, their final hypothesis, 'migration is likely to become linked to negotiations over preferential trade agreements when clandestine immigration is a substantial policy problem that cannot be addressed unilaterally' (Hansen et al., 2011: 11). Hansen and his colleagues present 'migration' as a neutral policy agenda, seeking to encompass both the states erecting barriers to inward movement and those trying to regulate and support outward movement. Instead of the pretence of a logical and 'fair' distinction between citizen and foreigner, interstate arrangements reveal the negotiations needed to identify the undesirable migrant. Instead of the in or out logics of the bordering nation, interstate cooperation necessarily calls into play a much more varied and complicated set of designations.

I do not suggest that this shift in logics of bordering takes place without any difficulty. Brexit, for example, has revealed the tensions between state-led xeno-racism, which seeks to allow movement for some in order to ensure bordering/incarceration/expulsion for others, and popular xeno-racism, which resents the erosion of perceived status and privilege associated with citizenship. For popular xeno-racism, 'foreigner' remains the counter-term that gives value to a citizenship so naturalized that it does not need to be documented. However, the negotiations between states to create cooperative machineries of containment and expulsion require an enhanced language of entitlement and disentitlement – being 'foreign' in itself is not enough; now we must learn to identify types and degrees of foreignness (for an instructive account of how this process plays out to multiply legalistic categorization and obscure or limit the rights of migrants, see Mourão Permoser, 2017). The machinery of bordering continues to operate as a set of mechanisms to anchor differential entitlement across the landscape of everyday life, conjuring up an ever-changing array of statuses, each translating into an approximation of identity and something close to raciality when dispersed through the interactions of everyday life (Forkert et al., 2020).

Why we should move beyond the 'age of migration' framework

As the twenty-first century proceeds, widespread and justified alarm about the extent and impact of climate catastrophe extends to encompass concerns about forced migration triggered by climate change. We are warned to expect 1 billion climate refugees by 2050 (Trimarchi and Gleim, 2020), with this projected number rising as time goes on. Whether or not there is widespread understanding of how climate catastrophe leads to population displacement, the broader sense that a greater proportion of the world is on the move and in circumstances not of their own choosing seems to have seeped into popular consciousness. This has included detailed discussion from the World Bank on likely numbers of people displaced by climate change within their nations, and the economic consequences of this (Clement et al., 2021), and signalling from the IMF that questions of global governance arise in the face of such widespread migration (Godefroid, 2021).

The world that is emerging is one where movement, and movement that, if not forced by persecution, is forced by circumstances, becomes a widespread experience. In response, there have been calls to address, with some urgency, the questions thrown up by a world on the move, including in the realms of health (Abubakar et al., 2018), social policy (Gingrich and Köngeter, 2017), and the alarming convergence of health, economic and climate crises (Vertovec, 2020). While the latter decades of the twentieth century already demonstrated the challenges of the so-called age of migration (de Haan et al, 2019), as the scale and depth of the challenges arising from climate crisis have become more apparent, the destabilizing impact of population movement on the arrangements of states and of business also has become a more urgent question of global migration governance (Betts, 2011).

We are entering an era where non-mobility no longer operates as the default norm. In fact, as scholars of migration have argued, once we move our gaze from cross-border movement to movement within territories, we may understand we have been in this phase for some time (for an overview of internal migration intensities across the world, see Bell et al., 2015). Such a realization reframes our thinking about the so-called response to the challenge or crisis of migration. Instead of regarding bordering policy and practice as an emergency response to a phenomenon understood as a crisis external to and apart from the normal business of states, we might understand the attempts to govern population movement as a shift in the spatial reach of (imagined) sovereignty. The attempts, often complex and/or apparently ineffective, to manage the movement of people on routes towards or spaces adjacent to a state's borders extend the aspirations of sovereignty beyond the sovereign space (for a discussion of the disruptive impact of national law on attempts to formulate and follow international law on migration, see Schindlmayr, 2003). Perhaps predictably, then, bordering increasingly describes a set of state-led actions that must be coordinated with other authorities, most often other states (Staring and van Swaaningen, 2021).

Bordering erects barriers against entry and machineries of surveillance designed to capture and expel those targeted as irregular or undocumented or undesirable (Parker and Adler-Nissen, 2012). Once states embark on interstate arrangements for bordering, the logic of insider and outsider is unsettled – in particular, the logic of xeno-racism. Scholarly research uncovering the working of the border in everyday life points to the manner in which state machineries coalesce with vernacular racisms to maximize the discomfort of those deemed irregular (Yuval-Davis et al., 2018; Forkert et al., 2020). In the process, the practices of the border squat within wider habits of racism from both state and society, extending the surveillance and suspicion to other racially minoritized groups (Yuval-Davis et al., 2019). However, as the machineries of bordering exclusion and containment become increasingly collaborative across states, the spectre of the unwanted foreigner also becomes less easily folded back into national stories of aversion. Instead, we see the emergence of a variety of global or regional 'foreigners' – Syrians and Rohingya, a return of the desperate Afghan, a normalization of the use of 'refugees' as an inclusive and racialized slur (Armas and Ruiz, 2021). This might involve an adaptation of popular racisms to accommodate the context of transnational bordering regimes, including through a stretching of established national racisms to take in new or adapted categories of racialized scapegoat (for a discussion of the emergence of distinct racism against Syrians, see Ozduzen et al., 2021).

Too often we can discuss the politicization of immigration as if national belonging is an automatic and natural experience, with aversion to the foreign other as equally automatic and natural. This has been an underlying logic in the mobilizations of the far right across Europe and elsewhere (for an examination of the communications strategies of the European far right on this issue, see Gould, 2010). Bordering, then, presented as the policy response to the overfocus on local nationalism expressed as xeno-racism, has had consequences for those attempting to mobilize against borders and for free movement. If borders are presented as an understandable, if misleading, response to the experience of aversive racism towards foreigners, then we challenge borders by appeasing and reassuring those suffering from such aversive sentiments. If borders are presented as tactical gestures designed to appeal to an anti-migrant electorate, then we challenge borders by re-educating the electorate to identify other, more apt, causes for their dissatisfaction than migrants. If, however, borders are presented as an indication of a realignment among the global ruling class and a set of agreements and accommodations designed to defend and maintain their class interests – what then?

The manner and content of attempts to institute transnational cooperation in bordering reveals the multiple interests in play.

- In some regions, we see the framing of 'human security' as a matter demanding interstate cooperation, with migration included alongside HIV and 'trafficking' as a risk to be managed and contained. Akaha (2019) suggests that this perception of urgent risk has opened moves towards cooperation between the nations of ASEAN and other East Asian countries, but that the weak adherence or antagonism towards international legal norms around the rights of migrants militate against more systemized cooperation.
- In others, we see a tussle over the leverage that might be achieved in other aspects of foreign policy through cooperation (or non-cooperation) on migration. The Visegrád Group – the Czech Republic, Hungary, Poland and Slovakia – drew anger from their close and powerful neighbour, the European Union, on the issue of refusing entry to those fleeing Syria. Both the Three Seas Initiative, to build economic cooperation between the north and south of Central Europe, and, more pointedly, the Slavkov Triangle of the Czech

Republic, Slovakia and Austria seek to achieve models of cooperation on migration and bordering that enhance and complement the free movement arrangements of the European Union while isolating threatening and uncooperative actors such as Hungary under Orbán (Jančošekovà, 2017).

- In still others, we see attempts to enable free movement for nationals of partner nations as part of enhancing economic growth and cooperation. The ECOWAS Common Approach on Migration to support movement between West African nations reflects such a goal, despite challenges arising from uneven institutional capacity (Attoh and Ishola, 2021). We might consider the ongoing and always fragile experiment with free movement with the European Union as a similar project (Recchi, 2015).

Bordering has become much more openly an aspect of foreign policy – explicitly linked to matters of security in both national and international rhetoric (Tucker, 2019; Barbé and Morillas, 2019). At the same time, local elites continue to battle to capture and retain control of the local state, although such control may, paradoxically, be the ability to make a deal about borders and migrants with a more powerful nation or bloc. The ability to control populations in movement becomes a kind of inter-state currency in the geopolitics of the twenty-first century.

The detail of regional cooperative arrangements reveals a dance between opportunistic responses to strands of populist nationalism among local/national populations and the pursuit of class interests across states. What is more difficult to understand is how these combined local interests come to be articulated in a formation that expresses a larger, non-local, if not yet global, set of interests. One approach to this mystery is to revisit the terms of racial capitalism. In my quest to persuade the reader that it is better to view challenges as puzzles, perhaps we might open the possibility that the complex accommodations of international collaborative bordering also represent a kind of mystery to be deciphered.

Interstate cooperation and the underprotection of populations in movement

The implementation of bordering practices has expanded to become a central aspect of relations between states (Shire, 2020). Inevitably, these negotiations and collaborations reflect the unevenness of resources and influence.

> The current system allows immigrant-receiving countries (core countries) to exert influence over changes to internal laws and policies of their neighboring, transit, and immigrant-sending countries (periphery countries). In doing so, core countries prevent not only immigration into their own territories, but the entirety of the migration movement. In a sense, they coopt the interests and policies of periphery countries, making them part of the core's regulatory system and converting them into a semi-periphery. (Stankovic, 2021: 258)

Through one lens, we might consider the ability to impose bordering machineries on another state as an aspect of our moment of neocolonialism. The ability to impose 'agreements' which cast other states into the position of the semi-periphery demonstrates domination of a kind, but this is not the neocolonialism of resource capture (for an account of neocolonial and post-Soviet regimes of labour control, see Bolokan, 2020). We might think of bordering agreements, however uneven in their power dynamics, as instruments designed to contain or manage risk. In this, migrants become akin to other portable risks, such as industrial waste (Clapp, 1994). Yet the irrationality of xeno-racism, including in its performative modes, runs alongside such expressions of apparent pragmatism (for a discussion of the racialized performance of neocolonial violence through deportation, see Fernández Bessa and Brandariz García, 2018). Bordering reveals some core contradictions of the contemporary state, torn between the theatre of sovereignty and the imperatives of pursuing class interests. As a result, we see highly amplified performances of expulsion operate alongside differently instrumental and often hidden delimitations of movement and rights leading to entry or movement, but with diminished status and protection. This combination of shouted racism with machineries that enable movement at the cost of social and legal status creates a global class of irregular migrants as systematically under- and unprotected populations.

What about cheaper labour?

I understand that some will ask why this would be the case. Surely all capitalists have an interest in access to cheap(er) labour and/or a desire to discipline domestic populations through nationalist rhetoric. Yet, at the same time, we see corporate defences of free(r) movement. 'Business leaders' have become increasingly vocal in their support of mobility for migrant labour. At the very least, these various pronouncements (often in bad faith) reveal the tensions among members of the dominant class on the issue of population movement. The point here is to understand that bordering, in itself, may not represent a straightforward asset to capital within one nation or across national spaces. Despite the justified complaints that there is always freedom of movement for capital but not for workers, the machinery of bordering may be better understood as arising from struggles within the capitalist class. And, as is so often the case, the temporary accommodations reached as an outcome of this moment of battling for ascendance reveal something of the direction of travel and, perhaps, of the class fraction likely to become dominant.

The ILO confirms longstanding tendencies in the employment experience of migrant workers, including a continuing inequality in wages that is difficult to explain. This includes very significant differences in average wages for migrant workers across forty-nine countries, with increasing wage gaps for low-skilled workers; a double wage penalty for women migrant workers, estimated as 20.9 per cent in high-income countries; and a greater negative impact on employment opportunities and wages for migrant workers in the aftermath of Covid-19 (Amo-Agyei, 2020). The notable exception to this overall trend to depress migrant workers' wages arises with the higher than average wages earned by migrant workers in low-income countries. This, however, appears to arise from the impact of relatively small numbers of very highly paid 'ex-pat' workers pulling up the average migrant wage very considerably. We understand the tendency for migrant workers to receive lower wages, both in contexts of difficult or limited movement and/or in systems where migrants are subordinated (for an influential attempt to unpack this 'vulnerability', see Jayaweera and Anderson, 2008; for a discussion of the particularity of labour migration, see Anderson, 2007). Implicitly, we may have understood this widespread outcome as an indication that global bordering regimes, whether or not coordinated between states, represent an attack on the global working class. Such an assumption, however, rests on a view of the world as not in movement – so it is those in movement who represent an opportunity for employers to segment the labour market and undercut wages. In our world, where the terms of stasis and the push to movement are in flux, perhaps these assumptions should be revisited.

What next after the 'international division of labour'?

There has been a reframing of the terms of the international division of labour, arising in the post-1991 period of the ascendance of 'the West', registering the impact of 'globalization', itself a term lodged in a very particular moment of debate (for some formative debates, see Fröbel et al., 1978; Cohen, 1988). Mittelman summarizes the key components of this reconceptualization:

> The familiar imagery of a core, semiperiphery, and periphery no longer applies to a new structure that envelops both vertically integrated regional divisions of labour based on the distinctive comparative advantages of different locations, and horizontally diversified networks which extend their activities into neighbouring countries as part of corporate strategies of diversification and globalisation. The old categories do not capture the intricacy of the integration of the world economy as well as the ways it constrains all regions and states to adjust to transnational capital. The global transformation now underway not only slices across former divisions of labour and geographically reorganises economic activities, but also limits state autonomy and infringes sovereignty. (Mittelman, 1995: 273)

The description helps us to imagine the spatial arrangements of a globally connected economy in constant motion. In the process, we are reminded of those other key elements of early globalization debates: a questioning of the power and reach of nation-states (Mann, 1997; Hirst and Thompson, 1995) and the demand to expand our analysis to consider the geographical reach and influence of emerging corporate forms (Suwandi and Foster, 2016). In fact, the claims about the diminishment of state sovereignty no longer seem so persuasive (for a discussion of the manner in which globalization remakes varieties of sovereignty that were never uniform and that always encompassed arrangements enacted by an array of parties, see Agnew, 2017). Writing in an earlier moment, Mittelman proposes an extension to the debate between analysts of the International Division of Labour (IDL) and the New International Division of Labour (NIDL), using the term Global Division of Labour (GDL). The Global Division of Labour, in this account, is remade by the movement of people and the restructuring of commodity chains:

> One element of reordering this hierarchical system is massive transfers of population from the Third World, Eastern Europe, and the former Soviet Union to the advanced capitalist countries, though there are also significant migratory flows within the South. Acting as magnets attracting imports of labour, global commodity chains form networks that

interlink multiple production processes as well as buyers and sellers. (Mittelman, 1995: 273)

Although this account is from an earlier phase of the analysis of globalization, the shift is away from an idea of an 'international division of labour' based around core and periphery towards one where we must consider 'multiple production processes' and a sense that buyers, sellers and production of all things spans the world in a multi-directional network. This shift in conceptualization allows us to imagine bordering as more than a wall around the rich world, however much it may continue to be this as well. With this shift, we can articulate more clearly the manner in which global bordering practices operate as a machinery through which populations are managed, with movement enabled or prevented, according to tightly delimited routes, temporalities and points of stasis. If the emerging world of racial capitalism operates through a system of differentiation of populations that is dispersed and tied far less to national logics, then this global machinery of bordering, despite the fragility and changeability of its arrangements, surely must be part of it.

This is not to say that matters of employment and the disciplining of labour are not enmeshed in bordering practices. No one now engaged in seeking to understand and dismantle borders should be unaware of the role of bordering practices as a technique stratifying labour markets through precaritization via irregular status (Anderson, 2010; Paret and Gleeson, 2016). This insight has transformed labour movement organizing around migrant rights, pointing to how intertwined the experiences of bordering and of precarious work have become (for a UK example, see IWGB, 2022).

However, the remaking of global relations through bordering and related interventions to limit and direct the routes of movement and containment across the globe suggests something more than a disciplining of labour markets. At the very least, we must be open to the possibility that bordering points us to an expanded conceptualization of the use of human life to capital. This might be regarded as a return to a central insight of the analysis of racial capitalism – that capital remakes itself by positioning humans as a variety of economic statuses and roles. Although the question of who can work for wages and where is important, it is not the only consideration. Humans might be subordinated to the imperatives of capital through a number of techniques, not only wagedness but also forced labour and bondedness, varieties of social reproduction and varieties of extraction, through the workplace and the place of non-work. If we understand the remaking of global capital to include, increasingly, modes of accumulation that expand or bypass the extractions of wagedness, then bordering on a global scale might be understood as a set of processes redistributing (often desperate) populations into this more extensive set of positionings. Questions of labour markets may be incorporated within this redistribution, including the familiar dirty and dangerous labours so often earmarked for those wilfully under- or unprotected roles in the workplace (Olvera, 2017). However, the violently policed positioning by borders should be understood in our time as pertaining to more than labour markets. If the question of how our lives are modified as resources for the remaking of capital extends to the arenas opened by platforms and indebtedness, then the question of who may move, and when, where and how, should be reframed to consider why some routes of movement and stasis may render populations legible and valuable.

Perhaps bordering in our moment reveals more starkly who can be regarded as future labour power and who cannot. Various civilizational discourses and other thinly veiled (if veiled at all) racisms deployed to argue for the apparent reasonableness of exclusionary bordering might be regarded as an instance of this (see, for example, the discussion of imagined civilizational threat as relating to real deaths and, importantly, real *births*, in Bialasiewicz, 2006; Carr, 2006, also offers a sobering but useful account of the attempt to essentialize cultural identity and delimit access to movement or to any rights on this basis). However, we might note that bordering both renders some disposable, sometimes in the most horrific of ways, disappearing people into open prisons or facilitating their deaths in the sea or in the desert (McMahon and Sigona, 2021; Heller and Pécoud, 2020; De Genova, 2021) and also parks some populations in an attempt to halt and contain particular migration routes (for an account of informal migrant camps as embodying legacies of empire, see Davies and Isakjee, 2019).

If we are trying to understand the shift into a global capital of logistics, then the agreements and instances of violence that together shape a global system of borders, routes and places of containment might be understood as a parallel to the global logistical order. Perhaps each is a component or branch of the other.

What if borders are not about nations and nationalism? Or, at least, not primarily?

The critique of bordering practices has tended to focus, understandably, on the place of popular nationalisms. The question of bordering has become both a question of the edge of the state and a question of how to dispossess some within the boundaries of the state. Whereas we have become schooled in understanding the incursion of bordering practices into the interior of national space (see Yuval-Davis et al., 2019), until recently this remained a formation targeting the foreign(er). Within this, we might understand that 'foreignness' was its own racialized fiction and highly moveable, with longstanding residents vulnerable to the accusation of non-belonging and subject to the violences suffered by those deemed not to belong (for a collection of pieces uncovering the machinery of unbelonging in play when groups are targeted for internment, a process operating through placing some outside of due process, see Myers and Moshenska, 2011). What changes in our time – or, perhaps, what returns – are processes to render some stateless and therefore out of place and vulnerable to bordering, despite not falling into more familiar categorizations of migrant or foreigner (to understand something of the process by which the implied reciprocity between sovereign and subject is eroded, see Pillai and Williams, 2017). This is not new, of course. If anything, it is textbook genocidal practice. However, to anticipate the cry that we are beyond such things and have learned better than the inhumanity of our forebears, let us note that, in the first decades of the twenty-first century, practices of bordering also become techniques of racialized violence against those who have never moved (for a detailed and illuminating discussion of India's recent histories of contested citizenship and belonging, see Roy, 2022; for a discussion of citizenship-stripping in Australia, Canada and the UK, see Pillai and Williams, 2017).

The migrant corridor and other fictional non-territories

Perhaps we are moving beyond imagining a jigsaw of adjoining nation-states, with the exercise of sovereignty saturating the space and with the end of one sovereign power signalling the opening of another. Increasingly, accounts of movement and forced stasis stretch towards other additional ways of conceptualizing the spatial terrain of migration (for a discussion of methodological nationalism in migration studies, see Wimmer and Glick Schiller, 2002).

There is already a considerable literature on the camp – with all of its implications of being on the border but outside the reach of sovereign space (Diken and Laustsen, 2005; Minca, 2015; Sigona, 2015). We have learned to understand the wilful construction of spaces of exception as an accompaniment to displays of sovereignty (for an overview of these debates, see Nair, 2021). However, and despite the importance of these insights, perhaps we have been encouraged to imagine the world of people in movement as segmented into spaces of sovereignty and spaces of exception. When we consider the practices arising from cooperation and/or agreements between states, we bring into play something other than this binary.

In fact, an important aspect of attempts to reorder global movement has been through an ordering of the spaces and practices between states. Of course, there is another strain of fictionality here. Whereas fictions of sovereignty imagine the world as tidily full of a jigsaw of adjacent sovereignties where no space falls outside the authority and order of some or other sovereign power, fictions of exception imagine a limit to the responsibility of states. Sometimes these second fictions intersect with tussles to offload responsibilities under international law, casting those fleeing into an unchartable void between sovereign spaces. It is this imaginary geography of spaces in between despite the lack of territory that fits this description.

However, and despite the considerable insights generated through scholarly excavation of a variety of spaces of exception, arrangements that create additional spatial imaginaries reveal the logics of collaborative bordering. In these arrangements we comprehend the spatial trajectory of migration, with agreements seeking to determine and delineate corridors or pathways (Pastore, 2019; van Reekum, 2016). In the emerging policy language of the migrant corridor, the term is presented as a neutral device to map a space of interchange.

'Corridors are used as a framing device and metaphor to understand the movement of people, goods, money, knowledge and skills between two places with sociocultural, economic, political and historical dynamics that transcend national borders' (MIDEQ, n.d.). This definition arises from a project to analyse South to South migration routes, including arrangements through which people might conduct their lives moving back and forth across one or more border. The implication is that the corridor represents a collaboration between equals, without imposition or inducement from either party. Yet despite this forwarding of the cooperative, MIDEQ's account of migration corridors includes a strong implication that governance arrangements of such practices of movement represent an example of the extra-sovereign.

The space of the migration corridor, a space that can be both elastic and shifting, identifies most of all the enabled route between two locations, mainly states, with a quiet acknowledgement that there are multiple factors that smooth movement along this 'corridor' – that is, factors that do not exist across all the possibilities of migratory space. The corridor, then, is a metaphor for a route that has other enabling factors. Much of the time, it is not a corridor at all and may not include the sense of unitary routes and stepping from one state to another. Spaan and van Naerssen (2017) point to the broader literature on migration industries as a lens through which to comprehend the notion of the corridor. The migration industry (MI), in this account, spans the illicit and the official, including both the services that prey on desperation in the face of ever-tightening border controls and varieties of official labour brokerages. At the same time, the authors point to the very particular tactics associated with outsourcing bordering machineries, as this process also externalizes responsibility for people if they are in movement:

> The appointment of non-state actors to administer some aspects of the sifting and selective mobility of bordering practices, such as the management of flows of migrant labour, reveals various functions of MI, namely (1) enticement, (2) facilitation and (3) control. As promoters, facilitators, organisers and controllers of migration flow, MI sets the conditions and boundaries of action. (Spaan and van Naerssen, 2017: 5)

This is a complex and multifaceted machinery, one poorly encompassed by the metaphor of the border. In fact, what is described as the migration industry here is focused as much on moving people to meet particular imperatives as it is on preventing entry. The addition of the concepts of enticement and facilitation remakes the available vocabulary of immigration control. The exercise of power and the demonstration of sovereignty rests, of course, on the ability to define the terms of movement (for more on transnational migration markets, see Shire, 2020).

The metaphor of the corridor implies a kind of order and ease of movement if within this designated route. However, the ascendance of the concept of the corridor here comes alongside the global experience of very large and very desperate flows of migration, often fleeing conflict but also increasingly fleeing the impact of climate catastrophe, whether direct or indirect. It is in this context that Bada and Feldmann (2019) suggest that the changing phenomenon of the migration corridor reveals the uncertain distinction between forced and voluntary migration in this moment, not least due to the numbers of people traversing in the corridor as 'survival migrants', a term they explain as 'people who leave their communities of residence to protect fundamental rights (life, liberty and physical integrity) threatened by violence, lack of economic prospects and/or environmental degradation' (ibid.: 58).

The concept of the survival migrant brings together the status of the refugee, including emerging understandings of climate refugees, with other movements borne of desperation, whether a desperation arising from a flight from violence or from a lack of access to the means of life. Implicit in Bada and Feldmann's account is the manner in which agreements about 'corridors' reveal collaborative arrangements by states seeking to limit or avoid their responsibilities under international law. The device of the 'corridor' presents an opportunity to expel some responsibilities beyond the space of sovereignty while retaining some collaborative management.

Alongside these collaborations to create ways of ordering spaces of population movement while retaining something of the fiction of the state of exception, as if desperate people move through spaces deemed 'corridors' or 'routes' but without ever touching spaces of sovereignty where their plight might become a responsibility of the sovereign power, we also see pretences of ordering that play a different performative function.

Whereas we have become accustomed to the rhetoric and practices of bordering as presented to domestic audiences, embodying one or other variety of populist nationalism, the performance of bordering for other states may call into play other considerations. There is, clearly, an element of seeking to demonstrate institutional competence. The display of constructing and administering a bordering machinery serves, in our time, to confirm particular state-like capacities. Perhaps the symbolic weight previously given to the administration of elections has passed to the administration of borders. Only those able and willing to contribute to the global machinery of border controls can enter the alliance of the civilized. This may include demonstrating an ability to corral (irregular) migrants into particular routes and/or rendering those in movement legible and/or promising to safeguard the territory of other (more powerful) states from unwanted incursions by those in movement. The theatricality with which any of these aspects are undertaken indicates their value in an arena of international political display.

The mutation of our time is the shift towards alliances of bordering, rendering bordering an extra-sovereign process. This raises some awkward questions for those seeking to assert national authority. If a state cannot manage its bordering practices without entering into a contract of cooperation, perhaps this can be accommodated as a mode of contemporary sovereignty. However, if a state finds that its bordering practices are determined by other, more powerful entities, the claim of sovereignty becomes less convincing. This is the argument forwarded by Stankovic above – without measures or the ability to regulate interactions between states, cooperative bordering becomes another aspect of peripheralization. We might go so far as to suggest that the ability to impose a particular bordering regime on neighbours, allies and others should be understood as a marker of geopolitical ascendance in our time.

Modes of cooperative bordering

To help us to map the terrain, let us consider the varieties of bordering cooperation beng enacted now. Obviously, this taxonomy does not exhaust the possibilities of the practice – but it does give some clues about the motivations and materialities shaping such transnational arrangements in this moment.

1 Folding immigration controls into crime or security

Since Stumpf (2006) coined the phrase 'crimmigration' to summarize the increasing convergence of criminal law and immigration law in a US context, there has been an exponential increase in similar measures across the world (for examples from Europe, see van der Woude et al., 2017; for Australia, see Billings, 2019). Bowling and Westenra argue that this convergence enables greater linkages between local and global systems of policing and bordering: 'The pursuit of the criminalized immigrant – a globally recognized "folk devil" – encourages communication, collaboration and coordination across a range of surveillant, coercive, punitive and carceral institutions in many countries' (2020: 3).

Perhaps the most established formulation of border collaboration has taken place under the cover of controlling crime or safeguarding national security. Between 1995 and 2000, the United States established bilateral agreements with twenty-nine states across the Caribbean and Latin America to collaborate to prevent the 'smuggling' of drugs and people. We might understand this phase of intensive diplomatic activity as a precursor to our moment of collaborative bordering. However, of course, this late twentieth-century rush represented an extension (or imposition) of US interests onto other states (Kramek, 2000). The approach established by the United States has led to 'agreements' which are 'essentially a compromise where the foreign State loses some sovereignty in exchange for limited security and protection by the United States against illicit traffickers ... it certainly jeopardizes long-term regional cooperation' (ibid.: 146).

The emergence of cross-national arrangements explicitly bringing together immigration control and other forms of policing of crime has led to so-called crimmigration – an increasing interpenetration of immigration enforcement and criminal law. In this framing, the movement of people is regarded as a criminal justice risk in itself, as breaches of immigration law come to be seen as affronts and perhaps as outright acts of violence against the state imagined as a form of personhood in which all citizens are incarnated. In addition, migrants are presented as more inclined to criminality, whether as a result of vulnerability or cultural predisposition (for an account of the impact of the belief that migrants are a criminal threat among the British population, see Stansfield and Stone, 2018). The emergence of crimmigration practices has ushered in aspects of bordering that now seem all but immoveable. For example, immigration detention in the United States begins in the 1980s as a supposed response to the threat of drug trafficking, adding the new phraseology of 'aggravated felony' as a trigger for automatic detention, but continues as a component of the state's bordering repertoire for all migrants (García-Hernández, 2018).

The machineries of bordering in single states and in collaborative agreements between states highlight the threat of criminal activity as a central justification for preventing and ordering movement. Such framings also merge now into machineries of anti-terrorism, a form of defensive practices which explicitly reference matters of nationality and culture when outlining 'threats'. One way or another, crimmigration serves as a way to turn migrants into a global threat, and one that it is justified to contain or expel.

2 The outsourcing of bordering arrangements to another territory

The strange and frightening innovations in bordering practices devised by Australia have been central to how we are able to think about this practice. As an early proponent of detention as a method to deter irregular migrants, Australia has had a system of immigration detention since 1992, with management of the detention centres outsourced to private companies from 1996 (for a discussion of 'offshoring' as a state practice, see Andrew and Eden, 2011).

> In 2001, the Howard government passed legislation that allowed them to excise certain external territories from their migration zone, including Ashmore, Cartier, Christmas and Cocos Islands. In the excised zone an 'unauthorised' arrival has no right to apply for a visa to stay in Australia, instead they are permitted to apply for refugee status with the UNHCR and asylum seekers have no recourse to Australian courts. (Ibid.: 221)

The invention of this zone of excision laid the basis for a bordering regime increasingly notable for its displacement of the border beyond its own national shores.

The arrangement with Papua New Guinea, leading to the detention there of those seeking asylum in Australia, is one precursor for the rich world's fantastical belief that unwanted migrants can be disappeared. Despite the ending of the agreement with Papua New Guinea (BBC News, 2021), Australia remains committed to offshoring the processing and detention of those seeking to enter Australia via irregular routes. This desire to offshore legal and perhaps moral responsibilities towards people in movement and refugees in particular can be seen in recurrent proposals such as building floating detention centres that can be housed at sea; forcing those in movement back to the 'first safe country' to make any application to regularize their status (UNHCR, 2016); and offshoring the administration and detention of those with irregular status to poorer and distant 'partner' nations (Urbina, 2021).

In more recent years, Australia has continued to lead troubling innovations in bordering practices, including in the deployment of funds to the International Organization for Migration as a method of containing people attempting to seek asylum in Australia in Indonesia – in effect incentivising the punitive incarceration of populations in movement. The International Organization for Migration has become integrated into UN structures, although still retaining its strangely contradictory mission both to build nations' bordering capacities and to undertake detention and to facilitate movement and initiate humanitarian work. As a result, Australia's push to outsource additionally punitive and poorly monitored treatment of populations in movement to Indonesia under the auspices of the IOM has been termed a form of 'blue-washing' – that is, using the pretence of humanitarian concerns to undertake repressive measures (Hirsch and Doig, 2018). Richer nations have adopted the language of humanitarianism when preventing and violently policing migration (Horsti, 2012). In parallel, we see, for example, the avoidance of the term 'refugee' in ASEAN agreements around collaborative bordering (Jati and Sunderland, 2018). In the unequal terrain of transnational agreements, deployment of ideas of complementary national interests and/or shared humanitarian goals create a landscape in which the combined actions of different states further erode the treatment of people in movement.

3 Tying bordering cooperation requirements to other aspects of foreign and/or trade policy

This last instance reveals the entrenched power imbalances between states. Although we might consider this set of practices as overlapping with outsourcing arrangements, the overt agreements reached through trade and aid agreements remain submerged in the wider and less explicit arrangements that make up relations between more and less powerful nations. These arrangements can be leveraged to pursue the domestic policy agendas of less powerful nations, in a process of 'reverse conditionality' (Tittel-Mosser, 2018). Arguably, the ability to contain or deflect migrants from their planned journeys towards affluent nations becomes a form of national product or industry. In addition, the linking of development aid to cooperation in immigration control has been used to further outsource responsibility for the welfare of migrants, as seen overtly in the case of the EU's infamous 'European Agenda on Migration' (Davitti and La Chimia, 2017). Interstate cooperation on bordering, where one party absorbs the administration, the containment and sometimes the removal of unwanted migrants, has become yet another dirty and dubious service undertaken by poorer nations.

Climate crisis and cooperative bordering

While we might consider the practice of bordering as the exemplary demonstration of state sovereignty, such an assertion must always rest alongside the recognition of the privatization of security practices, including those linked to bordering. In fact, the increasing use of private entities to enact the coercive function of states might be regarded as one important characteristic of the transforming capitalist state in relation to borders (Menz, 2011). Therefore, we might consider the changing risk and liability that arises from global agreements about the rights of refugees and asylum seekers, however poorly enforced such agreements are. In this iteration, people in movement represent a risk and a burden. Although there is some literature that seeks to identify the economic opportunities raised by displaced populations (for example, Clemens et al., 2018), in terms of the exercise of state power, this is sovereignty exercised as the containment of risk to the state. For much of the more affluent world, this takes the form of seeking to minimize liability, including through instituting the most restrictive and punitive interpretations of international law in relation to refuge and increasingly finding ways to offload or outsource the management, containment or expulsion of desperate populations to other states, sometimes through the mediation or intervention of private corporations (Akkerman, 2021). At the same time as this bundling, packaging and forced movement or forced stasis of refugee or refugee-like populations is taking place, there is an accompanying porosity of the border (Yuval-Davis et al., 2019). This is a porosity designed to enable exploitative stratification in the labour market. This is the border that creates and enables the shadow economy, that places a layer of desperate workers unable to access even the minimal protections available in law and which, through its operation, ensures a ready supply of workers who fall outside the terms of regulation and employment law, at least in practice.

Alongside all of this, there are other realms of movement and other kinds of population who remain mobile at a whim and who come to represent the demands of travel and mobility for those who are most fully enfranchised and who have most access to global resources. The world operates as if through these three realms of traveller – refugee, migrant worker, hypermobile global citizen – are distinct and will remain distinct forever. Yet what we are learning through the increasing rampaging reach of climate crisis, alongside other forms of life-defying crisis, is that we may all fall out of the happy category of 'traveller by choice', and it is likely that many more of us will be taking journeys of survival out of desperation, seeking either refuge or entry to some other means of accessing the resources of life. Given this likelihood and the precursor trends we are already living through, we might think again about the temporary enclosures of modern diplomacy and consider the emerging trajectory of 'migration diplomacy' (Adamson and Tsourapas, 2019). At present we seem to be at the fragile endpoint of one era, where something like functioning states with something like stable populations are able to make agreements about those sections of the world that no longer easily fall into those two categorizations. As the proportion of the world that might be regarded as the stable population of any territory changes, shifting the balance between those who regard themselves as settled and those who are unsettled beyond any peace of mind, the global machinery of bordering may be squeezed into a very different shape. The imagined coincidence between states and populations is already uncertain. As we come to understand that stasis can no longer be regarded as the default expectation for any human life, the statecraft of performing sovereignty at/through the border must also adapt.

We might consider this era of transnational agreement for the purposes of containing migrants as a parallel to the era of carbon offsetting or transnational waste disposal in response to a now unstoppable understanding of the fragility of the Earth and the deadly impact of cumulative human activity in the pursuit of profit. The containment of desperate people looks like another last-ditch attempt to safeguard the lifestyles and sense of safety of the few. Perhaps there is an understanding that this is a temporary measure, buying only a little more time, postponing the inevitable breaking point where the volume of the poor and the desperate and their barely planned movement for survival must overwhelm the enclaves of the rich or the richer. We might, then, understand our moment of capitalist crisis and class struggle as one where class domination is expressed as a will to safeguard the lifestyles of the few in the face of the imminent collapse of much of the planet. One aspect of racial capitalism in our time is best understood as the attempt to reconcile continued accumulation with the unavoidable limitations caused by climate crisis.

The standard arguments about the merits of bordering have tended to focus on what can be gained by the exercise of sovereignty at the border (Weiner, 1996; Sassen, 1996). As so much of what we understand as statecraft has become folded into the idea of economic management across the last hundred years or so, the issue of national prosperity and the issue of national security can become difficult to disentangle (Mastanduno, 1999). The policing of the border understood as the proper management of entry and departure of populations across national territories is presented as one necessary component both of managing the sovereign space over which responsibility and domination occurs and as a method to protect the terms of national labour markets. Across Europe and beyond, the alleged impact of migrants on pay and other terms within employment has become one of the central policy questions relating to immigration control (for a discussion of the alleged weakness of Italian and Greek bordering and the impact of this for other nations in the European Union, see Ambrosini and Triandafyllidou, 2011).

It is important to note here that this is a version of bordering rhetoric which can deny any racist motivation. Proponents of bordering for the purposes of controlling entry into labour markets may point to their antiracist credentials. At times, there may be claims made that only an insistent policing of movement on the border can prevent the further rise of racism within the national body. Either way, proponents of bordering for the purposes of labour market regulation can quite easily distance themselves from the varieties of cultural racism and/or longstanding nationalist antagonism that inform the anti-migrant sentiments of some other elements of the right. This is bordering as a pragmatic intervention. The bordering authority here acts as if it is indifferent to the identity, history and background of those seeking to cross the border. Although bordering activity increasingly tends towards extensive machineries of surveillance which scrutinize bodies and movement for signs of being out of place and/or less than human, the expulsion of the migrant in this logic avoids the explicit and overt racialization of some other modes of xenophobia. In the process we see a variety of political formations where other actors, particularly other non-elite actors, are called into a defence of bordering as an expression of their own self-interest. Bordering, then, encourages a certain uncomfortable alliance between those made desperate by the privations of the local labour market and those pretending to limit entry into the local labour market. There does not need to be any sense of identification between these two groups. If there is a nationalist project, it is stretched very tightly and leaves little sense of commonality between these two sets of parties. What there is, however, is a kind of bad faith alliance made as a way of keeping our heads above water and just about surviving in a world where every fresh human contact seems to threaten to be the competitive interaction that finally floors us. If there is a distinctive xenophobia of the twenty-first century, the question of whether the other is or is not 'like me' no longer seems pertinent. Instead, increasingly precarious populations across the world are offered the chance to cooperate with largely neglectful state apparatuses on the issue of bordering alone, and what this cooperation is based on is the limiting of competitive entries into landscapes already characterized by official neglect and a wilful denial of resources.

Bordering as accumulation through population placement

Bordering regimes arising from cooperation between states might be better understood as an accommodation between the largely nationalist imperatives and pressures of demonstrating sovereignty and the push to become incorporated into transnational systems where the ability to guide, monitor and position populations becomes an adjunct to accumulation. The positioning of populations here goes beyond the more familiar deployment of restrictions on movement as an aspect of disciplining labour, although this also continues. In addition, however, we see a variety of deals and business opportunities become tied to the administration of bordering between states. This includes the outsourcing of asylum from richer to poorer nations but also the potentials unleashed by demarcating limited paths of movement, enforcing stasis and rendering populations held within these disciplinary systems legible and, perhaps, as consumer markets. These tendencies reveal the extent to which statecraft takes place through an assessment of the political gains to be garnered from managing population movement within a global bordering regime.

In his wide-ranging and very scary book *Empire of Borders*, Todd Miller guides the reader through a tour of US-imposed bordering around the world. He argues, persuasively, that the US pursues its national interests through both the demarcation and violent policing of its own borders and also, by way of a variety of means spanning trade, diplomacy and war, dictates the bordering practices of others. While reporting the breathless excitement of those proposing the technological management of population movement, deploying facial recognition and data-tracking systems to ease the travel arrangements of the world's favoured classes, Miller identifies the dystopian undercurrent of the fantasy: 'Implicit in the dream are open borders for the elite and a caste system for everyone else' (Miller, 2019: 152).

A caste system is perhaps not quite the same as a global colour line, but it points to something similar in the attribution of status, worth and access to the means of life. The fantasy of high-tech frictionless movement, a fantasy expressed in trade shows and tech demonstrations in a time where the deadly risks of forced movement are apparent across the globe, must be understood as a wilful evasion of the question of mobility as a right or a need. These dreams of frictionless movement belong with the fictions of survival for some. They are ways of maintaining a pretence of business as usual for the most affluent in the world, while providing distraction and reassurance in the face of the rapidly spreading carnage of climate crisis. Miller goes a little further, proposing that we understand violent bordering as a global regime: 'The border apparatus has to be looked at as a global regime, reconfiguring before our eyes, a developing arsenal of the Global North sorting, classifying, and repelling or incarcerating people from the Global South, while employing and deploying countries of the Global South as enforcers' (Miller, 2019: 158).

It is the more affluent spaces of the world that sort and classify the desperate migrants of the poorer world as highly skilled or deserving of asylum (Aydemir, 2020). There has been an international architecture of selective movement in the service of the economies of the Global North since 1945 at least (Hollifield, 1992). What we seem to be seeing in our slightly different moment of crisis, however, is the emergence of a global machinery to manage populations in movement (or a series of regional machineries constructed with an eye on the practices of other regions; Geddes et al., 2019). While this machinery retains some aspects of local sorting mechanisms, what is being negotiated between states seems to go beyond this classification of economic and/or social worth.

It is through this analysis of the emergence of a global bordering machine that Miller argues for a need to think of empire as more than territorial expansion, instead characterizing empire in our time as 'the securitization of the global economy through . . . [an] emerging "harmonized" global border system' (Miller, 2019: 162).

How does thinking about cooperative bordering help us to understand racial capitalism?

Challenging bordering has become a central component of antiracist mobilizing in our time. While there was a period where it seemed that accounts of racism and how to fight it overlooked the place of border regimes, the folding together of the figures of the terrorist, the migrant and the racialized criminal (Bhattacharyya et al., 2021) forces a renewal of a more interconnected antiracism.

What seems to be happening in our moment is a reworking of bordering practices as a mechanism through which the global population can be placed, constrained and channelled into particular routes and spaces while being barred from others. This global map of where movement can occur and where it cannot is a matter beyond any one state. Even the most dominant of the world's powers are engaged in cooperation of a form in their quest to narrow and direct migration routes.

To comprehend this, we must both register the negotiation of interest that is taking place between states and at the same time remain alert to the power struggle between states that is played out in the process of negotiation/collaboration. To understand the role of bordering on a global scale in our adapting moment of racial capitalism, we need to remain open to comprehending the varied and contradictory actions undertaken to maintain particular class interests. Whereas we might have learned in a previous moment to consider the state as, on the whole, an entity embodying class interests within the nation with lines of activity relating to transnational alliances or interests, the question of the national border and its administration has tended to be viewed through the lens of national politics. And even if we have had the tools to adopt an alternative analytic approach to this question, *politically* the violence of borders has been addressed largely through a national lens. To be clear, there have been good reasons for this tactical choice, not least the reliance of the right on anti-migrant agitation within the terms of national debates.

More recently, movements for no borders bring us to a greater understanding of the international machinery of bordering (Bradley and de Noronha, 2022). As part of this, we have access to a better understanding of the interests involved in the world's interconnected border regimes, in particular through the mapping of corporate involvement in such processes (for an account of the state-corporate formations enacting corrosive control for women seeking asylum, see Canning, 2020; for an alarming but instructive account of the global security industry's role in bordering, see Lori and Schilde, 2021). At the same time, influential work by scholar-activists such as Harsha Walia reframes the global movement against borders as already and necessarily embedded in interlinking movements for Indigenous rights and climate justice (Walia, 2021). Increasingly, the question of bordering becomes a question about who lives and who dies. As such, we must recognize that, and despite areas of uncertainty or where the battle-lines are still emerging, bordering may constitute a central technology of racial capitalism for us, whatever might have gone on previously.

To understand this, we must move beyond only an attention to the exclusionary practices and partial inclusions of particular national spaces. These practices are illuminating as part of a global pattern. There is a different discussion to be had about the playing out of imperial histories of expropriation through the barring of movement, and some of the most inspirational writing of recent years addresses this issue (El-Enany, 2020; Walia, 2014; Trafford, 2020). However, and as always, the question for those seeking to understand the workings of racial capitalism is a little different. For us, the question is not why bordering is wrong, it is how bordering works to sustain racial capitalism. And, for our question to be addressed, we must find ways to lay out the global machinery of bordering as an element of class war.

In this racial class war, powerful actors are not united. They, too, have local interests and differences and differing relations to capital. Certainly, some of the lessons arising from early and prescient critiques of neocolonialism can help us to comprehend the interests at play in the still uneven and yet ever-expanding machinery of global bordering. What is central for our understanding is the ability to register the parallel disciplinings of space and movement undertaken in the name of bordering.

At the very least, we need to expand our thinking to consider both the border (always permeable by design) and the enabled routes. Both of these moments in the machinery of global bordering require collaboration between states, and the arrangements of individual states reveal both their alliances and their vulnerabilities.

So now it is almost explicit that the international 'management' of migration is a shared goal among the transnational ruling class, certainly as expressed through the representatives of formal government. This need to 'manage' migration continues to be narrated as a question of national interest, although this is a form of national interest presented as being held in common by all nations. In the process, the increasingly unstable spaces of the world where the maintenance of life is unreliable or outright dangerous are cast as a risk to the international community and a risk that is to be managed globally.

This is a set of interests centred around the terms of life – both the reproduction of capital and the maintenance of particular ways of life and access to resources.

I have written previously about how we might understand the impact of climate catastrophe on the international exercise of class power. As we enter the phase where there can be no going back, climate crisis becomes a trigger to remake global class interests as survival for some – and, it should be said, survival with little or no adaptation. The management of the supposed risk of migration falls within this account, with the combination of constrained and highly policed routes or corridors alongside differently permeable and cooperative bordering arrangements offering an updated machinery of global population management. What we see emerging are differential levels of being made surplus, not quite the total abandonment of a population that characterized the moment just passed, but still retaining the capability to divide humans into those who can and those who cannot make the journey, those who can and those who cannot contribute, those who can and those who cannot be seen as human.

Climate catastrophe racial capitalism requires a pivoting away from endless expansion and growth – even if this pivoting is barely acknowledged. The collaborative machinery of international class power now incorporates this new(er) imperative, whether explicitly or covertly. The convoluted arrangements that attempt to find common and workable interests between the very differently positioned elites of differing nations rely on this underlying assumption – that a lot of people must die for their ways of life to continue. Race provides the technique, so violently established over centuries, by which the distinction between those to be saved and those to be sacrificed can be enacted.

In our moment, this combines a superimposition of emerging imperatives onto longstanding racialized hierarchies and a flexibility that can open new or expanded populations to the violence of being rendered surplus. Within this, the push to maintain a version of business as usual within some spaces – what we might think of as the metropolis or the imperial centre but which are, in fact, themselves spaces in movement – demands increasingly complex systems of sifting and ordering of populations in movement, enabling some people to move via some routes at some times, but always under the murderous disciplines of the global bordering regime.

5

Prisons and the Carcerality of Transforming Racial Capitalism

What is the puzzle to be understood?

Carcerality has been embedded in the violences of colonial expansion and in the disciplining of populations into workforces (for an account of British, French and Italian colonial prisons, see Havik et al., 2019, and of colonial prisons in Guyana, Anderson et al., 2020; the seminal work outlining the interdependence of prison and factory systems is Melossi and Pavarini, 2018). In this much, carcerality is apparent both in the emergence of and in the maintenance of varieties of racial capitalism. A major component of our understanding of the structuring and operation of racial capitalism arises from the work of scholars and activists seeking to understand and dismantle systems of carcerality (see, as a heart-breaking but incisive example, Wang, 2018; much of this space of debate is shaped by the formative work of Ruth Wilson Gilmore, including her books published in 2007 and 2022). Prisons have operated as the always present threat neighbouring the factory (or the slum or perhaps the plantation), a reminder that resisting the demands of the productive economy risks more obviously violent punishment. As populations have resisted proletarianization and its assorted disciplines, carceral systems of imprisonment as well as other punishments have been constructed to corral resisters into the terms of compliance (Melossi, 1981).

We are accustomed to think of massive prison systems as a method of warehousing less enfranchised populations; a kind of fix to address over-accumulation and to undercut a regulated labour market; and a disciplinary formation with a knock-on effect on non-incarcerated workers and communities. Prisons, then, as we have understood them, play a useful role both for bosses and for the capitalist state. Most, if not all, of the time, this occurs through structures and practices of racialized differentiation and exclusion.

The question is what happens to these very established practices of incarceration in the service of one version of the capitalist state and employing class when both of those entities are undergoing (perhaps have already undergone) significant processes of remaking. Perhaps in some aspects these are no more than an intensification of what went before. In others, perhaps they represent a shift in the composition of 'the ruling class'.

More generally, such hints at a changing machinery of capitalist dehumanization reflect a broader suspicion that something about 'capitalism' is on the move. This work is an attempt to register this sense of something changing, something unfamiliar in what we recognize as capitalism, in order to think again about racial capitalism.

Still a world of prisons

Penal Reform International reviews the global map of imprisonment in the wake of Covid-19 and points to some troubling if predictable trends. A growing global prison population, with very large rises between 2010 and 2021 in the numbers of women in prison, recorded as increases of 53 per cent in Oceania, 50 per cent in Asia, 24 per cent in Africa, 17 per cent in South America, and 8 per cent in North America, with only Europe showing a decrease, of 29 per cent. Numbers in pre-trial detention have grown significantly, up globally by 30 per cent since 2000 (Penal Reform International, 2021; for a consideration of the longer history of imprisoning Black women, see Sudbury, 2002). Covid increased pressure on prisons, notably through high rates of infection among those imprisoned, a detrimental impact on mental health, and high rates of reported staff exhaustion.

In our collective quest to understand racial capitalism and the ugly world it has made, we have come to understand the centrality of carcerality as both systemic logic and elastic practice. It is through the work of prison abolitionists that we have become knowledgeable about the centrality of carceral systems to the (racialized) differentiation of populations and the segmented disciplining of economic spaces and processes which separate us into different kinds of opportunities for capital (for a demand to abolish prisons from the 1970s, see Holloway, 1974; for influential accounts of the argument for prison abolition as it has re-emerged from the late twentieth century, see Gilmore, 2007; Davis, 2011; for a British perspective, see Ryan and Ward, 2014). Prisons, perhaps, have been the exemplary institutional intervention of racial capitalism. So we understand already that:

- prisons have grown out of systems of unfreedom rooted in enslavement and in colonial violence. The construction of a status of a person beyond the protections of law and process has operated in different contexts to anchor systems of differential status (for an account of prisons as an exemplar of settler-colonial violence, see Nichols, 2017; for an account of prisons under the British rule of India, see Sen, 2012; for an account of prisons as a central element of the racial terror of plantation economies, see Childs, 2015). Prisons, in their incarnation as spaces determined by the exercise of law (as opposed to the differently mystified spaces of punishment instituted in the name of war or divine right), have worked to demonstrate the non-universality of law. The imprisoned person has forfeited their rights, including their right to be considered within the terms of legality. Well-known examples of this logic are the exclusion of prisons from the constitutional repudiation of slave labour (Armstrong, 2011); the exclusion of prisons from public health directives, including where this guidance is enshrined in law (Bradshaw, 2021; de Oliveira Andrade, 2020); and the removal of voting rights from prisoners and former prisoners (Rottinghaus and Baldwin, 2007).
- prisons have operated as a mode of disciplining labour, both through the threat of unfreedom and through the inclusion of coerced work as an aspect of prison punishment (De Giorgi, 2006). One of the rights removed from the imprisoned is the right to earn a wage or to claim the rights of a worker.
- prisons operate as one component of a carceral machinery spanning across institutions. They may occupy the role of embodied warning, and they may work to anchor other more diffusely carceral processes such as schooling or welfare in networks of punishment (on the school to prison pipeline, see Cuellar and Markowitz, 2015; on the restructuring of welfare as a mode of carcerality, see LeBaron and Roberts, 2010). However, the alteration or regulation or scaling back of prisons is not, in itself, a diminishing of carcerality (De Giorgi, 2015). It is

more helpful to think of carcerality as the manner by which punishment and the threat of punishment operates to discipline populations, including into and in work, in relations between individuals and within communities and in the overarching defence of private property and the interests of capital.

These three elements – instituting the space of exception, disciplining labour, and redirecting social forces towards the defence of private property and the interests of capital – have distinguished prisons as a particular form of capitalist institution. In this account, the prison is a counterpart to proletarianization; its meanings derive from the idea that somewhere else there is free labour and wagedness.

If once we felt sure that prisons divided the undeserving from the (potentially) productive, how do the far more variegated statuses of a changing moment of racial capitalism reframe incarceration? What work is done by this longstanding set of institutional practices when the surrounding landscape of both institutions and economic organization is remade? What may be altering in our time is the manner in which carceral processes come to be the pre-eminent expression of state power in economic landscapes where varieties of hustling have become a central component of everyday economic survival (Thieme, 2018; Ravenelle, 2019).

We might previously have thought of economic landscapes disciplined to enable and pin down particular formations of massification (including beyond mass production to the concentrations of capital and the human servicing of capital represented in the cities of the twenty-first century; Sassen, 2013b), with carceral systems demarcating spaces to police those within the populations of the metropolis, those moving in and out of the spaces of the metropolis, and those beyond the metropolis in the differently policed wastelands (Wacquant, 2008; Sanyal, 2014). This is the account of the interdependence of the factory and the prison, extended slightly to incorporate the insights of racial capitalism talk. The coercive authority legitimated by the claim of identifying, containing and punishing crime also anchored differential statuses of varying protectedness.

Carcerality as a set of interlocking processes orchestrated through an often unitary dominant power ranges across institutional spaces. Through the insights of activist-led scholarship, we can see more clearly the manner in which:

- the logic of the prison enters a broader range of public institutions, particularly in the manner through which attempts to access social goods are transformed into occasions of punishment (Wacquant, 2009);
- schooling lays out the pathways of racialized and classed dispossession through the funnelling of some young people into a pipeline to prison and punishment through an array of carceral institutions (Mallett, 2015);
- in a landscape of indebtedness and precarity, the poor and the racially minoritized can be captured by varieties of carcerality in ways that limit access to financial services, open vulnerability to predatory actors such as loan-sharks, and further constrain the kinds of work and work-like activity that can be accessed (Wang, 2018).

The grip of carceral logics over those lives deemed low status or low productivity or chaotic has tightened across the world, sometimes in combination with border regimes, sometimes in parallel to public services allocated through punitive logics (Bhattacharyya, 2015). At the same time, the global prison infrastructure has grown, including through the emergence of carcerality as a method of evidencing functioning statehood in the eyes of the international community (for a discussion of how the US imposes its models of criminal justice on others, see McLeod, 2010). These carceral systems emerge alongside and through a massive expansion of the global security industries, a development itself extending and amending the character of carcerality to encompass public–private arrangements and further blurring the boundary between state power and corporate interests (Tzifakis, 2012; Hönke, 2013).

This work tries to provide a map outlining both the shifts in the workings of capitalism in relation to corporate form and the position of the waged worker and the parallel burgeoning of an infrastructure of punishment and containment through increasing carcerality and bordering. This discussion is indebted to the work of William Robinson and his conceptualization of the global police state, although the emphasis of that analysis is slightly different to my own interests. Robinson identifies three interconnected nodes in the shift towards a global police state: mass surveillance and repression, including through military intervention and the reincorporation of militarized techniques into supposedly civilian space; the increasing reliance on industries of violence in the remaking of capitalism – what Robinson terms accumulation by repression; and the re-emergence of what he calls 'political systems that can be characterised as twenty-first century fascism' (Robinson, 2018: 80; for a fuller discussion, see Robinson, 2020).

All three elements run close to discussions of a re-energized and changing racial capitalism. This includes the seeping together of possibilities unleashed by digital capitalism and the global reach of the security industries and, alongside this altered configuration of the military-industrial complex, the dubious networks of interdependency and revolving-door interests between elected representatives, the arms industry and lobbyists, combined with a separate set of movements towards varieties of authoritarianism which may benefit from the first two trends but remain distinct. There is far too much to discuss in relation to the question of new populisms, the remaking of authoritarianism and the ongoing murderous threat of the global right (for some introductions to this large and ever-extending literature, see Traverso, 2019; Mondon and Winter, 2020). Here I point out only that the push towards mass death through economic and climate implosion and that through programmes of active (as opposed to neglectful) genocide are distinct and represent specific agents, alliances and agendas.

Despite the venerable tradition of antifascist writing uncovering the very particular and yet familiar class politics of fascist projects (for example, Mason and Mason, 1995), perhaps in recent years we have become more invested in understanding the resurgence of the organized right as a question of nationalism, read as affect and less as a matter of class politics articulated as economic interest (for example, see Rasmussen, 2021, on the cultural articulation of the organized right).

Robinson nudges us back into thinking authoritarianism and class interests together, framing our moment as one of accumulation by repression. In defining the term, he points directly to the assembly of repressive practices so importantly identified in discussions of contemporary racial capitalism: 'militarised accumulation, or accumulation by repression. The bogus wars on drugs and terrorism, the construction of border walls, the expansion of prison-industrial complexes, deportation regimes, police, the military, and other security apparatuses, are major sources of state-organised profit-making' (Robinson, 2018: 81). These are the techniques of state-sanctioned (although now often outsourced) violence that segment the spaces of legality and economics, positioning populations as variably protected and under- or unprotected, in the process determining the extent to which violence can be done. These are highly repressive regimes of violence, but they are unevenly so. Although the threat seeps through the whole of society, the enactment of violence is highly differentiated. The account of racial capitalism suggests that it is through this differentiated impact and enactment that capital is remade and valorization ensured.

Just as some forms of economic violence occur with the expulsion from social relations enabling exploitation, some forms of vulnerability occur with the expulsion from spaces overseen by institutional powers, even when those powers are themselves repressive. The logics of punishment may operate also by way of varieties of abandonment and banishment (de Noronha, 2020) through which the neoliberal or other state posits its 'edge' or 'outside'.

The lesson of carcerality is the reach of the prison into other institutional spaces and beyond. Prisons may well be becoming larger and more numerous, and this is something to note as we seek to understand the opening into a new era of amended horror. However, the insight of theories of the carceral is that the prison never operates alone. The criminal justice system as a whole never operates alone. Instead, the logic of punishment and containment roams across social relations in a carceral state (for an account of carcerality in the immigration system and the monetization of detention, see Bhatia and Canning, 2020). Institutions so often presented as (relatively) benign conduits of social reproduction, such as schools (training for life) or welfare (reproducing the population) or healthcare (tending the sick), are tied into networks of conditionality and outright punishment, sometimes serving to siphon the unruly or the unlucky into more overtly coercive institutional spaces, sometimes operating to ensure that punitive elements are intertwined in the response to any small claim for support.

As with so much of our conceptual repertoire when analysing state racisms, the discussion of carcerality relies heavily on a US literature and a North American framing of raciality. The particular interplay of settler-colonial states built with enslaved labour informs, rightly, how race and power appear in these debates. For the rest of the world, there are parallels – not least in the global repercussions of the Atlantic slave trade; however, the re-emergence of a moment of global carcerality cannot be understood through an Atlantic lens alone. To sketch out the implications of this perhaps too obvious remark, we might remind ourselves of the following.

• Penality is not based explicitly within slave logics everywhere, although many places and histories employ terms of arbitrary expulsion from humanness as part of the organization of penality.

- The terms of property, propriety and legal protection appear to operate as distinct racial logics in the spaces of settler-colonialism. On already stolen land, the terms of protection and punishment operate to render the settler into an always already vulnerable potential victim. The laws and punishments relating to property pre-emptively disallow native claims and position the Indigenous claimant as always criminal and punishable. Thinking about our moment of changing racial capitalism, we might think again about the implications of the supposedly impossible property claims of the Indigenous for other dispossessed and over-punished groups.

Although the legacy of colonialism marks the globe with a racialized logic, as described by Dubois' term of the global colour line, the global colour line does not necessarily or obviously translate into discernible or comparable racialized politics within each nation or region of the world. At the most obvious, the markers of community-level exclusion that accompany so many of the instances of disproportionate imprisonment are narrated through a variety of locally meaningful frameworks. While the United States, despite the ascendance of so-called colourblind racism, has tended to name race in its practices and structures of racism (for example, in the continuing shadow of plantation economics and forced labour through the prison system; Armstrong, 2011), other places have more disguised racisms and, perhaps, modes of exclusion and dispossession. One part of the puzzle of global carcerality is to ask the usefulness of the frame 'racial capitalism' in understanding the exclusionary violences of carceral states where the official language of a nation is non-racial or postracial or racialized differently.

The efforts of international human rights organizations suggest a pattern of systemic disadvantage among groups most likely to be imprisoned. For some spaces, this is narrated explicitly through the terms of raciality. For others, the attribution of arbitrary status echoes the arbitrariness of racialized ascription. So while we know that the prison population of the United States, still the largest in the documented prison population in the world at 2 million (ICPR, 2021), reflects the racialized violence of that country's formation, global audiences are less likely to consider the extreme carceral violences of India and China as matters of raciality. Yet of the 554,034 (at 31 December 2021; World Prison Brief, 2021) prisoners recorded in India's official figures, 77.1 per cent are recorded as pre-trial detainees/remand prisoners. In practice, pre-trial detainees and remand prisoners are imprisoned alongside convicted prisoners, for very long periods and in extremely dangerous and life-threatening conditions (Pretrial Rights International, n.d.). Indian prison kills, whether or not a person is awaiting trial (Ram and Kumar, 2021). At the same time, the convergence of state and popular violence against Muslim and Dalit communities reveals the logic of a racial state, including through the fostering of political speech exacerbating and sometimes excusing murderous violence against minorities (Alam, 2017). A prison system operated to punish before trial forms part of this wider constellation of unaccountable powers.

In parallel, the Chinese state deploys a political project based in the construction of a Chinese people no longer differentiated by earlier histories of region, language or faith. In addition to the 1.7 million sentenced individuals recorded as being held in Ministry of Justice prisons (at the end of 2018; World Prison Brief, 2018), it is estimated that 1 million Uyghurs are held in detention as part of the Chinese state's repression of this community (OHCHR, 2022).The carceral systems of India and China are not those of North America. However, in all three global powers we see the deployment of this particular mode of state violence as a means of marking the boundaries of national belonging and entitlement and concocting hierarchies of humanness which seep into other arenas of violence. In this particular moment of human tragedy and heartbreak, we might remember again that carcerality can be a technique to conjure up raciality.

Extractivism, penality and the decentring of the wage

I started this work trying to rethink insights from the work of Jackie Wang (2018). The ground-breaking and heart-breaking account of how poor racialized communities become fine-fodder, in the process propping up public services which target them as potential criminals who are always owing, was both transfixing and puzzling. The particular coordinates enabling this formulation of urban extractivism via the local state are not replicated in most other settings.

The particular racialized histories of US law, and the long shadow of this history, exist in somewhat different formulations elsewhere. In large parts of the world, it is the laws framed by former colonial powers that continue to cast their shadow over who and who is not eligible for humanness. In some others, local histories of racialized dispossession play out in the framing and reach of law. In yet others, a more open category of less-than-humanness is deployed to meet contextual demands.

But almost nowhere is there such an explicit thread linking the framing of laws designed to ameliorate the losses of slave-owners and defend the 'property' of settler-colonialists with present-day implementation to steal from the (often racialized) poor.

However, on reflection, I now think Wang's careful account of the mechanics of extractivism via fine regimes points us to a far larger insight about varieties of taxes on life. What Wang uncovers is a way of thinking about a highly mobile and shape-shifting extractivism no longer targeted on the treasures of 'free nature' alone but also innovating methods of extracting value from the very means of life. Whereas there is an extensive and painful literature schooling us in the intricacies of this barbaric process as a colonial violence, Wang pushes us to extend our analytic gaze to the innovations of extractivism within the metropolis. This shift in focus opens our comprehension of a recalibrated racial capitalism where it is the techniques of extractivism, not primarily those of exploitation, which degrade our lives and position us as desperate adjuncts to the remaking of capital.

Vagabondage

What we are living through is not the same ripping from the land of a previous moment of primitive accumulation. Despite the extensive literature reminding us of the continuation of practices of 'primitive' accumulation in contemporary capitalism (Glassman, 2006), there are of course many who are being ripped from their locations. In 2022, the UNHCR calculated that 89.3 million people were forcibly displaced, amounting to one in every eighty-eight people on Earth. This figure does not yet include the millions displaced by floods in Pakistan that year (Tunio, 2022). To comprehend this, it is useful to consider that, between 1991 and 2011, the number of people forcibly displaced across the world fluctuated between 40 and 50 million, falling below 40 million in 2011 and rising steeply since that year (UNHCR, 2022). We live in a world where ever greater numbers are forced into forms of catastrophe migration (flood, famine, war, pestilence) and where our established systems of ordering space and allocating 'rights' render such people as illegitimate interlopers disentitled from access to the means of survival. However, at the same time there is a less dramatic ripping from place happening across the world. We might consider this to be the end era of urbanization, where the enormous mega-cities of the Global South finally seem close to swallowing all that remains of the rural population, with only the very old and the very young left behind in countless empty villages and towns or in the shells of cities built to service a passing version of industrial organization. To understand what this kind of abandonment looks like, we might consider the spaces of infrastructural collapse.

Yet, as well as being the last hurrah of urbanization, this is something like the dispersal of the city, or a turbulence within the terms of urbanization, as the activities that were centred by economic infrastructure of existing cities become dispersed or wane or collapse.

I am calling this moment a form of vagabondage because I want to point to something distinctive about the violent move from one economic logic to another. I am attracted to the argument made so stylishly by McKenzie Wark (2019), and she and others have argued persuasively that we are living through a moment where capital is no longer what we might have thought it to be. I suspect that this transition is not yet decided. For now, we may have to be content to look upon the shifts in capitalist reproduction with a sense of openness and uncertainty, while recognizing the extent to which working people across the world end up being cut free from the anchoring infrastructure and institutions that previously made up the racialized geography of class.

The shift from one economic order to another does not happen in an instant. And neither does it mean that all elements of the previous order disappear. What it does signify is that the means of life can no longer predictably be accessed through the previous arrangements of living, of working, of spatial positioning. In this period where life cannot be remade by most with any sense of security, there is a throwing up in the air of where and how people may pursue their quest for survival. When Marx is writing of a moment of pre-capitalism, he looks back into the archive to uncover a kind of marauding free for all – a not yet proletariat seeking to innovate other less ordered and controlled ways of life, despite the violent imposition from above by the powerful, without thus far having the means to articulate a class consciousness. Marx points to the many ways in which ordinary people resist the attempt to colonize their life-worlds, to take over their time, and to transform them into beasts who live only to work. The vagabondage of that moment is part displacement and part escape. People are seeking not a stable home but the ability to live freely.

In our time there are two slightly different moments of vagabondage. One is the more familiar uprooting of human populations, not only because war and disaster force people to flee but also because the means of life may no longer be accessible in the time and space and rhythm of life of where we previously were. The city does not yet have a new way of life for these new vagabonds (for a painful catalogue of lives broken by forced movement arising from climate change, see Rahman and Sohag, 2011). There has not yet been a transition from the old to the new. Yet what there is comes from this new era of vagabondage, perhaps combined with indebtedness and leading to new sets of quite unpredictable ways of life or near life.

When we think of the vagabond, we think of the individual human cut free from the expectations and constraints of a social order embedded in a material infrastructure (Baumann, 1996, argues that these are the victims of postmodernity). Another thing that changes in our moment is the crumbling of one phase of social ordering linked to this form of material infrastructure (for a discussion of the impact of failures in urban infrastructure which encourages an understanding of urban spaces as made up of flows, not structures, see Graham, 2009). As bordering operates to limit the access to movement of so many of the world's poor, ours is also a vagabondage where the instruments of capital are the ones to go travelling. This is not to say that there is not a movement in both directions and a spitting out of human populations into a variety of new wastelands (Wacquant, 2008), in parallel with a simultaneous flightiness of productive processes, now so ephemeral that the term 'productive' barely seems to fit at all. These two movements together create a landscape where humans are constantly seeking to find the moment of contract or agreement or connection with some other actor who can provide access to the means of life (Graham and Anwar, 2019).

When I call this phase the phase of vagabondage, I am not trying to romanticize a moment where it seems that the balance of power between the capitalist class and ourselves seems too skewed for survival. What we see is a widespread uncertainty about how the terms of life can be found and sustained. I am thinking here both of apocalypse talk (Mitchell and Chaudhury, 2020; Wolf-Meyer, 2019) and of the varieties of survivalist expression (Bounds, 2020; Ford, 2019). This sense of unease extends far beyond those who face racial subordination. It is, however, a moment that points to the ongoing and violent work of racialized subordination as the machineries of imprisonment and bordering rest on top of this new landscape of vagabondage, spreading the fear of punishment among all of those on the move (Zatz, 2020; Mayblin, 2019; Golash-Boza, 2016).

Old and new carcerality

Much of the existing literature about mass incarceration charts some continuity between colonial models of oppression and what we might understand as neoliberal expansions of industrialization. The prison returns as a mass technique in the moment in which the massification of the labour force stalls (for an account of the turning inwards of the punitive arm of the Keynesian project, see Gilmore, 1999). If we imagine the world as it is now as populated by highly fragmented groups far less tied to the imperatives of large-scale production but instead giving up value through piecework forms of employment, differently constituted social reproduction practices and the extension of value scraping into the priorities of leisure and media use, then the role of mass incarceration may adapt to this shifting context. What we have been describing as the proletarianization of this new moment does not seem to require the containment of significant sections of the population in the ways offered by mass incarceration. Yes, there is still routine production-line work that can be obtained very cheaply and compliantly through the use of prison labour, and I do not wish here to underestimate the role of this particular form of brutal exploitation in some of our key commodity chains (for allegations of prison labour in the production of global sporting goods, see Lund-Thomsen et al., 2012; for the continuing use of prison labour in the United States, see Cao, 2019).

However, the combination of the platform and indebtedness presents a different set of coercive bargains for a capitalist class seeking to extract value from other human beings if we assume that the dispersed, disaggregated workforce of a time of platform isolation and debt may throw up some different mechanisms of disciplinary organization. Some established models designed to discipline working populations into particular forms of time management, household arrangement and geographical distribution seem no longer to be in play, or at least to not be in play so insistently. Given this, the kinds of disruption of proletariat discipline which mass incarceration seemed designed to punish or contain seems somewhat different. It may be that what we are living through is closer to a period of reproletarianization, as the reshaping of capitalism contracts some established economic and social arrangements while working to force human life into new regimes of degradation in the service of capital.

When Marx talks about the intensive violence required to birth the proletariat, he points to the extreme resistance of human beings to succumb and submit to the total disciplines of capital accumulation. People don't want to be told what to do, where to live, when to work. Neither do they want to know and be told that their whole lives must be subsumed into a version of work that must be undertaken in order to live, on terms that are never their own. In response, people run away, abscond, engineer any and every escape possible. They return endlessly to pre-capitalist timeframes of activity, bunking off, taking holidays, pleading faith or pleading nothing at all. As we see work transformed into something that perhaps has an echo of a much earlier moment in capitalism, and where the established contracts of employer and worker are in flux and cannot be easily relied upon, perhaps the particular violences of incarceration start to make a different sense.

Instead of considering mass incarceration to be a kind of adjunct to the productive economy, it might be more helpful for us to consider these techniques of the platform and debt and of the border and the prison as together forming an intertwined disciplinary net to hold populations in particular places without there being an overarching author of this global arrangement. The actions of individual states clearly have a tendency towards particular outcomes, including when these outcomes arise as part of an association with other states and other local contact. The prison then becomes one other important component of this machinery of population management that, in itself, makes little sense but when articulated alongside other multiple disciplines plays its part in constraining human populations claimed by no employer and, often now, in only the most tendential manner by any state.

The transformation of racial capitalism that I am trying to describe, knowing full well that transformation is too large a word, a word for what may well be only a far more modest adaptation to maintaining a certain kind of status quo – that transformation is a transformation away from understanding the economic ordering of the world as centred around an easily identifiable and bounded productive economy, perhaps reliant on what we might still understand as a process of industrialization. Saying this does not in any way discount the continuing role of manufacturing sectors or the factory form. We can see all over the world variations of this continuing or springing up anew. However, we have not been seeing the move towards large-scale massified production-line manufacturing across all regions and across all sectors in a way that perhaps, even in the twentieth century, many of us expected. Instead, we see an industrial economy that seems to be making itself smaller in its units, not larger, but which increasingly outsources many tasks in ways that seem to make invisible the employment relation – and, most surprisingly of all, which seems to have abandoned many of the innovations of coordination and efficiency that were charted so carefully in the last decades of the twentieth century. It seems clear that the major technical forces of capital are no longer attending to creating more efficient networks of production and instead have been turned elsewhere, to what the next phase of most profitable endeavour will be or already is.

Industrial production continues, and it is difficult still to imagine a world without it. But the centre of gravity of capitalist innovation and expansion and investment is not in smoothing the production lines of major manufacturing goods. There was a moment when our collective attention did seek to understand the shift in that global productive network. In particular, the assessment of the very rapid deindustrialization of some locations in the Global North alongside an assessment of what newer upstart regions appeared to be doing. Japanization (Wood, 1993) and the rise of the 'tiger' economies pointed to a need both to understand production as it could be organized most efficiently transnationally and across borders *and* to appreciate the melding of information, productive technology and supply chains. That moment, however, seems to have passed, and we see a turn away from seeking competitive gains by increasing the efficiency of manufacturing. What there is instead is a return to a kind of workshop manufacturing which services a large machinery of data-capture/prediction-logistics that overwhelmingly gain their competitive advantage through their systems of storage and delivery, including anticipatory relations to consumer behaviour (for an account of the data capture enabling this shift, see Sadowski, 2020). The benefits that come from the larger factory-style production appear to wane here, because the major platforms are sourcing goods for many, many different places of a huge variety and seek most of all to get these to another place or the right place quickly. The shift is from an industrialization imagined around industries such as the car industry and an industrialized world where many things are made at many scales in many places, and yet the massification is not at the point of production but at that of distribution.

Although the United States has typified the punitive state that shrinks all activity apart from an increasingly bloated penal system, the growth of prisons and prison-like practices is not at all limited to one country. If, instead of circling the pretence of 'liberal democracies' versus the rest of the world, we consider the largest global economies, it becomes apparent that carcerality appears alongside the rapid emergence of the world's new rich and still rich. If we consider state infrastructure, increasing and increasingly harsh carceral practices are identifiable in highly industrialized societies with functioning political institutions, in states engaged in protracted conflict, or resisting occupation, or in the long aftermath of violent conflict, and in varieties of authoritarian capitalism. If there is such a thing as a neoliberal/post-neoliberal moment that can describe the world with any efficacy, then carcerality is one of its recurrent phenomena.

At a common-sensical level, this succeeds. If 'neoliberalism' marks a shorthand for the incursion of a particular model of economic and political organization in which the gap between the rich and poor increases (Fiorentini, 2015), with the poor cast into ever more extreme penury and any last vestiges of the caring or redistributive state are dismantled (Sowels, 2019), then we can see why it might be convenient to expand the prison population. This, in fact, comes very close to the analytic framework of prison abolitionists (Ryan and Ward, 2014; Saed, 2012), leaning heavily on the earlier work of Angela Davis and Ruth Wilson Gilmore (Davis, 2011; Gilmore, 2007). This is the account that argues that prisons 'disappear' inconvenient populations – those who have been displaced and dispossessed, those who cannot be easily absorbed into the productive economy, those who pose a disruptive threat (in part arising from the first two characteristics) (Gilmore, 1999). There is little that is *necessarily* racialized about such categorizations. Yet the sedimented cumulative dispossession that shapes the landscape of racial capitalism cannot be separated from the landscapes of carcerality. Cumulative dispossession exacerbated by systemic racism spits people out into highly constrained possibilities of survival. Whereas once these might have been the wastelands alongside and beyond the productive economy, the dispersal of economic activity via platforms also informs a new dispersal of human communities. Perhaps the carcerality of our moment represents an attempt to contain and corral errant humans, curtailing their attempts at wriggling away from the diminishments of proletarianization.

6

Platform Capitalism as a Remaking of Racial Capitalism

What is the puzzle?

The rise of the platforms opens a number of renewed puzzles for us all. How does this economic model reach into so much of our lives while, apparently, disrupting the possibilities of solidarity between us? With the platform, it seems capital has discovered at last how to combine the will to subordinate all human (and other) life to the logic of accumulation with processes of dispersal and atomization that postpone class consciousness and, perhaps, class agency. It is mass production, but not as we have known it.

The framework of racial capitalism encourages us to think not only of the manner in which longstanding histories of racism and dispossession become folded into each new moment of capitalist development but also of how each new iteration of capitalist remaking might adjust techniques of racism for its own ends.

The rise of platforms includes a number of intriguing shifts in corporate behaviour. What changes is not the core logic of capital – to strip value and accumulate, to reconstitute itself, to tend towards the monopolistic. Instead, what changes are the means and approaches to pursuing these ends.

The analysis of the platform form has burgeoned in recent years, offering a whole new literature linking questions of corporate form, employment practices, consumer reach and logistical connections.

I cannot and do not pretend to offer new insights overlooked in this scholarship. Instead, I try to utilize the insights of this scholarship to consider three questions pertinent to an understanding of racial capitalism:

- What shifts in this corporate form and how does it remake or unmake racialized differentiation?
- What happens to the terms, character and organization of work and with what relation to previous racialized segmentation of the labour market?
- How does the rise of platforms reshape the economic terrain, amending the racialized dispersal of populations and the racialized framing and status of economic activity?

For our purposes, the task is to reorientate our understanding of racial capitalism to incorporate what we have learned about platform capitalism. Inevitably, what follows here is schematic but, I hope, sketches a way forward for further discussion.

Why thinking about platforms is important for an understanding of racial capitalism

This volume is an attempt to reorientate the question of racial capitalism to our current circumstances. If capitalism continues to operate by dispersing us into racialized segments, with hierarchical value attributed to racialized categories and this whole system of differentiation acting as a central (constitutive not incidental) aspect of the remaking of capital, then we should be at least slightly curious when the organizational forms of capitalism alter. The advent of the platform asks us to reconsider what we understand by 'the firm', 'the corporation', 'logistics' and 'infrastructure' – and a reconsideration of these previously core terms in the lexicon of capitalism demands a reconsideration of what we may previously have understood as the logics and techniques of racial capitalism (for an instructive overview of the business structure of platforms and what this implies for our future understanding of business growth and innovation, see Kenney et al., 2019; for a schematization of the characteristics of logistics platforms which spans both established regional platforms and the continuities with the emergence of newer transnational platforms, see Cote et al., 2021). Exciting scholars of colonial infrastructure and its legacy have taught us of the manner in which the disciplines of capitalism in its colonial incarnation operated through infrastructural means, building on the debate-shaping work of Daniel Headrick placing the role of technology in imperial practices (Headrick, 1981; Bhattacharyya, 2018). Increasingly, scholars of settler-colonialism point to the centrality of infrastructural projects in the extractivist violences of settler projects, in one swoop stealing from, dispossessing, displacing and erasing Indigenous communities (Glenn, 2015; Cowen, 2020; Curley, 2021). However, it is only with the rise of platform capitalism that the consequences of folding together corporation, logistics and infrastructure fully enter our collective consciousness.

This, then, is one key insight to digest. The platform corporation operates by extending the business of the firm into what we might previously have considered as 'infrastructure', and it is this extension and capture of the networks of organizational form that together create the possibility of the valorization of capital that signals something unfamiliar. As more established accounts of racial capitalism have tended to point to varieties of racialized segmentation of space and time, this reshaping is significant (we might think here not only of Cedric Robinson, 1983, but also of the energetic attempts to chart the history of racial capitalism including Leroy and Jenkins, 2021).

The rise of platform forms blurs the boundaries between the corporation and economic infrastructure. Whereas perhaps previously our economic analysis sorted entities into production, transportation, storage, distribution, retail, marketing – now platforms span these sectors, in the process remaking the infrastructures of energy use and transport, blurring the boundaries of communications and retail, embedding their operations into every cranny until we can no longer distinguish between what is a transaction and what is just living.

In the process of the expansion of the reach of platforms, we not only see more and more of the spaces of everyday life become included in the purview of corporate interest, we also find that our everyday lives rely increasingly on an infrastructure of services and connections embedded and sustained by corporations. This is not the taking over of public space or public infrastructure by private interests, although it may include this as well. Plantin and his colleagues suggest this is 'a "platformization" of infrastructure and an "infrastructuralization" of platforms' (Plantin et al., 2018: 3). In important instances, this is a remaking of the infrastructure of everyday life as indistinguishable from corporate logistics. We might think here of the remaking of the infrastructure of public higher education by Amazon (see Williamson et al., 2022) or the ascent of Facebook to the role of gatekeeper to an uncountable number of online services

(Ko et al., 2010). In both instances, we learn to recalibrate our lives through the logistical machineries developed for corporate interests.

Immediately, this adaptation – akin to driving on a road system built by car companies for the development and transportation of cars – encourages us to reconsider the terms of racial capitalism. The embedding of everyday life into the infrastructure of platforms seems to militate against the textured differentiation of populations we have known from other moments of racial capitalism (for an enlightening account of the racialized urban political economy of global cities and the deadly consequences for those deemed 'surplus', see Danewid, 2020; for an exemplary account of the processes of rendering surplus enacted through urban planning in Brazil and South Africa, see Melgaço and Coelho, 2022). Unlike previous understandings of the concentration of productive forces, the process of underpinning practices of everyday life allows platforms to extend their reach, incorporate greater numbers into their 'markets' and not be reliant on standardizing or homogenizing human populations. While we see plenty of indication that humans continue to be rendered surplus or expendable or 'less than human', the economic logics surrounding these outcomes are in flux. That movement, where humans are made surplus but in differently unpredictable patterns, is part of the puzzle of a changing racial capitalism.

Digital capitalism and the differentiation of populations

The age of platforms and of digital capitalism raises some questions for our understanding of the differentiation of populations that is such a core characteristic of racial capitalism. There is an extensive and persuasive literature informing us of the manner in which digital capitalism operates by capturing and monetizing our leisure and private lives (Sadowski, 2020; Canpolat, 2021). This, we have quickly learned, is a process that also re-creates and amplifies cultures of racism and othering, including by siphoning users into explicitly racist trails arising from the embedded racist associations of predictive online searches (Noble, 2018; Benjamin, 2019). However, and perhaps against our habit, anticapitalists should be wary of accounts that over-focus on the excesses and moral failures of particular corporations. Instead, and in order to assist our attempts to see racial capitalism as it is remade today, we might consider platforms as the corporate form of a particular phase or moment in capitalist history (famously proposed by Srnicek, 2016; among other influential accounts is Langley and Leyshon, 2017).

> Platforms are responsible for the management of digital markets, which open new cycles of value extraction and capital accumulation. . . . we consider platforms as part of a larger socioeconomic order in which they assume a leading role, but in coordination with the wide range of institutions that take part in the digital economy. In this regard, the performance of platforms is deeply dependent on their relation to financial markets and government policy. (de Rivera, 2020: 726)

This summary helps us to conceptualize what shifts in the economic landscape: an altered corporate form operating in a differently constituted and weakly regulated market, enabled through the need of finance capital to siphon funds somewhere and inadvertently protected by the mismatch of state policy designed for an earlier set of economic formations. Rather than in Google or Uber or Amazon, our interest is in the nature and logic of this socioeconomic order.

To be clear, this is not a wholesale shift in economic arrangements. What we see, as is perhaps the case in every phase, is an uneven landscape where older forms of profit-seeking and profit-making exist alongside the formations of the digital economy. Key to this is the manner in which the machineries of scraping value via personal data appear to flatten differences between populations and zones. Far from differentiating, this is a moment where the poor and the displaced may constitute sources of value and valuable data in a manner almost identical to more obviously lucrative consumer markets (for an instructive account of data-scraping activity in refugee camps, see Madianou, 2019). We seem finally to have entered a moment when the market makes us interchangeable, perhaps also reaching towards that perpetual promise of capitalism, to make every human life valuable, albeit valuable only in market terms. The differentiating processes of the just passing phase of racial capitalism, reliant on differing positioning in relation to the wage economy and differential (and enforced) reliance on the realm of social reproduction to sustain life, now operate alongside this additional logic of interchangeability via the digital economy.

Disconcertingly, this is a set of processes based on a model of personalization (Kalpokas, 2019). Whatever similarities of process or experience arise, these are not processes that can bring us together. This is not the massifying force of the factory; we are not the assembly line. Our atomization is embedded in the business model. In fact, if we are not atomized, we cease to be so valuable and our data ceases to be a source of insight. This is not quite the argument arising from the suggestive term of 'beta lives' and the identification of our constant interplay within a complex system where our data and activity at once disrupt and consolidate the working of the whole (Kalpokas, 2021). Capitalism for us, therefore, represents a moment where the desire to automate and standardize seems magically to be coupled with the simultaneous push towards individualization, differentiation and the breaking of social bonds.

All of which I think requires at least a moment of our consideration.

Datafication of all our lives

Our question here is: What does the emergence of accumulation via datafication do to landscapes of racialized differentiation and inequality? The possible strands of such a discussion might include:

- access to work: platforms transform the entry points to the labour market, often rewriting the terms of employment and serving to occlude the role of the employer. Famously, some of the most powerful and visible platforms have attempted to refuse the responsibility of employer. Vallas and Schor argue that platform work is highly variegated and cannot be generalized, including at least the five key types of technologists of platforms; cloud-based freelancers; gig-workers engaged via platforms; microtaskers employed on a range of online tasks; and content-producers and influencers (Vallas and Schor, 2020). However, despite the variety of roles and entry points, platforms remain resistant to existing frameworks to combat racism and discrimination (Piracha et al., 2019). More than this, the practices of platform work mobilize the pre-existing landscapes of dispossession and exclusion, leading to what Gebrial (2022) calls racial platform capitalism.
- character of work: datafication has opened questions about where and how profit can be made. Building on the highly anxious debates of the later twentieth century linked to the imagined death of manufacturing, discussions of datafication and work tend to revolve around the loss of jobs (Hester and Srnicek, 2017). Alongside this, there is a more fundamental question about what the economy does if, as we are led to believe, it no longer makes things. Of course, these anxieties can be misleading. Manufacturing may be reconfigured, but the capitalist world remains one teeming with stuff, made, extracted, adapted, exchanged. The stuff seems to be drowning us, not disappearing. Better then, instead of pointing to a shift from something

called manufacturing to something else altogether, to think again about how we conceptualize different moments of economic history characterized by altered configurations between manufacturing, services, logistics, communications and data (for a discussion of the increased role of logistics in the shift to data capitalism, see Tang and Veelenturf, 2019). If, as seems likely, we have not moved beyond the dominance of the commodity, then perhaps it is more useful to think again about the machinery of economic activity that arises in differing moments of commodification.

- the incorporation of the realm of social reproduction: a variety of feminist scholarship and activism has instructed the broader anticapitalist community to recognize social reproduction work as the always necessary supplement to the productive economy, with variations in the arrangement of social reproduction reflecting (often local) battles around the rights of women, the provision of welfare and the changing demand for (formal) labour (Katz, 2001; Bakker, 2007; Ferguson, 2016; Federici, 2020). What the advent of data capitalism does is amend and perhaps extend the possibility of re-routing the value production of the realm of social reproduction into the circuits of capital in ways that (further) bypass the wage relation. In particular, as the configuration of waged work shifts, the incorporation of the work of social reproduction is important to understand.
- the economics of consumption: this element of becoming a capitalist subject seemed to fall away from interest in the first years of the twenty-first century. After considerable discussion of the politics and processes of consumption as an alternative lens through which to understand our formation as capitalist subjects (Featherstone, 1990), the expansion of consumer-like behaviours into many, if not all, spheres of life displaces the language of consumption from our analytic discourse. After an interlude where attempts were made to meld together insights from accounts of both production and consumption (Ritzer and Jurgenson, 2010), our collective attention has turned to the manner in which our consumer desires, habits and practices are collated as part of our overall data footprint (Zuboff, 2019). Whereas previously theories of consumer culture might have tracked attempts to shape consumer desire, in the process shaping the kinds of desiring subjects that could emerge in any moment of capitalist existence, data capitalism moves away from the will to standardize our consumer desires. Instead, the proliferation of pathways to capitalist subjecthood, each now captured as the carefully documented biography of a

life lived in constant interaction with an economy mediated through data, recentres consumer desire as the traceable element of an economic landscape built on endless differentiation.

Raciality as a compensation for atomization

One part of the puzzle is how insistently resurgent racism seems to be. If anything, it seems that the violent divisions of racist cultures and of racist movements seem to thrive in the arena of data capture and data sharing (for an account of the use of global online cultures by white supremacist organizations, see Daniels, 2009; for an exploration of the experiences of those targeted in online racism, see Ortiz, 2021). The logic of zero-sum, where no one can win unless somebody else loses, pushes us into the most defensive of arms (for an account of the active resurrection of the terms of 'culture wars' as a tactic of right-wing media forms, see Davis, 2019; for a review of research examining the role of social media in increasing political polarization, see Kubin and von Sikorski, 2021). There is a collectivity being remade through the digital sphere, but all too often it is a return to the most offensive and unsettled forms of nationalism. At the same time, we see the highly punitive policing of spaces of living, casting some out into the new wastelands of the beyond, of the border, of encampment, of imprisonment (Mbembe, 2019). The fantasy of a global homogenized workforce-cum-consumerforce, where every human being can be brought to the altar of the market to render up their value, and where humanity may, at long last, forget the different divisions between ourselves as we find out that we are all equally serfs in the new feudalism, that fantasy remains remote. All of which demands that we register both the familiar ways in which our particular moment of capitalist adaptation does not erase older racisms and the manner in which it inhabits new racisms in new ways, conjuring up new forms of difference, which ultimately are both dangerous and endanger us all.

How platforms remake waged work and the segregated labour market

Thanks to the rapid and insistent work of many scholars, activists and activist-scholars, collectively we know quite a lot about the manner in which platforms remake waged work (Graham et al., 2020; Jones, 2021; Altenried, 2020; van Doorn, 2017; Woodcock and Graham, 2019). Our interest here is in understanding how these shifts in the nature and organization of work in their turn remake racial capitalism, with the understanding that the impacts of such changes on the landscape of inclusion, exclusion or partial exclusion from the labour market, the formal economy or the (fantastical) realm of the productive are still emerging and remain undecided. Our interest, then, is not to chase down the moment of 'racism' and point triumphantly. Instead, let us try to remain open to what is puzzling about this moment, in the hope that learning how platforms position workers in ways that do and do not replicate familiar racisms might help us to battle a little more effectively for our collective survival.

To do this, we return again to the question of waged work and its reframing through the entry of platforms. There are two key elements to this reframing. One is the concerted attempt to dismantle, obscure and deny the employment relation. The second is the incursion of work for/through platforms into 'non-work' arenas. Both tendencies blur the edges of 'employment' and further collapse the boundaries between the arenas of production and of social reproduction.

Platforms automate the process of bringing the fruits of labour to market – we might understand a number of early success stories, not least those of Amazon and Uber, as exercises in redirecting capital away from seeking improvements in production and towards pursuing competitiveness by capturing the space of distribution. In the process, 'jobs' are increasingly reframed as 'tasks' (or 'gigs', or even as 'microwork').

The business model embedded in this shift to modern-day piecework is well understood already (Lehdonvirta, 2018; Alkhatib et al., 2017). In the face of employment legislation and/or worker organization and/or social norms that seek to ensure the most minimal rights and protections for workers, innovative employers seek to remake their businesses in ways that occlude or deny the role of the employer (Williams and Horodnic, 2019). Perhaps more than a response to legislative regulation (which is patchy and challenging to enforce in any case), the dispersal of 'jobs' into 'tasks' indicates an altering conception of the place of workers in the planning and administration of the business. Labour conceived as a series of discrete tasks as opposed to a workforce, or even as a set of contracted workers, leads to some well-documented changes in the presentation (if not the reality) of the employment relation (De Stefano et al., 2021). The disciplines of work skew increasingly towards incentives and checks based in reputational management, with the employer pretending to be no more than a broker between worker-producer and consumer. As a result, the highly intrusive surveillance and disciplinary systems of platform work are narrated as varieties of self-management or, even, self-development (Sannon et al., 2022). The gamification of work (Cardador et al., 2017) and the (pretended or, at least, only partial) automation of management can work to obscure the operation of workplace racisms. Sometimes the workplace itself is disappeared in favour of varieties of screen-based organization of tasks where, it is made to seem, no one but the worker themselves is responsible for any aspect of the working environment or any other work outcomes (Jones, 2021). The audacity of abolishing bosses in the name of good business is a move that demands some attention.

Early and ground-breaking research on this form of employment has pointed to the manner in which some forms of platform work exacerbate racialized divisions and hierarchies in the labour market (for a suggestive account of the remaking/continuation of racialized labour markets via platform work, see Altenried and Bojadzijev, 2017; for a ground-breaking account of labour organizing in Uber, including to address racism, see Aslam and Woodcock, 2020). Perhaps most notably, accounts of driving work and lift platforms point to the over-representation of some of the most underprotected segments of the labour force in these jobs, both reflecting the pre-existing patterns of driving work and revealing a tendency for emerging and further deregulated forms to be saturated with workers, with few other routes to regular employment (Chihara, 2022).

It is worth pausing for a moment here to consider what we mean by 'racism in and through work'. I say this not to underplay the extreme and challenging forms of aversive racism that scar the working lives of many. My point is not to proclaim that only some things (structural, leading to measurable detriment) are really racism and others (discomfort, threats to safety, humiliation) are not. My point is only to seek to slow our rush to denounce the racism of platform capitalism so quickly that we do not pause to consider what and how this particular inflection of racism through capitalism might be.

In the most schematic of ways, I try here to lay out what the distinctive racisms of platform capitalism might be. As always, I am indebted to the scores of researchers who have shared their insights in a manner that allows this speculation.

Varieties of racism at work – platforms and changing labour markets

It can be easy to speak of workplace racism as if it is one thing, always recognizable and with an implication of uniform and predictable impacts. It is hard to escape the quiet assumption that we all know what workplace racism is and that what we 'know' has the same referent (for an insight into the range and extent of varieties of racism in UK workplaces, see Ashe and Nazroo, 2017). It might be more helpful to think of the varieties of workplace racism made and enabled through shifts in the organization of work.

Some simple starting points – and readers may wish to focus on understanding the kind of barrier or detriment racism can be at work before seeking to sort such detriments into a hierarchy of importance – might be:

- entry into work. We know there are racialized barriers to entry in a wide range of jobs deemed covetable because stable, or relatively well paid, or because representing the main or only form of ongoing employment in the vicinity. Sometimes this occurs through explicitly racialized networks of entry, such as industries which have required an introduction by a current worker or where tests of racialized belonging are disguised (thinly) as requirements for entry (Guo, 2015). More often in recent times, these barriers to gaining a particular form of employment rely on a network of informal racisms, with individual discriminatory actions enabled or encouraged by systems designed to appear 'colour-blind' while replicating workplace hierarchies. Employment via platform operates, for some, as a method of circumventing the overtly racialized barriers to accessing work. In fact, we see some infamous platforms operating predominantly in the less enfranchised sections of the labour market, promising entry to well-paid work without the hurdles or barriers erected to limit entry to more regulated forms of employment (van Doorn et al., 2020). Despite the riskiness of the work in many cases (Moore, 2018), employment via platform can unsettle the established racialized barriers to entering the labour market.
- distribution of tasks within the workplace. We might consider this as a Fordist mode of workplace racism, with dirty, dangerous tasks allocated to racially subordinated groups who continue to have lesser protection in the workplace. Infamously, this has included unionized

workplaces where unions have aligned themselves with employers in order to maintain the racialized privileges of their membership or a portion of their membership (Butler, 2006). The outsourcing of the distribution of tasks to digital platforms disrupts the relationship between employer and employee, a disruption exploited by employers in order to offload risks to the employee. Employment via platform corrals the worker into the management and distribution of their tasks, albeit with penalties or incentives or nudges for those unwilling or unable to take up the 'offer' (Scheiber, 2017). In the process, the status attributed to differing tasks becomes more difficult to read. We might think of this, also, as an aspect of the 'wages of whiteness' that is in flux.

- progression within work. How a person can and cannot gain greater recognition and pay as their working life progresses has become an important element of the landscape of workplace racisms (Ashe and Nazroo, 2017). The partial erosion of ethnicized barriers to particular industries, in part enabled by the reframing of hiring triggered by equality legislation (itself an outcome of struggles over access to work and services), opens another battle-line of workplace discrimination. In workplaces and industries where there are fewer racialized barriers to entry (and in many or most former colonial powers these continue to exist to varying extents across industries), treatment within the workplace becomes a central technique of continuing differentiation. In the workplace remade via platforms, the structures of progression are pushed back onto the worker. Sometimes, enragingly, workplace progression is gamified (Woodcock and Johnson, 2018). At the same time, the statuses arising from a seemingly more static and knowable landscape of racial capitalism become more elusive, and sometimes may become meaningless.

Racial capitalism through platforms, 1: performing the racialized self

I begin with this because it is this interaction between customer and worker, so often disciplined by the use of ratings, that has garnered popular attention (Chan, 2019). As the sectors of work that have been remade via platforms most visibly fall within varieties of personal service, the manner in which performances of self are hampered or remade by the dynamic of interpersonal racism has been noted (Rosenblat et al., 2017). Rogers summarizes the challenge with reference to Uber drivers:

To stay above a certain rating, drivers may need to be friendly, and perhaps a bit servile. Cab drivers, in comparison, can afford to be themselves – which may involve venting their frustration at long hours and low pay. Such emotional labor may impose a disparate burden on racial minorities. Minority drivers, to retain high ratings, may need to overcome white passengers' preconceptions, which can involve 'identity work.' (Rogers, 2015: 98)

The framework of ratings operates to transform every aspect of human contact into an aspect of the transaction or service. Performing self, and here a self that is simultaneously efficient and friendly yet servile, becomes an urgently important element of maintaining access to work. Of course, no attempt to 'rate' the satisfaction derived from the interaction with the worker giving you a service can be torn free of the dangerous traps of racialized social meaning (Piracha et al., 2019).

A whole set of platforms (although not all) base their business on the illusion of a form of brokering. Platforms adopt the language of enabling, with a pretence of empowerment for consumers and workers. They might pander to our weakness for 'rating' goods and services, another sign of the contraction of our political imaginations to an accountability that is little more than the online equivalent of complaining to the manager. Removing the direct supervision of many workers, instead inserting the surveillance of the app, platform-mediated services speak to our sense of being demeaned, overlooked and underserved (as, of course, we are) and weaponizes it as a technique of horizontal consumer–worker disciplining. The super-rich become less visible than ever, with one or two eccentric representatives hogging headlines and the larger class obscured by the revamped commodity fetishism of the platform form. At the same time, we, poor saps, turn on one another, as if we now truly believe that the sorrows and disappointments of our disrespected lives arise from a too-slow delivery or a disappointing demeanour when served and not from the subordination of human life to the imperatives of capital.

Racial capitalism through platforms, 2: squatting in the divisions of a racially divided labour market

Despite the understandable interest in Uber as an exemplar of platform work, others argue that an over-interest in Uberization occludes other forms of platform work and other types of platform worker (for a discussion of carework platforms and the distinctive experience of women workers operating via platforms as 'cultural entrepreneurs', see Ticona and Mateescu, 2018). The implied gendering of Uber and Deliveroo drivers, imagined as lone male workers, often migrants, tied into modes of work that are masculinized in particular ways owing to the valorization of temporal and spatial flexibility and the disregard of possible risks arising from mobile lone working, impacts on how we can conceive of mobilization in the face of platform capitalism.

Theorists of the platform have schooled us in this adaptation of the available approaches to valorization (for an admirably illuminating account, see van Doorn and Badger, 2020). Although only a few years ago the workings of platforms may have appeared mysterious, not least in our understanding of the business model in play, now every person with a passing engagement with the online world understands what is being bought and sold.

> The 'capitalism of the platforms' begins to be structured. We refer to the ability of companies to define a new composition of capital capable of managing in an increasingly automated way a process of dividing data according to the commercial use that may derive from it. It is based on the participation, more or less conscious, of individual users, now transformed into prosumers. (Fumagalli et al., 2018: 66)

Much remains mysterious in this formulation, not least the manner in which this compartmentalized data can be put to commercial use. However, the recognition of deployment of data as a mode of business, as opposed to a mode of marketing alone, has entered both scholarly and popular understandings. Fumagalli and colleagues propose a distinction between digital work and digital labour, with the first referring to the diminished versions of waged labour undertaken through digital technologies and the second referencing the 'human activity used by other platform-based business models . . . that rely on a new composition of capital capable of capturing personal information and transforming it into big data' (ibid.: 67).

This distinction between digital work and digital labour arises in recognition of the increasingly degraded quality of waged work undertaken via platforms. Some have argued that this mode of buying labour power represents a shift away from 'jobs' and towards varieties of task-based or piecework (Dubal, 2020; Potocka-Sionek, 2022). While we might doubt claims of an end to work or employment, it is hard to see how established structures of hierarchization and differentiation in space and time within the labour market can be maintained in a world of discrete tasks for pay. Although it seems apparent that the most notable and noticeable sectors of intensively platform-mediated work have been those already occupied by racially minoritized and/or migrant workers (Gebrial, 2022), we might surmise that this early entry to some sectors reflects most of all the limited employment protections in play in these segments of the labour market. The ability of platform corporations to enter, transform and capture some forms of work such as driving or delivering does not mean that other less historically subordinated forms of work are immune from the transformations and degradations of platformization. And, as we see such shifts enter a range of workplaces, we might also wonder whether the racialized segmentation of work as we have known it until recently can be sustained. Or sustained in the same way.

Schor et al. (2020) characterize platform work as described in one of the following three modes: precarity, efficiency and algorithmic control. In response, they argue that platform work must be understood as a combination of these three aspects, leading to a highly heterogeneous workforce who cannot be understood as overwhelmingly precaritized or as self-managing, and that workers occupy differing labour market positions which amend the apparently colour-gender-status blindness of algorithmic control. In addition, the authors show that platform labour can include highly differentiated experiences of work both between platforms and across one platform. Yet across types of work, workers increasingly lose the small protections of previously familiar employment relations. 'Platform labor intermediaries are active "infrastructural" agents in the reconstitution of labor relations and the nature of work, further institutionalizing the tenuous post-Fordist social contract that forces workers to shoulder the risks and responsibilities of social reproduction' (van Doorn, 2017: 5).

When we think about shifts in the organization of work and corporations, it is easy to imagine a wholesale change that happens all at once. One day there was smallholding agriculture, the next there were factories; one day there was Fordist production, the next there was disorganized capitalism morphing into platform capitalism as the deployment of data overrides all other business approaches. While this chapter focuses on the impact of platform economics on patterns of racial capitalism, these shifts occur alongside a continuation of other older economic arrangements. The realignment we are living through arises from this overlapping of differing arrangements, with new economic forms squatting on top of far older formations, perhaps even reliant on these remnants of a world just passing. Whereas Schor and colleagues argue that platform work relies on the existence of more stable and rewarded work in the form of the much mourned standard employment, such modes of work are in decline both globally and within more local labour markets. We might speculate that what comes next is not an extension of platform work as we now know it to all sections of the labour market, but instead, perhaps, a further mutation of work to encompass a variety of platform work, some on demand but some constituted in other still emerging ways.

The racist representations of digital capitalism

As a small detour, and to reveal once again my own intellectual trajectory, data-tracking is also a representational practice. However extensive and various the elements, data form a symbolic representation of the person in question – no more a reduction than any other representational form (a painting, a photograph), but, nevertheless, a necessarily partial account.

For the cultures of racialization rehearsed through digital data mapping, this means that we lack an everyday language of representational critique. The demeaning racialization of more established forms of media is well documented (Jacobs, 2000; Titley, 2019). We have learned to challenge these practices. We know (we think) the impact of such representations on social relations. We know that some representational tactics are bad and damaging to the social esteem and status of some groups (Morris, 2000). We may even argue that the propagation of such demeaning representations is itself an issue of struggle.

Of course, the strong consciousness of viewing a representation is largely absent from our encounter with data. The everyday aesthetics of data representation are still being learned by most audiences (for an account of virtual literacy that goes beyond instrumental considerations, see Dengel, 2018; for a collection that opens the question of aesthetic and algorithmic literacy, Schulze Heuling and Filk, 2021). Although we are learning all too quickly that our lives are infiltrated, logged and stored, the extensive repertoire of popular interpretation (and alternative construction and reading) that accompanies older and more familiar representational forms has yet to emerge for digital data of the everyday.

Noble highlights the role of representation early in her groundbreaking and widely read work *Algorithms of Oppression*: 'Think about the impact of algorithms on how people are represented in other seemingly benign business transactions . . . how business owners are revolting due to loss of control over how they are represented and the impact of how the public finds them' (Noble, 2018: 95). The work of Noble and, differently but connectedly, of Zuboff (2019) frame the challenges of surveillance capitalism as a set of discriminations to be fixed. By discrimination, I am trying to indicate the view of racism as an anomalous behaviour to be corrected, with the implication that society has a default of frictionless and non-discriminatory interaction between social actors. In this instance, we can understand this to be the distinction between wishing more and better regulation of the internet and viewing the racialized workings of the internet as a technique of racial capitalism.

So, if we revisit the challenges of our data-driven age through this lens, we need to think about how the predictive use of data works to remake the inherent differentiation of racial capitalism.

To review why this is a tricky thing to think about:

- The predictive use of data clearly replicates some aspects of what we might understand as racial profiling. However, the accumulation of data is presented as individualization. No pattern of background data can be the same for any two individuals – and therefore, we are encouraged to believe, such blunt descriptors as 'race' disappear in the face of this new mode of imagining and representing the connections of human life.
- The analytic framework of racial capitalism is not one focused on representation or, even, 'ideas'. This is a mode of thought seeking to uncover the practices and structures that disperse, segregate, differentiate and hierarchize 'populations'. In fact, I would go so far as to suggest that it is these combined disciplinary processes which conjure up 'populations', transforming human beings into categorizable and placeable bundles. However, the tools or machinery (or whatever metaphor for exerting power we use here) of predictive data use rest on practices of representation. We might consider this particular mode of representational practices as a new terrain of exploitation or value extraction, not least because this takes us to the question of how this disembodied and highly dispersed set of practices can become a vehicle for the differentiating processes of racial capitalism.
- Even if we accept the contention that predictive data use constitutes a new frontier of value extraction, previously existing economic landscapes remain. In the main, it is these residual structures arising from work and non-work, metropolis and periphery, and the necropolis in the metropolis that place us in our differentiated yet interconnected nightmares. We need to think more about how data-informed modes

of value extraction work alongside and on top of this longer-standing formation.

Capitalist (and anticapitalist) subjects

Platforms require a certain self-training and information awareness from consumers – this, in effect, is the basis of their reach. Yet, as the world of platforms proceeds, consumer knowledges also become a form of class consciousness, perhaps not yet organized but certainly not straightforwardly compliant. The knowing consumer of platform services and products has an awareness of the value of their personal data and the manner in which data collection has been built into practices of consumption. We know this, in part, from the additional services available to minimize or swerve such data collection. Of course, knowingness about the workings of platforms creates a customer base for services which can allow users to disguise their online and consumer activity.

We might think of this unsettled accommodation and simultaneous disruption as an aspect of the tussle that takes place when a new mode of control and subjugation is threatening to emerge. We have come to understand more clearly the extent to which proletarianization demanded intensive violence and also the variety of ways in which people ducked and dived and avoided and ran away and chose to exit from the constraints of wage labouring. Our histories of work, waged and unwaged, include a documentation of disruption by workers, from shirking to sabotage. However inescapable the machine of data-led prediction may appear, perhaps we are in the very first moments of this encounter, before people learn to become invisible or differently visible, or before we learn to disrupt the process of data collection through using 'consumer practices'. Perhaps in this early moment the terms of our subjectivation remain to be decided.

In this context of rapid renegotiation, where the imposition of techniques which strip value from what we might have considered 'private' or 'non-productive' activity in the past creates new arenas of the economy, the question of how any of us might become a political agent remains. I take this to be one organizing question of McKenzie Wark's entertaining but alarming message in *Capital is Dead* (2019). Wark describes a world where the vectoralist class has become predominant, controlling the flow of ideas and knowledge in a way that subordinates other segments of the economy. What we might understand as capitalist production is still around, but it is not in the ascendant – in fact, it is in decline, representing a set of social relations that are in the process of being superseded.

Racial capitalism through platforms, 3: the question of logistics

Our interest here is not so much in the potential flattening of experience through the automation of key processes of distribution. Although there is an engaging and persuasive body of work arguing against automation and for varieties of new Luddism (Benanav, 2020; Mueller, 2021), I attempt to remain agnostic about the impact of technological change. As has been asserted and demonstrated repeatedly, the racializing and racist impacts of the digital turn arise not from some glitch within the technology but from the human inputs on which all algorithms rely (Fountain, 2022; Benjamin, 2020).

Our interest, then, is not so much in the racist deployment of new technologies by actors who have a long history of racist deployment of everything. Instead, our task is to try to understand if and how platformization remakes the racialized segmentation of economic life in all its forms. To be clear, this remaking may include both a replication of longstanding racialized divisions and hierarchies and a disruption of previous landscapes of racial capitalism. This disruption can amend or adapt existing patterns of status and entitlement and access but, equally and simultaneously, can erode previous expectations of racialized privilege and the comparative security that can bring.

The intriguing and instructive lesson for us here is to shift our gaze from the question 'How does the employer seek to cut the costs of labour and remove employment protections?' to 'How do platform corporations attend to the question of logistics as the central operational and business concern, and how does remaking of the logistical infrastructure then remake the landscape of racial capitalism?'

Despite the often disastrous impacts on workers, the rise of platforms pushes us to relearn ways of understanding corporate behaviour that may not centre the employer–worker relationship (Drahokoupil and Fabo, 2016). I say this not at all to diminish the urgent questions about working lives in a time of platforms – questions that are extending into new sectors daily (Eurofound, 2018; Krzywdzinski and Gerber, 2020). Incorporating logistical capacity into the platform and utilizing this capacity as a central aspect of the business is a development that shifts the manner in which populations are positioned in the service of capital. To understand the scale of this rebalancing towards logistics, it is helpful to be reminded of the rapidity and scale of Amazon's transformation into a logistics-led endeavour. Amazon, 'instead of relying on UPS and FedEx, . . . created "Amazon Logistics" delivery service in 2018 to gain better control of the last mile delivery performance (speed, reliability, and cost). In 2018, the company's fulfillment and shipping expenses amounted to $34.0 billion and $27.7 billion respectively, up from just over $1 billion each in 2007' (Tang and Veelenturf, 2019).

Felix Richter, writing for Statista, identifies an increase in Amazon's logistics costs that amount to a near doubling between 2019 and 2021. In 2021, Amazon's fulfilment and shipping costs came to $151.8 billion, representing 32.3 per cent of the net sales. At the same time, Baidu, Alibaba and Tencent have extended their logistical capability in collaboration with the Chinese state's Belt and Road Initiative (Su and Flew, 2021), in the process folding corporate aspirations into the push to construct a new silk road, combining physical and digital infrastructure.

We might understand the platform as an organizational form that shapes the economic landscape through control of logistical networks, with workers distributed across this network as one more moveable resource (for some consideration of the questions raised for economic geography, see Kenney and Zysman, 2020). Whereas the emergence of massified production demanded massification of human residence, with the whole business of the (often violently abbreviated) life-course huddled around nodal points of production and the segregated statuses of that shape of racial capitalism mirroring segmentation of the working populations, platformization suggests different spatial and temporal arrangements. If platforms subordinate human life to the demands of accumulation, then this is done through a logic of logistical network, not productive centre, or not productive centre alone (for a discussion of this for the global labour market, see Graham and Anwar, 2019). In the process, how we work and live to work comes to be organized and differentiated in slightly amended ways.

Whereas perhaps the moment of high industrialism imagined the human body as an adjunct to the factory machine – and the elements of social reproduction grudgingly accommodated in the outcome of struggle reflect what might be required to remake the adjunct to the machine (Ware, [1924] 1964) – the moment of populations dispersed to serve the logistical chain implies something else again.

For our habits of thought, this slight disruption from productive centres to logistical networks might appear to unmake the differentiating terms of racial capitalism. In the economy, where logistics are central to an ascendant logic of accumulation, the work of racialized differentiation plays out in other patterns, but this is not a flattening into sameness (Alimahomed-Wilson and Reese, 2021; Danyluk, 2021). Whatever we might wish, the unmaking of elements of the knowable racialized hierarchies of work and place and sector and residence of a just passing moment does not mean we are entering, at long last, the time of ecstatic and automatic unity and non-differentiation among the global working class.

Rather than thinking of the moment of platformization as a transformation, we might better think of it as a rebalancing or amendment in emphasis. Something like logistics was already part of the productive forces – and perhaps has been since humans have engaged in more complex collaborative forms of production. One account places the violent instrumentalization of social relations at the heart of racial capitalism, with logistics functioning as the reframing of people as things and operationalizing the genocidal slow and fast death of slavery and colonialism (Cuppini and Frapporti, 2018; Harney and Moten, 2013). Certainly the advent of mass production required logistical surrounds for both sourcing raw materials and distributing goods to market. What changes in our time is the greatly increased proportion of corporate resources devoted to logistical matters.

There are two components to the enlargement of platforms to incorporate logistical capacity. One is the price and time advantage gained from streamlining logistical aspects leading to production – and we might think of this as exemplified in a slightly earlier phase where discussion of 'just in time' approaches to production begin to identify sources of competitive advantage arising from logistical operations as opposed to massifying production or technical innovation (Steinberg, 2022). The other is the ascendance of distributive capacity as an asset that can lead to the absorption of former competitors and create relationships of almost unavoidable dependency for others in your sector, including new entrants.

The moment of 'just in time' revealed a shift where at least part of the process of capitalist innovation moved into logistics and elements of logistics moved into the firm (Sayer, 1986). One component of what we come to know as platform corporations emerged in this earlier time (for the role of time in structuring platform businesses and work, see De Stefano, 2015; Chen and Sun, 2020). To note, this also runs alongside the transnational dispersal of production, another factor that leads to a renewed focus on logistical capacity (Dekkers, 2009). Arguably it is the differentiations of an earlier phase of racial capitalism that make the dispersal of production a matter of competitive advantage – with enforced segmentation of populations leading to uneven landscapes of employment protection, organized labour power and wage levels. To pursue this advantage, it becomes increasingly necessary to invest in communication, transportation and other associated activity that enables cost-effective transnationally dispersed production.

We have been encouraged to think of data capitalism as a new moment in capitalist transformation. For some, this is a whole new mode of production, a new moment in the ways in which accumulation can take place. However, I wonder if it might be more helpful to think of data capitalism not so much as a change in the mode of production as an expansion in the realm of logistical possibility.

Perhaps also there is something about our moment of climate crisis that adds an unevenness and disruption to this universalizing tendency. On the one hand, datafication offers up a set of techniques that should be able to reach a universality never before seen in the history of capitalism. The wish and the capacity to capture, document and process data about each and every human life in the interests of business do represent a significant shift (on attributing value to all personal data, see Malgieri and Custers, 2018; for a helpful if alarming discussion of personal data as the 'new oil' and the implications of this, see Spiekermann and Korunovska, 2017). However, alongside this highly inclusive and predatory mode of population capture, we also live with increasingly fraught knowledge of climate collapse. Perhaps everyone can be included in the global economy, as data, but we have not yet found a way to include all those data sources as living bodies. The mismatch between the efficient universalization of data capture and the erratic and dangerous and collapsing materiality of a world on fire seems impossible to reconcile. In previous work I have suggested that some of the contortions of racial capitalism we have been living through are responses to the disruptions of climate crisis (Bhattacharyya, 2018). It is no longer audacious to suggest that capitalism is seeking ways of surviving as a system – to say that, while the world collapses, capitalism is busy turning its attention to how capitalism can survive even if the world as we know it does not (Rice et al., 2022). The question is, for us, to understand what capitalist survival is imagined to be and for whom and for which regions of the world (Tuana, 2019), because it is climate crisis that marks the limit of universalist aspirations.

If we think of the differentiation of populations through economic activities as one of the key aspects of racial capitalism, then perhaps we are imagining the capitalist world as a variegated jigsaw in more than two dimensions. Pieces might overlap, but it is a complex picture in which the distinctiveness of particular racialized economic positions can be discerned, even if people kind of slot up and down against one another. Importantly, if the differentiation of populations means that differently positioned people get to do different things, then we might imagine in a moment of global logistical crisis that the glitches in supply chains could also be understood as local mishaps or local struggles within one of the spaces of differentiation. Previously we might have thought of this as a bottleneck – perhaps even a point of leverage for class struggle (for exciting insights into the possibilities of organized industrial disruption through a mapping of supply chains from below, see Hartman, 2022).

Historically this has been one of the reasons why labour organizations in industries such as freight and haulage have had very considerable industrial power (to be inspired by the organizing of dockworkers in San Francisco and Durban, including the pivotal role of this section of organized labour in the battles against apartheid and for civil rights, see Cole, 2018; for an encouraging account of European dockworkers' resistance to workplace erosions, see Turnbull, 2006). What is more surprising is that, after these decades of reorganization, where capital has sought to lessen its reliance on these key moments of transfer of goods, of storage and of transport, so that we, poor workers, have no moment of leverage where we can stop things happening because there is always someone else to do it somewhere nearby, somehow still we are getting the glitches. Perhaps not with the articulated intention of previous dockworkers' disputes or previous logistics workers' disputes, but with the same disruption to the chain. And that disruption demands a revisiting of the interconnectedness of racial capitalism where space is not flattened but differentiated, by populations that are not interchangeable but are highly differentiated in hierarchical ways. Through all of this capitalism remakes itself as a series of interconnected actions, but not as a series of interchangeable actions.

We may think of the landscape of interconnected sectors or segments of a global economy – partly spatial, partly temporal, partly mediated through other social and political barriers – which enables the differentiation of populations that remakes racial capitalism. If we think of that landscape as always requiring a kind of supplementation from the so-called non-productive economy, or the spaces which cannot be seen by the productive economy, we might imagine a changing politics of abandonment in which the broader spaces of global social reproduction contract, change, or experience a different level of ecological crisis to those spaces still lauded as the nodal points of the productive economy (for a devastating account of the vulnerabilities created through sedimented dispossession in the aftermath of Hurricane Katrina and the politics of abandonment that fails to remake structures of social reproduction after a disaster, see Katz, 2008). We might think, for example, of the rapid expansion of urban spaces, especially but not only in the Global South, and what this has done to the rhythms and arrangements of human lives (for a discussion of the symbiotic relationship between the growing informal sector and the formal economy in mega-cities, see Daniels, 2004; for a view of the risks of mega-cities from the perspective of the insurance industry, see Munich Re Group, 2004).

This is the enormous expansion of cities as spaces of intensive work – work that increasingly demands a falling away of previous domestic arrangements, work that sucks migrant workers, internally and internationally, into urban landscapes that function as enormous factories of variegated labour (for an account which presents the city as factory as an opportunity to renew solidarity and community, see Greenberg and Lewis, 2017). What we have seen is that the money-making endeavours, the things that are most celebrated in the global city, also require moments of contact with varieties of the postcolonial wasteland (Sanyal, 2014), or the necropolis within the metropolis. This might be as simple as access to quick and tasty snacks on your journey to work – think of the trade in portable snacks delivered through car and bus windows in traffic jams across the Global South (for discussion of these services among others as globalization from below, see Mathews et al., 2012). It might also mean access to a cooked lunch, perhaps a lunch that is delivered to a workplace that offers you so little respect that there is no chance of eating unless the food comes straight to your door. It might mean the ways in which the streets and spaces of a city cannot quite hold such a rapidly growing population, particularly a rapidly growing population which has outsourced its social reproductive practices elsewhere. So, no time to clean, no time to pick and carry, no time to tidy up after itself and/or too few spaces in which to remake cleanliness.

That kind of space requires the occasional precarious person, probably non-waged, probably resident elsewhere most of the time, to be able to be sufficiently mobile and innovative and in the right place at the right time to provide a supplement of something like social reproduction for a workforce that is squeezed so tight that these matters of maintaining the body can no longer be squeezed into either their living arrangements or their working day (for an account of the fragile systems of survival social reproduction created by precarious urban migrant workers, and the only barely workable supplement offered through community groups, see Martin, 2010; for a discussion of the gig work and domestic work, see Sedacca, 2022). The question, then, is what happens to this very fragile set of arrangements when the spaces of the necropolis or the wasteland become truly uninhabitable and subject to ecological collapse (for a discussion of the challenge of maintaining a safe water system in megacities, see Alves et al., 2021). What happens to the chain of informal services when this happens?

When the reproduction of capital does not coincide with the reproduction of life

Despite the extreme degradation and death carried out in the pursuit of profit, we have seen a longish period where the reproduction of capital occurred in formations which also enabled the reproduction of (some) life (see Ausubel and Herman, 1988). This may have occurred despite capital's indifference to human well-being and despite the push to reduce our lives to nothing more than adjuncts to the reproduction of capital. However, this almost coincidence between the needs of capital and the needs of human society – for some, for a while, in some places – arose from an earlier phase of production. Lauren Berlant identifies the emergence of a dangerous mismatch between the needs of life and the collapsing/dispersing infrastructure of capitalist reproduction as a 'glitch', in the process reminding us that everything is always in transition and that infrastructure is 'the living mediation of what organizes life' (Berlant, 2016: 393).

In particular, the emergence of the capitalist city and the associated infrastructure of such a formation has shaped thinking about the infrastructure necessary to remake life. From sanitation to energy to transport to the built environment, our thinking about how (at least some of) the resources of life can be stolen back from capital and organized towards our collective survival references the city and its associated spatial formations (on sanitation, see Schultz and McShane, 1978; on urban infrastructure, see Hanson, 1984). Even as we kick against the monsters of accumulation that global cities became, it is hard to imagine modes of sustaining massed life without reference to the city form (to revisit an influential formulation of the horror and the possibility of the city, see Massey, 2007). Since a much earlier phase of urbanization, although perhaps also including the more recent rapid urbanizations of the Global South, we have come to think of the infrastructure required for the remaking of capital as a machinery that resides in spaces accessible to the concentration of human population (Mitchell, 2014). The city may be structured to meet the needs of capital, but, despite itself, in the process it also amasses capacities needed to meet the needs of human populations. Sometimes this has been planned for, as in the moment of Keynesian-Fordist welfarism (for an influential account of spatial Keynesianism and its crisis and demise, see Brenner, 2009). More often, capital collects a looser population around itself, hoovering up the resources of society but, in the process, enabling human populations to build lives in and around the landscape created.

In a time of platforms and climate catastrophe, we witness a breakdown in these former accommodations. The infrastructure created and maintained to remake capital is in a process of flux as capital tries out ways of remaking itself differently (for an instructive discussion of the impact of financialization on UK water infrastructure and the suggestive argument that transforming basic infrastructure into profit-seeking endeavours renders us all renters of the means of life, see Loftus et al., 2019). One terrifying aspect of this manifests as the breakdown of previous infrastructural arrangements such as water supply or arrangements to anticipate and contain flooding and wildfires. Whereas the twentieth century coded such instances of abandonment as natural disasters, suffered largely by populations distanced from the metropolis, now the landscape of disaster is patterned differently across the world. The long-established unevenness in vulnerability to early death continues, whether mediated by the actions or inactions of states or through non-state shaping of economic positioning. We see it in the numbers of those displaced and dying and those surviving but struggling. Yet, at the same time, the terms of vulnerability to early death become less certain. It is harder to predict where and how life-endangering events will occur. Instead, we all try to learn how to navigate a world where the quest to stay alive is constrained by the dispersal of economic life via platforms alongside the combined but uneven coercive forces of bordering, incarceration and indebtedness.

Conclusion: Fun and Games

No account of capitalism is complete without some reckoning with the pleasures of capitalist subjectification. For us, it is difficult to imagine a world other than that in which we know ourselves through the lens of capital. As we live in a world where every human relationship and sense of self has been remade in the image of capitalist reproduction, perhaps it is no longer possible for us to distinguish between what we do to remake our humanness and what we do to remake capital. While this may take the form of what Lauren Berlant names 'slow death', where the interruption/distraction of passing pleasure at once disrupts and confirms our subjugation to the imperatives of capitalist remaking, this is still also a remaking of our lives (Berlant, 2007). More than this, our sense of our own humanness, our unique abilities to remember, to anticipate, to love and to rage, all of them seem so intertwined with what capital makes us that it is no longer easy to think of any existence that does not also remake the beast in and through which we live. That of course is what people have meant when they paraphrase Fredric Jameson's still hilarious aside that it is easier (and, the joke is, less traumatic) to imagine the end of the world than it is to imagine the end of capitalism (I wavered between attributing Jameson and Žižek – and also the retelling by Mark Fisher. Perhaps we need to accept that the joke that exemplifies the late late capitalist moment is multi-authored as all the best jokes are). The aphorism indicates a kind of dampening of the imagination, and I do see how apt that feels as an account, echoing both

Mark Fisher's description of the sensibility of capitalist realism (2009) and Jodi Dean's account of the challenge and necessity of articulating the communist horizon (2012).

However, and while recognizing the resonance of these accounts, I want to remember that capital not only suppresses but enables, presenting itself as the best and only vehicle of our desires and our hopes. In fact, we learn to articulate our desires and hopes in the cyborg interface between ourselves and the reproduction of capital. It is in this hybrid machine that human capacities and sensibilities are endlessly reincorporated into a process that ultimately strips us of life and transforms our life-force into an abstracted value elsewhere. I say all this only to remind ourselves that being a capitalist subject, with all of its difficulties, contradictions and outright hardship, is not a location of unabated misery, and, more than this, the unlikely pleasures of subjectification must always be part of what we keep in mind when we seek to understand the capitalist project (for a very different but enlightening account of these questions, including the contention that late capitalist consciousness should be understood as 'love of the love of self', see Roberts, 2021).

How, then, might we think of the admittedly ambiguous pleasures of racialized subjectification? The phrase sounds like an apology for racist supremacism. And of course that also does exist, those fantasies of belonging to a master race where people learn to love the trappings of differential power and the suggestion that, whatever violences are inflicted upon them, they too can inflict violence (to understand this dynamic in Hindu nationalism, see Bhatt, 2001; in European anti-Roma racisms, Fejzula, 2019; in the white supremacist strand in Trumpism, Inwood, 2019). That, however, is not the everyday currency of capitalist reproduction, and neither is it an honest account of how living under capitalism makes us feel as racialized subjects. The texture of racialized consciousness cannot be reduced to its supremacist registers. Instead, there is something in the coming to self under capitalism, with self here spanning the range of identity formations and more precise biographical details that every human life must, that represents our most intimate affective investments. This is how we understand the very ability to take pleasure or to desire, through this imperfect vehicle that must always remake the murderous machine as we remake ourselves. Capital creates us in such a way that we cannot help but want and long for the very beast that is stripping us dry.

Although it may seem contrary, my suggestion is that our racialized selves are also part of this dynamic.

Although we say so rarely, lest our words are used against us or, even more painfully, against others like us, racially subordinated identities also have their intoxicating pleasures. We also see and love and enjoy our selves through the prism of a racial capitalism that may position us as outside full humanness. We remain in love with our racialized selves, because these are the only selves we can have known. I am inspired in this thought by bell hooks's repeated injunction that we must love ourselves but with seriousness (1998, 1999, 2004) and by Audre Lorde's complicated but urgent insistence that we excavate the power of eroticism (1984), as well as by the countless masses, young and old, who move through the world and online spaces sharing a joyous fabulousness and delectation of themselves and others. At the same time, I understand, with sadness, that any threat to the remaking of racial capitalism can feel like a threat to our own sense of self.

Changing repertoires of racialized identity making

My sense is that the materials available to construct racialized identities and, more importantly, to differentiate racialized identities are becoming more haphazard, thin and unpredictable. We can discern this from the various anxious pronouncements of those who appear frightened of losing a certain kind of racialized privilege (for a report of an alarming incarnation of such accounts, see Moses, 2019; for an insightful narrative of the racialized and class claims of Trumpism, see Davis, 2017). In so much of this noisy complaint, the loss of privilege is folded into the loss of identity, as if there is nothing at all to be if it is not a being which has its boot on someone else's neck. However, I also think that there is a kernel of rational recognition in the strange (largely white) anxieties about what has been lost in a racial order that seems to be almost passing. Yes, there is the out of control unreason of the colonizer, but there is also a registering of unsettling change in the components that have previously anchored familiar racialized hierarchies. Many of the components of racialized hierarchies that have established the structures of institutional racism as we know it are in some flux. The segregated labour market that could be relied upon to complement segregated residence, the ways in which a disproportionate lack of protection in the workplace and in society more generally could combine to segment working lives and living lives and leisure lives – these things may be less available than they were. For example, see the discussion by Deganis, Tagashira and Yang (2021) laying out the need for an amended framework for employment rights that can fit the unsettlements of changing working practices, including the changes brought about through platformization. These shifts represent an erosion of employment protections for all, a fragmenting and/or decline of previously regulated arenas of work and an unsettlement of the living arrangements that arose in a time of more stable and predictable spatial arrangements of work. This is not to say that habits of racialized segmentation and segregation do not continue. They very clearly do, including in the odd interaction between online and in-person spaces. To be clear, I am not arguing that racialized differentiation is disappearing or that we have entered even the most shallow kind of postracial culture. My point is that the machinery of racialized positioning appears to be shifting, and with this shift there are adaptations in the manner in which racialized outcomes occur.

There is clearly a continuation of longstanding and established racialized patterning across a range of social sites, including in the call from popular media and the participation in different media forms and in the many kinds of work that are more and less precariously dangerous (for an international account of who is likely to be concentrated in risky precarious work, see Kalleberg and Vallas, 2017). None of that has passed. However, I wonder if what is beginning to pass are the structures and processes that gave rise to that relatively predictable landscape of racial hierarchy with components that allowed a certain differential privilege to some groups: stable work, secure housing, an expectation of living with a certain amount of protection and ease in your lifetime, perhaps even an assumed contract with the state that allowed a sense of safety when illness or death came to call (for a discussion of South Africa's move beyond racial Fordism, in a context where the social wage was tied explicitly to the status of whiteness in the apartheid era, see Makhulu, 2016; for an account of 'aggrieved whiteness' in the face of the restructuring of public spending and automation of some industries, see King, 2017). Those components seem unattainable regardless of racialized identity now, and in the places where some remnants of that social organization remain there are the most fraught and unpleasant battles about who might be entitled to such social goods (for a discussion of the deployment of 'welfare chauvinism in the political approach of far-right parties in Sweden, Norway and Denmark, see Finnsdottir and Hallgrimsdottir, 2019; for a discussion of media coverage of questions of immigration as a threat to Scandinavian societies, including to welfare systems, see Hovden and Mjelde, 2019). So in a world where some populations age and others move, where the economy can no longer be easily located in the large centres of production within one nation, but instead seem strung across a series of fragmented production units, logistical networks, transport and storage hubs, all linked together through the business of data, in this context what might previously have been understood as the wages of whiteness do seem to be ebbing away.

If we imagine an economic landscape in which our previous certainties appear to be in the process of being uprooted and moved around (Kenney and Zysman, 2020), and in this process of tumultuous change human beings are offered the ability to regenerate themselves and their status through the most localized and atomized version of self (Preciado, 2023), we might start to understand the odd configuration of our shifting racial capitalism. We are witnessing a digital capitalism that appears to offer an endless array of individual possibilities of being (Hu et al., 2021), while simultaneously eroding, fragmenting and making precarious all of the material underpinnings necessary to sustain life (Foster and Suwandi, 2020).

Although this tension between the imaginative promise of what we might become through capital and the lived reality of what is required to stay alive is not new, for us both the element of cultural possibility and the element of material precarity have been in flux. Again, what this means is not that capital is not remaking itself (we have not won yet), but that the processes and techniques of capitalist reproduction are in a moment of recalibration. While there are clearly some bridges between the realm of articulation and the realm of bodily existence, very different logics appear to be in play in our moment. The new forms of value placed on and/or scraped from our atomized engagement with the digital sphere link to the shift away from a previously more static and mapped form of global economy, because we are living through a disordering of racialized identities occurring at the same time as the re-entrenchment of racialized dispossession. The digital reorganization of our hopes, fears and selves must be understood to be part of this.

I have tried to argue previously that people may long for their own subjugation (Bhattacharyya, 2018). And if subjugation is folded into inclusion, survival, or recognition, this doesn't make people stupid, but it does make the will to mobilize against evil more complicated. However, now I am not so sure that what we are witnessing is a desire for subjugation in the name of inclusion. That model perhaps worked in relation to a more stable belief in wagedness as the ultimate economic destination of the world's population. In a wage-centred economic imagination, some forms of subjugation are indistinguishable from some forms of inclusion, and that particular couplet of subjugation–inclusion exhausts the space of what becoming an economic subject might be. But if that particular moment is in flux, passing, transforming, fragmenting before our eyes, then we may need to think again about what people are longing for when they throw themselves into habits of self-narration that seem to accept a subordinated role in the world. The untying of the material grounding and the superstructural articulation here makes it hard to understand what the occupation of social identity can be understood to be for us.

Although the analysis of racial capitalism also agrees with a wider range of scholarship in positing race as a complexly and socially constructed fiction, my interest in the manner in which people may desire their own racialized categorization and even subordination is not a call to think ourselves beyond race. A discussion of racial capitalism is precisely an attempt to bypass this over-focusing on the realm of the ideational or what is spoken. Race may well be constituted and reproduced through discursive means, with discourse ranging as widely as we have understood discourse to reach, but it is not a matter of 'unlearning'. The very considerable pains of racial capitalism will not be ameliorated by shifting ideas or talk about race, and neither will it be dismantled by persuading people to love themselves in non-subordinated ways. Instead my interest in the desire to be racially contained arises from a belief that we need to understand these impulses and how they play out in the world if we are to understand how racial capitalism remakes itself. What is revealed is not the foolishness of false consciousness but, instead, the machineries of reproduction that arise through these particular impulses now, in our time, as the racialized geography of the global economy has been undergoing some alteration. Yes, there continues to be an all too violent and obvious division between Global North and Global South, between centre and periphery, and we see the most excessive violences enacted on spaces of containment whether named ghetto, camp or border. However, within this seeming familiarity, there are shifts in the ways in which work and the economy function, and these also change the patterning of what positioning in a slightly amended phase of racial capitalism might be. We need to remember here that positioning in racial capitalism is a kind of shorthand for the way in which a whole network of racializing processes split us into status/identity/categorization. This is an accumulation of some familiar aspects, such as disgust, but also of other important attributes, such as labour market position, residential position, access to mobility, temporal positioning in the world of the economic, and of levels of social and legal protection or underprotection, both in the

CONCLUSION 153

labour market and in wider society. It is a positioning that spans vulnerability to state violence, popular violence and the likelihood of entering some labour markets and not others. All of this together can be understood as positioning in racial capitalism, and it is a way of thinking that helps us to understand the process of racialization as always contextual and open to change but also always spanning these quite instrumental violences and far more nebulous and fantastical incarnations of social fear and arbitrary power. So when I want to think about an active desire to be positioned in one way or another in the landscape of racial capitalism, I am also reaching to understand how people want and, even more, actively enact particular ways of being racialized which must always also mean inhabiting these other difficult spaces.

If what has changed for us is the certainty of how the spaces of racialization are anchored in economic processes, then the question of the articulation of racialized identity does become more pressing. In reality, much of what we discuss within the field of antiracist scholarship returns to the space of articulation; furthermore, it is true that the racists have been talking a lot and in horrible ways, and it is hard for us not to be fixated on the need to respond and challenge the stream of bile (for a discussion of online hate speech, see Castaño-Pulgarín, 2021). In truth, much of the discussion of the cultural articulation of racialized identities in contexts of racist violence divides these two moments of expression and subordination, splitting away the languages and practices and pleasures and joys of a cultural existence that is, yes, overwritten, constrained and demarcated by the experience of racialized subordination and occurs despite and in response to the violence. There is some kind of symbiotic or dialogic relation between these two moments, but they are not quite the same. The joy has its own autonomy. And it is precisely those intoxicating glimpses of a different utopian existence, clung to and celebrated even in the most hostile circumstances, that reveal that history does not disappear, whether expressed as joy in the divine (Stewart, 1997), shared memory and emotion through music (Baraldi, 2021), or pleasure in mutuality through invention (Lu and Steele, 2019). The expressive cultures of the African diaspora and of others facing ethnic cleansing and the threat of genocide continue to circulate as resources of hope and sustenance. It is not a mistake to find joy in such things.

However, as the landscape of racist violence changes, not in a way that lessens the violence sadly, but in a way that makes the pattern of incidents and enactment of that violence more unpredictable, I wonder if there are also some convolutions going on in the realm of cultural articulation. A major shift, of course, is the capture of the realm of articulation in all its most everyday forms into practices of value scraping. Digital capitalism devises techniques to colonize the life-world that go far beyond anything previously seen. The mediation of our everyday lives, both the practical elements of tasks that must be done to live and the frippery of what we do to entertain ourselves, all passes through techniques of recording, calculation, data scraping and reuse for the purposes of prediction. This occurs even for those who are not insistently online, and furthermore our sense of self and connection is recalibrated to seek affirmation through precisely these interconnected processes. So in a time of differently escalating racist violence, with a shutting down of some previous routes to access the means of life and a disruption of the certainties of what work and life might mean, I wonder if the realm of online articulation and its offshoots might come to occupy a differently disciplining status in anchoring us to a new phase of racial capitalism. All of which is to say not much more than they make us want it, but also to remind ourselves that this question of what we want and are made to want is always an important question when we try to understand how systems of domination and dehumanization both continue and are continually remade. We are in the machine, and we need to understand how that happens and what it means.

When the masses laugh – jokes and the will to survive

I want to make a case for the place of jokes in our collective survival. Not always the jokes which have a formal structure (a comrade walks into a bar and finds three factions, and the bartender says we all end up at closing time in the end). Much more I am talking about the ways in which lightness and laughter are necessary to our interactions and to our lives. Perhaps not all the time, and, of course, there are so many things that seem beyond the smallest amusement and joy. But I still like to think that, when the masses laugh, power quakes. And even if the other side did not quake, it remains important that we had a laugh. Partly for this reason, I want to make the case that the reproduction of racial capitalism also requires both the unsettlement and that which is unsettled by the laughter of the masses.

Capital seeks to instrumentalize all our lives and to dehumanize us, but to dehumanize us differentially. In this process our lives become hollowed out, for many in the most violent and physically challenging of ways. And the quest for life becomes collapsed into the demand that we service the needs of capital. What the frame of racial capitalism adds to this account is to explain both how we are hollowed out in these ways in different but parallel processes and that the enforced or policed or staged differentiation between these different processes of dehumanization acts in a way to make it hard for us to see one another, and in a way that segments what we might understand as the global working class. It also differentiates us in a way that confounds some of our ideas of political agency or representation, and it encourages some to consider themselves as of the metropolis and therefore as more human and more deserving than those of us who remain invisible within the metropolis, or who survive at its edges or its hinterlands or its wastelands.

However, despite all of this, up until this moment there has been widespread agreement that capital does require social reproduction to take place – because capitalist reproduction and social reproduction are intertwined. There may be an ongoing political battle about how the social reproduction will be sustained, who will pay, where the balance of contribution will be between what recompense we get through the wage or other mechanisms of monetary transfer and what is absorbed into the world of so-called non-work, that huge iceberg of unacknowledged sup-plementarity to capital. However, there are few who doubt that capital does require these processes of social reproduction. What comes into question then is, What is the requirement from social reproduction, what must be remade? We have lived through some periods quite recently where there is a sense that the remaking of the labour force and of the consumer force is most efficiently achieved for capital if human life is limited down to its most debased level. In this conception, the object of labour lives only to work, survives only barely, has no boundary between work and life, because life is only this moment of work and can be cast aside when depleted to the point of death.

We have seen that the end point fantasy of mass production is based around something close to this idea of the disciplining of the worker. It was the case in the factory system described by Engels in the mid-nineteenth century, and it remains the case in the unregulated workshops of production that squat on the edge of the formal economy today. And yet, even in these most abject spaces, the role of sociality remains an ongoing question and challenge. The dormitory-factory attempts to construct the trappings of free time and social pleasures while squeezing down the available time for such pastimes. Incorporating day-to-day social reproduction such as meals, leisure and sleeping arrangements into the workplace blurs the boundaries of the working day. This is, of course, an echo of Fordist dreams of the total workplace, and, it should be remembered, there have been instances of gains for workers ensconced in such wraparound arrangements (schools, social clubs, healthcare).

Yet the different energies and distractions and entertainments that arise when human beings are together, which surely are part of how we are able to continue our lives, is an input wiped out by all sides. Care here is translated into the most instrumental of relations, as if I wipe your bum and your nose and push the food into your mouth in the same way that I would maintain a machine given to my care. All the other things that human beings do with one another – sing and josh, scold and remind – all of that is lost in that telling of social reproduction, and with that loss we forget again how much the oceans and centuries of human laughter and imagination contribute to the remaking of capital and how little capital registers of this endless supplement that can never be repaid.

We have understood for some time that the remaking of life is more than a purely material endeavour. Although earlier discussion of domestic labour focused almost exclusively on the material aspects of care – the reproducing of the body, the provision of essential services to remake life (Vogel, 2013) – increasingly we have understood that care spans the material and the emotional, and both aspects are crucial for the business of social reproduction to take place (Doshi, 2017; Katsikana, 2021). However, despite this recognition in many places, there has been less attention to the role of emotional labour in producing value or perhaps contributing to the production of value (Arcy, 2016). There are good reasons for this. It is painful to think that our affective lives are also redirected to the reproduction of capital. However, one of the lessons of Marx is that all human life becomes subordinated to the imperatives of accumulation. Things that we might previously have done for ourselves alone now also are redirected to this other machinic logic. That doesn't mean that we do not live and love and laugh as humans have always done, but it does mean that a force outside ourselves, but through which we live, also has an interest in these seemingly mundane and non-economic activities.

Racial pleasure

There has been a more recent return to the question of racial pleasure. In a critique of the wilful narrowing seen in the definition of legally comprehensible racism, Gotanda (2011) returns to the suggestion of racial pleasure indicated in earlier debates. This is a suggestion of racial

CONCLUSION 157

pleasure as a kind of sadistic delight in the ability to subordinate, with the racially subordinated serving as a fetish object that makes the articulation of pleasure possible. Such forms of racist irrationality, where the violence of subordination might reveal no objective other than an opportunity to enjoy the process of subordinating an other, appear to sit outside the analytic framework of racial capitalism. And yet the attempt to make sense of the durability and adaptability of racism has returned to this question often – perhaps too often in the psychologizing of racism as a form of disorder (for the sadistic pleasures of racism, see Giroux, 2010; Goldberg, 2010; for recent psychoanalytic discussion, see Reynoso, 2021; for some of the formative work on this question, which continues to be central to our collective understanding of racism, see Memmi, [1957] 2013; Fanon, [1961] 2001, [1952] 2021).

The difficulty is, of course, how overt some forms of sadistic and irrational racism can be. We might consider, for example, the manner in which participants in violent racial orders have fixated on the imagined sexual power of the subordinated, with additional barbaric violence unleashed as a result (Collins, 2004; Bhattacharyya, 2008). The most well-known documented instances relate to lynching (Wiegman, 1993; Ore, 2019) and pogroms (Dekel-Chen et al., 2010), but we might consider other instances of brutalization in colonial and other contexts as being linked to a similar logic (Ward and Dawdy, 2006; Sigal et al., 2019).

These forms of overtly racist violence cannot be registered within the legal framework of discrimination as it has been decreed in the operation of US law. In response, Gotanda proposes racial pleasure as a form of racialized violence, where the process of racially subordinating an other yields the very particular pleasure of racialized domination:

> Rather than the disparate treatment of neutral racial categories, the idea that racial pleasure is subordination is grounded in the difference in position between the subject and the object of pleasure derived from raced bodies. Within racial pleasures, I suggest two divisions. There is a legal normative distinction between permitted racial pleasures and illicit racial pleasures. Second, there is a legal distinction between racial pleasures and commodified racial pleasures. (Gotanda, 2011: 288)

There is something useful here for us. Beyond the psychological account of pleasure as arising from interpersonal subjugation, we are offered a way to think about commodified racial pleasures. This is racism as commodity or racism as an added value to other commodities. 'As a commodity, we participate most fully in racial pleasure at the moment that the racialized commodity is consumed. The moment of celebration or humiliation of a raced body is the moment of racial pleasure and the moment of the consumption of racial pleasure' (Gotanda, 2011: 294).

That some may take pleasure from racially subordinating another – an imagined scenario which still reduces racism to a moment of contact between individuals – is a convincing suggestion on account of the documentation of racist cruelty and its excesses (Baer, 2020; Hasian and Paliewicz, 2020; Mukherjee, 2020; Bhattacharyya, 2008). What has been far more dangerous to suggest, so dangerous I barely dare to write it here, is that those who are racially subordinated may also take pleasure or sustenance from this process. In this, I do not mean the sexualized pleasures of being constrained, or humiliated, or of playing out the most egregious instances of murderous racism in an attempt to work through or survive the knowledge of these histories. I appreciate that the bizarre and bloody histories of racial trauma seep through our lives in unexpected ways, including by infecting our erotic and/or emotional responses (Oddie, 2022). However, this is not our concern here. Our interest is not the manner in which the irrational excess of racism can bleed into the space of pleasure and sexuality, at least not quite and not quite here. For our argument, what is more immediately pertinent is the manner in which we become invested in our racialized identities, even when these ascriptions are subordinating and lead to barriers and hurt. I am taking this investment as a kind of pleasure in the self, in precisely the racialized self. Such a pleasure may be fraught, uncertain and contradictory, as Keguro Macharia explains through the use of the term 'frottage' to image the African diaspora, 'to suggest diaspora as a multiplicity of sense-apprehensions, including recognition, disorientation, compassion, pity, disgust, condescension, lust, titillation, arousal and exhaustion' (Macharia, 2019: 5).

If we were to try to chart the antecedence of this structure of feeling, we could point to the active rehumanizing of racially subordinated identities in the face of violence and threatened or actual erasure. The ability to love yourself, including your racialized self, has been part of the repertoire required for survival (this can include trivial and mediocre representations, as suggested by Nguyen, 2018, and also the seriously joyful and defiant love of self suggested by Hurston, 1979).

Through this, we come to take pleasure in subordinated identities as an aspect of the remaking of capital. We might think of this as a kind of adaptation of hegemonic practice. The ideas of the dominant class may remain mysterious, but the intertwining of our sense of self with the differentiating demarcations that remake capital, in the process extending its reach into ever greater spaces, represents a further blurring of the boundary between self and capital. We become invested in defending, celebrating and remaking the self shaped by the violences and teasing promises of capital. As the material landscape of racialized positioning becomes more uncertain, and certainly less obviously mapped, the investment in the racialized self may become more intense. Or perhaps just more visible as a necessary mark of allegiance in the face of racialized exclusion and dispossession and arising in ways that can feel untethered from previous fixities of racialized positioning.

Race can be a precious part of how we love ourselves – can be part of the deep pleasure of being with others like ourselves, or imagining ourselves as whole and gorgeous despite all we know of dehumanization and suffering.

The question of atomization vs the question of racialized division

For some time, we have been subjected to political and economic processes that appear to atomize, as opposed to massify. Much of the cultural theory of the later twentieth century revolved around this strange challenge (for an account of the move away from possessive individualism to individuation and fragmentation and, possibly, back to authoritarian collectivism, see Turner, 1988; for some influential accounts of the cultural shifts of late capitalism, see Foster, 1983). Whereas hopes had been pinned on the belief that capitalism could not help but bring us together, unable to avoid creating the massed assembly and collective consciousness that would lead to its own downfall, as the twentieth century progressed we seemed to be more alone than ever. Somehow capitalism had learned to isolate us from one another and still keep going. Even where mass workplaces remained, capital colonized other spaces of life to create a subjectification based on atomization, aloneness and the pursuit of individual interest/survival (for an indication of this landscape, see the necessary but troubling project of feminist loneliness studies, Magnet and Orr, 2022).

One of the great victories of capitalist culture has been to persuade so many of us that this aloneness, in both life's joys and its sorrows, is an inevitability written by nature.

What is interesting is the extent to which raciality forces forms of collectivity against this. Of course, collectivity can be an ugly thing as well, and the collectivities of raciality can be those of the mob, the nation in defensive mode, the chanting stadium, the imagined community under attack, whether by grinning picaninnies or swamping immigrants or unassimilable Muslims (for an intriguing account of the links between histories of racist mob violence and approval for contemporary racist politics, see Abbott and Bailey, 2021; on the long shadow of Enoch Powell, see Hirsch, 2020; on the politics of Thatcherism, see Hall and Jacques, 1983). Yet, despite the ugliness of what is articulated in the name of the racial collective, none of these is the atomization of the capitalist subject made whole only through consumer relations. The language of race forces us into association with one another. Instead of lone subjects, busy with the various practices of self-authorship, we become members of this or that group, engaged in this or that antagonism, battling over this or that group interest.

Racial capitalism inhabits these divisions between groups, however fictionally drawn. Although discrimination and exclusion, even expulsion, may be experienced as an attack against an individual (calling up all of that talk about aversion and otherness, quite rightly), such attacks on the person arise from assumed group affiliation. Racism necessarily collectivizes the other, if not in the minds of the othered (who may be unaware of these fantastical kinships), certainly in the articulation of the racist and their racisms.

This must mean that within the terms of racial capitalism there is a tension in the subjecthood of those marked as the/a racially ascendant group. On the one hand, they, more than any, are supposed to be the most successful capitalist subjects, alone in the world with their capacities and their possessions, authors of their own selves. On the other, and this is the case whether or not they themselves embrace the logics of raciality, their capacities and destinies are collectivized, but only as a racial destiny.

In an extended moment (but no more than a moment, because what seems immoveable and timeless to us will also pass) of what, for want of a better term, we might call consumer individualism, the practices of racial capitalism reposition us into teams of racially categorized types. The fact that the categorization is provisional and may change is irrelevant here – no one will be recategorized into a group of one; raciality will never register our delicious individuality in the way that the market promises to do. Yet in a world of shifting connections between people, where the terms of economic and social status, of work and the infrastructure of liveability that might be constructed around work all seem in question, raciality may emerge as one of the more durable languages of collectivity. We may cling to the 'fact of race' as a bulwark against being alone. As new modes of dehumanizing extractivism emerge and extend, turning to our own raciality as our remaining gesture of collectivity is (nothing like) what is needed.

Thinking again about the remaking of capital

This work is inspired by the urgency of critical infrastructure studies (Cowen, 2014) and the analysis of capital's operations (Mezzadra and Neilson, 2019), although the preceding discussion is hampered by the limits of my own education and expertise. The remaking of economic arrangements via platforms places logistics at the heart of a differently dispersed landscape of accumulation. Whereas previously we understood the remaking of capital to require massification or, later, a disorganization that retained mappable supply chains siphoning resources and profits back to the metropolis, now we are living through a different readjustment.

Previously, I have suggested that we are witnessing forms of deproletarianization and reproletarianization as the resource limits of a planet on fire impact on the available routes to reproduction for capital (Bhattacharyya, 2018). Varieties of expulsion and abandonment have disrupted access to the wage economy as it was, casting large sections of the Earth's population beyond the terms of humanness as worker-citizens. This set of processes, revealing the overlapping outcomes of changing industrial forms, uneven development, and the emergency economic adaptation to a geography changed by climate crisis, threatens to render many more of us 'surplus', but not in predictable ways. Indications include the collapse of the infrastructure of life in former industrial cities such as Flint, Michigan; the abandonment of populations in the aftermath of ecological disaster as in the floods in Pakistan; and every terrifying instance of climate apartheid.

Whereas the period of massifying production enabled some coincidence between the infrastructure required to remake capital and the infrastructure required to remake life, the infrastructural components of the reproduction of capital in this moment no longer ensure these previous modes of the reproduction of life. Instead, the demassification of production accompanying the platformization of the economy hails us as workers and consumers but bypasses much of what we might have expected as the infrastructure of both economy and life. In this period of transition, established practices of racialized exclusion and stratification are also in flux. As so many of us are expelled from one model of productive economy and/or worker-citizen and reintegrated unevenly into a shifting/emerging economic landscape, the patterns of racial capitalism also move around. For some, historical marginalization in the labour market may lead to early, if temporary, inclusion in new forms of work. For others, established structures of differential entitlement, particularly when accessed through social goods, become increasingly unreliable. None of us enters a postracial world, but the wounds and eruptions of raciality in economic life become more unpredictable.

In this time of new enclosures, there is an echo of previous moments of disruption, displacement and expulsion. In particular, the disciplinary machineries of the capitalist state also adapt to the changes brought by platforms and indebtedness. In this period of transition, away from what has been known and towards what is not yet quite known, the ramping up of international cooperation through carcerality and bordering reveals a reinvigorated concern from above about the unruly masses. The assorted machineries of discipline, containment and surveillance continue to be shaped by the needs of capital, while also reflecting the tussles within the capitalist class. As we struggle to survive in this new time of horror, it might help us to understand how such disciplinary regimes work to sew us back into the imperatives of capital, supporting again attempts to discipline human and other lives to adapted processes of remaking capital. In our time, this may include curtailing or funnelling new modes of vagabondage into spaces and ways of living that can be incorporated into the adapted logistics of a transitioning global capitalism. All of which is a way of saying that maybe we need to map carefully how we are positioned to be useful to capital and remain alert to new techniques to organize our lives towards this feeding of the machine. The questions of racial capitalism help us to see how we are made into instruments of capital through differentiation – and it is an approach to understanding that becomes more urgent in those periods where capital shape-shifts again.

Maybe none of us is immune to the seductive sensation of our racialized self?

It is a hard but urgent task to be attentive to the logics of raciality that have made the ugliness of the world while simultaneously remaining open to surprise in the unexpected rearticulation of race in service to an altering phase of capitalist remaking. We have to learn to look backwards and forwards at the same time, registering the sedimented horrors of history and their weight while alert to the possibility that the coming dangers might be quite new and apparently unfamiliar.

It is understandably tempting to focus our energies on comprehending the racial capitalism that has brought us to this place and to agitate for reparations to address this violent past and present. Of course, this must be part of the work of racial capitalism talk – how we come with our different but parallel wounds to this place is undoubtedly central to the question of whether and how we survive. However, at the same time, an over-focus on the harms already done can distract us from the harms just about to be done. This requires us to remain open to the moving techniques of raciality, so that we can see, hopefully before it is too late, not only the genocides of the past but also those beginning to unfold before our eyes.

I suspect that there is something in the pleasures of racialized identity that can be mobilized to sew us into shifting modes of capitalist subjectification. I have run out of road to chase down this particular argument, but I hope that even the passing suggestion can serve to inform some next conversations. It may be useful to think again of identity as a technology or as an outcome of the melding of the affective, the material and the historical. The awkward dead-ends that identity talk may lead us down may not disappear in the face of good argument. As the world spins out of control and other coordinates of social life wobble, we may find our collective addiction to raciality hardens because we do not know any other way to be ourselves. Digital capitalism's personalized intrusion into our most private worlds also mobilizes this understanding, pushing our predictable pleasure buttons, telling us how to be our familiar selves again. As we work together to survive the carnage and destruction of our time, we need to understand both the manner in which capital remakes itself by setting in motion new and old processes of differentiation, segmentation and dispersal *and* the manner in which our understandable (and perhaps unavoidable) love for our racialized selves is mobilized to embed us in the machine remaking capital. If we struggle to imagine the end of capitalism because that would be to imagine the end of our selves in any form that we can recognize or feel, then this is also part of the challenge to our collective survival.

I have said before that I write books to quieten the noise in my head, and I know some of you also look out at the horrors of the world and hear something like that same cacophony. I hope some of what I try to map here not only helps to illuminate the new ways our lives are being wrecked but also uncovers possibilities for us to be together and survive. I hope it very much.

Afterword: Being Ridiculous

As I finish this brief work, which, despite its brevity, has caused me such heartache (again), there is a joke circulating via social media. It arises from the filmed arrest of a Russian 'antiwar' protester – arrested for the temerity to protest in public with a completely blank placard. What are they for or against? Why are they there? None of that is stated in the terms of the protest. But the cops know. The joke is told as something along the lines of:

> Someone stands in a Hamburg street in 1918, holding a sign saying 'The king is an idiot.'
> When arrested he says, 'No, I meant the British king.'
> The police say, 'You can't fool us, we know who the idiot is.'

I had hoped this time to include a book within a book here – 'Racial Capitalism's Big Book of Rib-Tickling and Side-Splitting Gags' – but the jokes of racial capitalism do not lend themselves easily to such anthologization. After all, the gags of survival times are not meant to be repeated at all. Certainly not tied down to one telling or one author. Not least because all the laughter is squashed out with the scholarly but boring quest to document the resistance cultures of the downtrodden.

So readers will have to use their imaginations here. Concentrate hard. Hear the eruptions of giggles in the crevices of racial capitalism. The guffaws that continue even though the sighs are more numerous. All of the laughter that shows, again and again, that no human life can be completely subjugated to instrumental ends. Amid all of the blood and waste and labour and displacement and every form of bodily hardship, people have lived and snatched back fragments of their life-force from the jaws of a machine that reduces them to expendable stuff.

At the same time, I want to claim the space of the ridiculous. Not only because the audacity of hope demands a tolerance of things that come close to silliness, although that is also true. Although you would not know it from most accounts, I think the terms of racial capitalism demand an openness to looking ridiculous. This is a way of thinking that acknowledges both the overarching connectedness of capitalist violence and the endlessly fragmented and localized enactment of this violence. It is an analytic frame that points to the shape-shifting character of capital. We learn that the remaking of capital includes disruption of totalizing narratives, tricking us into non-recognition of the continuities between parallel but distinct forms of capitalist violence. The fragmentation of the beast of capital, each poisonous dragon tooth springing up to form a new monster, unsettles our analytic repertoire. Each time we try to get a handle on the dynamics of racial capitalism, we must risk ridiculousness again.

Endings, beginnings, threats and survival

In the first half of this project, my previous book (2018), I ended feeling that the whole work had acted as a preamble to being able to ask the *question* of racial capitalism. To ask it in a way that made space for uncertainty and difficulty, to ask the question of why and how capitalism disperses and divides us while retaining the hope that a better world is possible.

In this work, again, it feels like the effort of delineating what is at stake has taken all my energies. I have tried my best to point out the shapes in the water, in the hope that my account can help others piece together what is happening and how we might survive. But we end with little more than a suggestion of where we might turn our heads.

How hard it is to learn anything at all

I am invited to speak at a meeting of those working in heterodox economics. When I preface my talk with the view that economics attends to the question of how resources can be distributed and by what mechanisms, there is some irritation in the room. How dare I reduce this noble science to such a banal question?

Of course, the discipline of economics has been devoted to creating models to both describe and predict economic behaviours and outcomes, but isn't the underlying question still much as I described it?

When we imagine a new world beyond the horrors created by capitalism, the question of how resources will be distributed arises, but rarely as a question of economics. The dismal science has been so tightly tied to capitalist imperatives that it can be hard to imagine a place for an anticapitalist/postcapitalist economics. What would be measured or predicted if accumulation and speculation are removed from the equation?

But increasingly I think we must also try to imagine a little of what an economics might become after capitalism. Perhaps this is an economics which will forward questions of logistics and effectivity, with both of these things 'measured' through markers of collective well-being. Perhaps we will devote our energies to conceiving and creating methods of meeting the needs of humans and others and the planet itself that harness and distribute resources in non-extractive ways. Perhaps we will revisit systems of complex barter or of money alternatives. Most of all, perhaps we will be able to think seriously about how all who live can access the means of life, with the arena of 'economics' intertwined with our accounts of desire and our accounts of ethicality, returning our collective practices of learning and knowing to these questions of how and what it is to live, questions that range beyond any disciplinary boundaries. The questions of racial capitalism of our time, and perhaps of all times, are questions of our collective survival. Regardless of discipline or training, the challenges of racial capitalism demand that we turn our collective energies towards repurposing our habits of study, research and imagination to this end.

Will the most pompous inherit the Earth?

One way that capitalism seeks to remake itself is by degrading intellectual life – making ideas no more than another realm of commodified entertainment (often without too much entertainment). Persuading us that ideas are useless or pretentious or irrelevant plays its part in limiting our ability to imagine and build another world. Unless we devise ways to understand how the evils of the world occur, how can we ever hope to resist? The attempt to understand how racial capitalism works is part of this quest.

However, as the shelf-loads of work on racial capitalism here, there and everywhere pile up, a person might wonder where this is all going. My hunch is that at least two things are going on.

- In the world of academic fashion, the term 'racial capitalism' appears to resolve a number of longstanding concerns. It brings together an attention to multiple histories and positioning while also bringing an analysis to the workings of global power. It rescues us from a world of competing identities and speaks more directly to a politics focused on collective survival. I, too, feel all of this.
- The terms of racial capitalism allow you to feel that you are finally getting ahead of the curve. The horrors of the world can seem more comprehensible, perhaps can even be anticipated. Sometimes the language of racial capitalism can seem to offer the most meta of meta-theories, at last sewing together the variegated ugliness of the world in a way that can be narrated as one story, however segmented. However, it is at this point that we should remind ourselves of the question(s) of racial capitalism. The question(s) offer an entry point to understand the uneven and differentiated eruptions of an always mutating racial capitalism, but not the answers of how racial capitalism operates in any location or instance. Whatever the phrase might suggest, 'racial capitalism' cannot be a totalized theory, at least not in the manner we have been used to such things previously. Instead maybe we might think of this as a set of questions which takes seriously both the historical and the materialism of historical materialism, but which also is attentive to the range of agency uncovered through the Black radical tradition.

This work has tried to point towards the emerging landscape of racial capitalism as the spatial and temporal dispersal of economic life remakes and repositions human lives. Alongside the emergency relocations of climate catastrophe, the different dispersal of an age of digital capitalism resurrects a network of disciplinary interventions. Here I have summarized these forces as bordering, carcerality and indebtedness, not because these terms exhaust the possibilities of a remade racial capitalism but because, together, they help us to understand the changing parameters of state activity and the adapting accommodations with the different dispersals of digital capitalism. Whereas a just passing incarnation of racial capitalism seemed reliant on familiar patterns of segregation, placedness and differentiation in relation to an idea of standard work that also conjured up its own infrastructural surrounds, none of that seems stable now. Instead, we see an erosion of the infrastructural scaffolding that was linked to an earlier moment of capitalist remaking, a dispersal and sometimes displacement of populations as the quest to access the means of life becomes more desperate for more of the world's humans and a different patterning of capitalist capture of the energies of human lives as platform economics also reorders the productive economy. The logics of racial capitalism remain discernible: populations are differentiated and placed differently in their access to the means of life: some are rendered surplus, others are parked as future opportunities for the market – raciality seeps through all of this. Yet the manner in which racial capitalism remakes itself in our time is not wholly familiar or predictable. Somehow we must retain our openness to surprise in the face of endless but changing horror, because we must be able to fight the monsters as they are rather than as we remember or imagine them to be.

Our collective understanding of the mutating and variable but interconnected landscape of racial capitalism can help us to see a different future. This is a useful strand in the development of our antiracist imaginations. What it is not is an intervention in the language, articulation or expression of racism. Although I understand and want to give space to all the efforts to build acknowledgement and respect and love between us, because how we are able to be with one another is an important and necessary element of slaying the beast, these efforts are not, I think, part of understanding how racial capitalism makes the landscape of violence and possibility in our lives.

Instead, the question of racial capitalism remains, How does the remaking of capital occur through the differentiation of populations, even in circumstances where previous attributions of status or privilege seem unavailable? How does this differentiation operate in ways that enable and safeguard the reproduction of capital, even as the evolution of capitalism shows us increasingly starkly that capital does surely hate us all? When the invocation of 'racial capitalism' passes from fashion, placing die-hard adherents as stuck in the political preoccupations of the second and third decades of the twenty-first century, my hope is that some trace of the serious quizzicality of this way of thinking remains among people of goodwill. Until such a time as we are able to build another world or destroy absolutely the planet that exists, capital will continue to remake itself through modes of expansion that include differentiation. As we have learned, painfully, these modes of differentiation may position us in such a way that our claims to humanity and survival are pitted, despite ourselves, against the claims of others who are our class kin.

Whatever comes next, we will need to stay alert to how this happens. Pretending it does not happen will not help us to win, or to survive. The question of how capital has built a dispersal and unmaking of the class subject into the processes of capitalist reproduction must be included in our thinking about remaking the world.

I don't think it matters whether or not we think of this as an analysis of racial capitalism.

Because in the end, of course, the only thing that matters is whether the forces of life can win.

References

Abbott, R., and Bailey, A. K. (2021) Historical mob violence and the 2016 presidential election, *Annals of the American Academy of Political and Social Science*, 694(1): 172–88.

Abubakar, I., Aldridge, R. W., Devakumar, D., Orcutt, M., Burns, R., Barreto, M. L., Dhavan, P., Fouad, F. M., Groce, N., Guo, Y., and Hargreaves, S. (2018) The UCL–Lancet Commission on Migration and Health: the health of a world on the move, *The Lancet*, 392: 2606–54.

Acosta, A. (2013) Extractivism and neoextractivism: two sides of the same curse, in *Beyond Development: Alternative Visions from Latin America*. Amsterdam: Transnational Institute, pp. 61–86.

Adamson, F. B., and Tsourapas, G. (2019) Migration diplomacy in world politics, *International Studies Perspectives*, 20(2): 113–28.

Adkins, L. (2017) Speculative futures in the time of debt, *Sociological Review*, 65(3): 448–62.

Agamben, G. (2005) *State of Exception*. Chicago: University of Chicago Press.

Aggarwal, N. (2022) The new morality of debt, in J. Mökander and M. Ziosi, eds, *The 2021 Yearbook of the Digital Ethics Lab*. Cham: Springer International, pp. 112–18.

Agnew, J. (2017) *Globalization and Sovereignty: Beyond the Territorial Trap*. Lanham, MD: Rowman & Littlefield.

Aguiar, L. M., and Herod, A., eds (2006) *The Dirty Work of Neoliberalism: Cleaners in the Global Economy*. Oxford: Blackwell.

Akaha, T. (2009) Human security in East Asia: embracing global norms through regional cooperation in human trafficking, labour migration, and HIV/AIDS, *Journal of Human Security*, 5(2): 11–34.

Akkerman, M. (2021) *Financing Border Wars: The Border Industry, its Financiers and Human Rights*. Transnational Institute and Stop Wapenhandel, www.tni .org/en/publication/financing-border-wars.

Alam, A. (2017) Is lynching the new normal in India?, *The Conversation*, 7 July, https://theconversation.com/is-lynching-the-new-normal-in-india-80415.

Alexander, N. (2003) *An Ordinary Country: Issues in the Transition from Apartheid to Democracy in South Africa*. Oxford: Berghahn Books.

—— (2013) *Thoughts on the New South Africa*. Auckland Park, South Africa: Jacana Media.

Alexander, S., Konanova, Y., and Ross, D. (2010) *In for a Penny: The Rise of America's New Debtors' Prisons*. New York: American Civil Liberties Union.

Alimahomed-Wilson, J., and Reese, E. (2021) Surveilling Amazon's warehouse workers: racism, retaliation, and worker resistance amid the pandemic, *Work in the Global Economy*, 1(1/2): 55–73.

Alkhatib, A., Bernstein, M. S., and Levi, M. (2017) Examining crowd work and gig work through the historical lens of piecework, *Proceedings of the 2017 CHI Conference on Human Factors in Computing Systems*, pp. 4599–616.

Alliez, E., and Lazzarato, M. (2016) *Wars and Capital*. South Pasadena, CA: Semiotext(e).

Altenried, M. (2020) The platform as factory: crowdwork and the hidden labour behind artificial intelligence, *Capital & Class*, 44(2): 145–58.

—— (2021) Mobile workers, contingent labour: migration, the gig economy and the multiplication of labour, *Environment and Planning A: Economy and Space*, 52(8): 1643–61.

Altenried, M., and Bojadzijev, M. (2017) Virtual migration, racism and the multiplication of labour, *Spheres: Journal for Digital Cultures*, 4: 1–16.

Alter, A., Feng, X., and Valckx, N. (2018) *Understanding the Macro-Financial Effects of Household Debt: A Global Perspective*, IMF Working Paper WP/18/76.

Alves, E. M., Geere, J. A., Gutierres Arteiro da Paz, M., Jacobi, P. R., Grandisoli, E. A. D. C., and Sulaiman, S. N. (2021) Water security in two megacities: observations on public actions during 2020 in São Paulo and London, *Water International*, 46(6): 883–99.

Ambrosini, M., and Triandafyllidou, A. (2011) Irregular immigration control in Italy and Greece: strong fencing and weak gate-keeping serving the labour market, *European Journal of Migration and Law*, 13(3): 251–73.

Amin, A., ed. (2011) *Post-Fordism: A Reader*. Chichester: Wiley.

REFERENCES

Amin, S. (2014) *Capitalism in the Age of Globalization: The Management of Contemporary Society*. London: Bloomsbury.

Amin, S., and van der Linden, M. (2008) *Peripheral Labour: Studies in the History of Partial Proletarianization*. Cambridge: Cambridge University Press.

Amo-Agyei, S. (2020) *The Migrant Pay Gap: Understanding Wage Differences between Migrants and Nationals*. Geneva: ILO, www.ilo.org/wcmsp5/groups /public/---ed_protect/---protrav/---migrant/documents/publication/wcms _763803.pdf.

Anderson, B. (2007) Battles in time: the relation between global and labour mobilities, in *New Migration Dynamics: Regular and Irregular Activities on the European Labour Market*, International Conference, Antipolis, France, 6–8 December, pp. 5–24; https://documentation.lastradainternational.org /lsidocs/03_TravailDomestique.pdf#page=5.

—— (2010) Migration, immigration controls and the fashioning of precarious workers, *Work, Employment and Society*, 24(2): 300–17.

Anderson, C., Ifill, M., Adams, E., and Moss, K. (2020) Guyana's prisons: colonial histories of post-colonial challenges, *Howard Journal of Crime and Justice*, 59(3): 335–49.

Andrew, J., and Eden, D. (2011) Offshoring and outsourcing the 'unauthorised': the annual reports of an anxious state, *Policy and Society*, 30(3): 221–34.

Arcarazo, D. A., and Geddes, A. (2014) Transnational diffusion or different models? Regional approaches to migration governance in the European Union and Mercosur, *European Journal of Migration and Law*, 16(1): 19–44.

Arcy, J. (2016) Emotion work: considering gender in digital labor, *Feminist Media Studies*, 16(2): 365–8.

Armas, Á. D., and Ruiz, A. S. (2021) Provocative insinuations, *Daimon: Revista Internacional de Filosofía*, no. 84: 63–80.

Armstrong, A. C. (2011) Slavery revisited in penal plantation labor, *Seattle University Law Review*, 35: 835–76.

Ashe, S., and Nazroo, J. (2017) *Equality, Diversity and Racism in the Workplace: A Qualitative Analysis of the 2015 Race at Work Survey*, https://hummedia .manchester.ac.uk/institutes/code/research/raceatwork/Equality-Diversity -and-Racism-in-the-Workplace-Full-Report.pdf.

Ashforth, B. E., and Kreiner, G. E. (1999) 'How can you do it?' Dirty work and the challenge of constructing a positive identity, *Academy of Management Review*, 24(3): 413–34.

Ashiagbor, D. (2021) Race and colonialism in the construction of labour markets and precarity, *Industrial Law Journal*, 50(4): 506–31.

Aslam, Y., and Woodcock, J. (2020) A history of Uber organizing in the UK, *South Atlantic Quarterly*, 119(2): 412–21.

Atkinson, A. (2021) Philando Castile, state violence, and school lunch debt: a meditation, *New York University Law Review Online*, www.nyulawreview.org/online-features/philando-castile-state-violence-and-school-lunch-debt-a-meditation/.

Attoh, F., and Ishola, E. (2021) Migration and regional cooperation for development: ECOWAS in perspective, *Africa Review*, 13(2): 139–54.

Ausubel, J. H., and Herman, R., eds (1988) *Cities and Their Vital Systems: Infrastructure Past, Present, and Future*. Washington, DC: National Academies Press.

Ayazi, H., and Elsheikh, E. (2019) *Climate Refugees: The Climate Crisis and Rights Denied*. Berkeley, CA: Othering and Belonging Institute.

Aydemir, A. B. (2020) Skill-based immigration, economic integration, and economic performance, *IZA World of Labor*, https://wol.iza.org/articles/skill-based-immigration-economic-integration-and-economic-performance.

Bada, X., and Feldmann, A. E. (2019) How insecurity is transforming migration patterns in the North American corridor: lessons from Michoacán, in A. E. Feldmann, X. Bada and S. Schütze, eds, *New Migration Patterns in the Americas: Challenges for the 21st Century*. Cham: Springer, pp. 57–84.

Baer, A. S. (2020) *Beyond the Usual Beating: The Jon Burge Police Torture Scandal and Social Movements for Police Accountability in Chicago*. Chicago: University of Chicago Press.

Bakker, I. (2007) Social reproduction and the constitution of a gendered political economy, *New Political Economy*, 12(4): 541–56.

Bandyopadhyay, R. (2009) Hawkers' movement in Kolkata, 1975–2007, *Economic and Political Weekly*, 44(17): 116–19.

Baraldi, F. B. (2021) *Roma Music and Emotion*. Oxford: Oxford University Press.

Barbé, E., and Morillas, P. (2019) The EU global strategy: the dynamics of a more politicized and politically integrated foreign policy, *Cambridge Review of International Affairs*, 32(6): 753–70.

Barrientos, S. W. (2013) 'Labour chains': analysing the role of labour contractors in global production networks, *Journal of Development Studies*, 49(8): 1058–71.

Bauman, Z. (1996) Tourists and vagabonds: heroes and victims of postmodernity. Vienna: Institut für Höhere Studien, www.ssoar.info/ssoar/handle/document/26687.

BBC News (2021) Australia ends controversial asylum detention deal with Papua New Guinea, 6 October, www.bbc.co.uk/news/world-australia-58812578.

Beer, D. (2019) *The Data Gaze: Capitalism, Power and Perception*. London: Sage.

Bell, D. N., and Blanchflower, D. (2010) Recession and unemployment in the OECD, *CESifo Forum*, 11(1): 14–22; www.cesifo.org/DocDL/forum1-10 -focus3.pdf.

Bell, M., Charles-Edwards, E., Ueffing, P., Stillwell, J., Kupiszewski, M., and Kupiszewska, D. (2015) Internal migration and development: comparing migration intensities around the world, *Population and Development Review*, 41(1): 33–58.

Benanav, A. (2020) *Automation and the Future of Work*. London: Verso.

Bengtsson, E., and Ryner, M. (2015) The (international) political economy of falling wage shares: situating working-class agency, *New Political Economy*, 20(3): 406–30.

Benjamin, R. (2019) Assessing risk, automating racism, *Science*, 366(6464): 421–2.

—— (2020) *Race after Technology: Abolitionist Tools for the New Jim Code*. Cambridge: Polity.

Bennett, M. (2005) Indigeneity as self-determination, *Indigenous Law Journal*, 4: https://ssrn.com/abstract=2603932.

Bent, P. H. (2017) Historical perspectives on precarious work: the cases of Egypt and India under British imperialism, *Global Labour Journal*, 8(1): 3–16.

Berlant, L. (2007) Slow death (sovereignty, obesity, lateral agency), *Critical Inquiry*, 33(4): 754–80.

—— (2016) The commons: infrastructures for troubling times, *Environment and Planning D: Society and Space*, 34(3): 393–419.

Bernstein, H. (1977) Notes on capital and peasantry, *Review of African Political Economy*, 4(10): 60–73.

Betts, A., ed. (2011) *Global Migration Governance*. Oxford: Oxford University Press.

Bhatia, M., and Canning, V. (2020) Misery as business: how immigration detention became a cash-cow in Britain's borders, in K. Albertson, M. Corcoran and J. Phillips, eds, *Marketisation and Privatisation in Criminal Justice*. Bristol: Policy Press, pp. 262–77.

Bhatt, C. (2001) *Hindu Nationalism: Origins, Ideologies and Modern Myths*. London: Routledge.

Bhattacharyya, D. (2018) *Empire and Ecology in the Bengal Delta: The Making of Calcutta*. Cambridge: Cambridge University Press.

Bhattacharyya, G. (2008) *Dangerous Brown Men: Exploiting Sex, Violence and Feminism in the 'War on Terror'*. London: Zed Press.

—— (2015) *Crisis, Austerity, and Everyday Life: Living in a Time of Diminishing Expectations*. Basingstoke: Palgrave Macmillan.

—— (2023) *We, the Heartbroken*. London: Hajar Press.

Bhattacharyya, G., Elliott-Cooper, A., Balani, S., Nişancıoğlu, K., Koram, K., Gebrial, D., El-Enany, N., and De Noronha, L. (2021) *Empire's Endgame: Racism and the British State*. London: Pluto Press.

Bhattacharya, T. (2017) *Social Reproduction Theory: Remapping Class, Recentering Oppression*. London: Pluto Press.

Bia, M. T. (2004) *Towards an EU Immigration Policy: Between Emerging Supranational Principles and National Concerns*, EDAP–European Diversity and Autonomy Papers, 2/2004.

Bialasiewicz, L. (2006) 'The death of the west': Samuel Huntington, Oriana Fallaci and a new 'moral' geopolitics of births and bodies, *Geopolitics*, 11(4): 701–24.

Biermann, F., and Boas, I. (2010) Preparing for a warmer world: towards a global governance system to protect climate refugees, *Global Environmental Politics*, 10(1): 60–88.

Billings, P. (2019) *Crimmigration in Australia*. Singapore: Springer.

Blanchflower, D., Costa, R., and Machin, S. (2017) The return of falling real wages, *CEP Real Wages Updates*, 6; https://cep.lse.ac.uk/pubs/download/rwu006.pdf.

Bolokan, D. (2020) Recruitment infrastructure within the agricultural and agri-food sector: post-Soviet and neocolonial entanglements between 'Eastern' and 'Western' Europe, *Social Change Review*, 18(1): 39–77.

Bonefeld, W. (2011) Primitive accumulation and capitalist accumulation: notes on social constitution and expropriation, *Science & Society*, 75(3): 379–99.

Bounds, A. M. (2020) *Bracing for the Apocalypse: An Ethnographic Study of New York's 'Prepper' Subculture*. Abingdon: Routledge.

Bowling, B., and Westenra, S. (2020) 'A really hostile environment': adiaphorization, global policing and the crimmigration control system, *Theoretical Criminology*, 24(2): 163–83.

Bowyer, G., and Henderson, M. (2020) *Race Inequality in the Workforce: Exploring Connections between Work, Ethnicity and Mental Health*. London: Carnegie Trust.

Bradley, G. M., and de Noronha, L. (2022) *Against Borders: The Case for Abolition*. London: Verso.

Bradshaw, E. A. (2021) Do prisoners' lives matter? Examining the intersection of punitive policies, racial disparities and COVID-19 as state organized race crime, *State Crime Journal*, 10(1): 16–44.

Brand, U., Dietz, K., and Lang, M. (2016) Neo-extractivism in Latin America – one side of a new phase of global capitalist dynamics, *Ciencia Política*, 11(21): 125–59.

Braunstein, E., Bouhia, R., and Seguino, S. (2020) Social reproduction, gender equality and economic growth, *Cambridge Journal of Economics*, 44(1): 129–56.

Brenner, N. (2009) Urban governance and the production of new state spaces in Western Europe, 1960–2000, in B. Arts, A. Lagendijk and H. van Houtem, eds, *The Disoriented State: Shifts in Governmentality, Territoriality and Governance*. Heidelberg: Springer, pp. 41–77.

Brewer, M. (2020) Household debt and children's risk of food insecurity, *Social Problems*, 67(3): 565–84.

Bright, L. K., Gabriel, N., O'Connor, C., and Taiwo, O. (2022) On the stability of racial capitalism, http://philsci-archive.pitt.edu/20664/1/Racial_Capitalism_Project.pdf.

Brown, G., Dowling, E., Harvie, D., and Milburn, K. (2013) Careless talk: social reproduction and fault lines of the crisis in the United Kingdom, *Social Justice*, 39(1): 78–98.

Bryceson, D. F. (2019) Transnational families negotiating migration and care life cycles across nation-state borders, *Journal of Ethnic and Migration Studies*, 45(16): 3042–64.

Butler, G. A. (2006) *Disunited Brotherhoods: . . . Race, Racketeering and the Fall of the New York Construction Unions*. New York: Iuniverse.

Byrd, J. A., Goldstein, A., Melamed, J., and Reddy, C. (2018) Predatory value: economies of dispossession and disturbed relationalities, *Social Text*, 36(2): 1–18.

Canning, V. (2020) Corrosive control: state-corporate and gendered harm in bordered Britain, *Critical Criminology*, 28(2): 259–75.

Canpolat, E. (2021) Smartphones and exploitation in the age of digital capitalism: ordinary aspects of the transformation of everyday life, *tripleC: Communication, Capitalism & Critique*, 19(2): 424–37.

Cao, L. (2019) Made in the USA: race, trade, and prison labor, *New York University Review of Law & Social Change*, 43: 1–58.

Carbó, S., Gardener, E. P., and Molyneux, P. (2005) *Financial Exclusion in the UK*. London: Palgrave Macmillan.

Cardador, M. T., Northcraft, G. B., and Whicker, J. (2017) A theory of work gamification: something old, something new, something borrowed, something cool?, *Human Resource Management Review*, 27(2): 353–65.

Carr, M. (2006) You are now entering Eurabia, *Race & Class*, 48(1): 1–22.

Castaño-Pulgarín, S. A., Suárez-Betancur, N., Vega, L. M. T., and López, H. M. H. (2021) Internet, social media and online hate speech: systematic review, *Aggression and Violent Behavior*, 58, https://doi.org/10.1016/j.avb.2021.101608.

Castles, S. (2011) Migration, crisis, and the global labour market, *Globalizations*, 8(3): 311–24.

Castree, N., Charnock, G., and Christophers, B. (2023) *David Harvey: A Critical Introduction to His Thought*. Abingdon: Routledge.

Cavallero, L., and Gago, V. (2021) *A Feminist Reading of Debt*. London: Pluto Press.

Chagnon, C. W., Durante, F., Gills, B. K., Hagolani-Albov, S. E., Hokkanen, S., Kangasluoma, S. M., Konttinen, H., Kröger, M., LaFleur, W., Ollinaho, O., and Vuola, M. P. (2022) From extractivism to global extractivism: the evolution of an organizing concept, *Journal of Peasant Studies*, 49(4): 760–92.

Chan, J., Selden, M., and Pun, N. (2020) *Dying for an iPhone: Apple, Foxconn, and the Lives of China's Workers*. Chicago: Haymarket Books.

Chan, N. K. (2019) The rating game: the discipline of Uber's user-generated ratings, *Surveillance & Society*, 17(1/2): 183–90.

Charbonneau, M., and Hansen, M. P. (2014) Debt, neoliberalism and crisis: interview with Maurizio Lazzarato on the indebted condition, *Sociology*, 48(5): 1039–47.

Chen, J. Y., and Sun, P. (2020) Temporal arbitrage, fragmented rush, and opportunistic behaviors: the labor politics of time in the platform economy, *New Media & Society*, 22(9): 1561–79.

Chen, M., and Carré, F. (2020) *The Informal Economy Revisited: Examining the Past, Envisioning the Future*. Abingdon: Routledge.

Chen, M. Y. (2012) *Animacies: Biopolitics, Racial Mattering, and Queer Affect*. Durham, NC: Duke University Press.

Chihara, M. (2022) Radical flexibility: driving for Lyft and the future of work in the platform economy, *Distinktion: Journal of Social Theory*, 23(1): 70–93.

Childs, D. (2015) *Slaves of the State: Black Incarceration from the Chain Gang to the Penitentiary*. Minneapolis: University of Minnesota Press.

Clapp, J. (1994) The toxic waste trade with less-industrialised countries: economic linkages and political alliances, *Third World Quarterly*, 15(3): 505–18.

Clark, I. (2001) *The Post-Cold War Order: The Spoils of Peace*. Oxford: Oxford University Press.

Clarno, A., and Vally, S. (2022) The context of struggle: racial capitalism and political praxis in South Africa, *Ethnic and Racial Studies*, doi: 10.1080/01419870.2022.2143239.

Clemens, M., Huang, C., and Graham, J. (2018) *The Economic and Fiscal Effects of Granting Refugees Formal Labor Market Access*. Center for Global Development, Working Paper no. 496.

Clement, V., Rigaud, K. K., de Sherbinin, A., Jones, B., Adamo, S., Schewe, J., Sadiq, N., and Shabahat, E. (2021) *Groundswell*, Part 2: *Acting on Internal*

Climate Migration. Washington, DC: World Bank, https://openknowledge .worldbank.org/entities/publication/2c9150df-52c3-58ed-9075-d78ea56c 3267.

Cobbinah, S. S., and Lewis, J. (2018) Racism & health: a public health perspective on racial discrimination, *Journal of Evaluation in Clinical Practice*, 24(5): 995–8.

Cohen, R. (1988) *The New Helots: Migrants in the International Division of Labour*. Aldershot: Gower.

Cole, P. (2018) *Dockworker Power: Race and Activism in Durban and the San Francisco Bay Area*. Champaign: University of Illinois Press.

Collins, J. L., and Gimenez, M., eds (1990) *Work without Wages: Comparative Studies of Domestic Labor and Self-Employment*. Albany: State University of New York Press.

Collins, P. H. (2004) *Black Sexual Politics: African Americans, Gender, and the New Racism*. New York: Routledge.

Cooper, M. (2012) Workfare, familyfare, godfare: transforming contingency into necessity, *South Atlantic Quarterly*, 111(4): 643–61.

Corredor, E. S. (2019) Unpacking 'gender ideology' and the global right's antigender countermovement, *Signs: Journal of Women in Culture and Society*, 44(3): 613–38.

Cote, M. A. A., Polanco, D. F. S., and Orjuela-Castro, J. A. (2021) Logistics platforms: trends and challenges, *Acta Logistica*, 8(4): 341–52.

Coulthard, G. S. (2014) *Red Skin, White Masks: Rejecting the Colonial Politics of Recognition*. Minneapolis: University of Minnesota Press.

Cowen, D. (2014) *The Deadly Life of Logistics: Mapping Violence in Global Trade*. Minneapolis: University of Minnesota Press.

—— (2020) Following the infrastructures of empire: notes on cities, settler colonialism, and method, *Urban Geography*, 41(4): 469–86.

Cresswell, T. (2016) The vagrant/vagabond: the curious career of a mobile subject, in T. Cresswell and P. Merriman, eds, *Geographies of Mobilities: Practices, Spaces, Subjects*. Farnham: Ashgate, pp. 239–54.

Cuellar, A. E., and Markowitz, S. (2015) School suspension and the school-to-prison pipeline, *International Review of Law and Economics*, 43: 98–106.

Cuppini, N., and Frapporti, M. (2018) Logistics genealogies: a dialogue with Stefano Harney, *Social Text*, 36(3): 95–110.

Curley, A. (2021) Infrastructures as colonial beachheads: the Central Arizona Project and the taking of Navajo resources, *Environment and Planning D: Society and Space*, 39(3): 387–404.

Cutts, A. C., and Van Order, R. A. (2005) On the economics of subprime lending, *Journal of Real Estate Finance and Economics*, 30: 167–96.

Danewid, I. (2020) The fire this time: Grenfell, racial capitalism and the urbanisation of empire, *European Journal of International Relations*, 26(1): 289–313.

Daniels, J. (2009) *Cyber Racism: White Supremacy Online and the New Attack on Civil Rights*. Lanham, MD: Rowman & Littlefield.

Daniels, P. W. (2004) Urban challenges: the formal and informal economies in mega-cities, *Cities*, 21(6): 501–11.

Danyluk, M. (2021) Supply-chain urbanism: constructing and contesting the logistics city, *Annals of the American Association of Geographers*, 111(7): 2149–64.

Darychuk, A., and Jackson, S. (2015) Understanding community resilience through the accounts of women living in West Bank refugee camps, *Affilia*, 30(4): 447–60.

Datta, K., and Aznar, C. (2019) The space-times of migration and debt: re-positioning migrants' debt and credit practices and institutions in, and through, London, *Geoforum*, 98: 300–8.

Davies, T., and Isakjee, A. (2019) Ruins of empire: refugees, race and the post-colonial geographies of European migrant camps, *Geoforum*, 102: 214–17.

Davis, A. Y. (2011) *Are Prisons Obsolete?* New York: Seven Stories Press.

Davis, J. (2008) Selling wares on the streets of Accra: a case study of street hawkers in Ghana's capital, *Focus on Geography*, 51(3): 32–6.

Davis, M. (2006) *Planet of Slums*. London: Verso.

—— (2017) The great god Trump and the white working class, *Catalyst*, 1(1): 151–72.

—— (2019) A new, online culture war? The communication world of Breitbart.com, *Communication Research and Practice*, 5(3): 241–54.

Davitti, D., and La Chimia, A. (2017) A lesser evil? The use of aid funding to foster immigration control, *Irish Yearbook of International Law*, 10.

de Haan, H., Castles, S., and Miller, M. J. (2019) *The Age of Migration: International Population Movements in the Modern World*. 6th edn, London: Bloomsbury Academic.

De Genova, N. (2021) Anonymous brown bodies: the productive power of the deadly US–Mexico border, *From the European South*, 9: 69–84.

De Giorgi, A. (2006) *Re-Thinking the Political Economy of Punishment: Perspectives on Post-Fordism and Penal Politics*. Aldershot: Ashgate.

—— (2015) Five theses on mass incarceration, *Social Justice*, 42(2): 5–30.

de Noronha, L. (2020) *Deporting Black Britons*. Manchester: Manchester University Press.

de Oliveira Andrade, R. (2020) COVID-19: prisons exposed in Brazil's crisis, *British Medical Journal*, 370.

REFERENCES 181

de Rivera, J. (2020) A guide to understanding and combatting digital capitalism, *tripleC: Communication, Capitalism & Critique*, 18(2): 725–43.

De Stefano, V. (2015) The rise of the 'just-in-time workforce': on-demand work, crowdwork, and labor protection in the 'gig-economy', *Comparative Labour Law & Policy Journal*, 37, http://dx.doi.org/10.2139/ssrn.2682602.

De Stefano, V., Durri, I., Stylogiannis, C., and Wouters, M. (2021) *Platform Work and the Employment Relationship*. ILO Working Paper no. 27.

—— eds (2022) *A Research Agenda for the Gig Economy and Society*. Cheltenham: Edward Elgar.

De Vito, C. G., Schiel, J., and van Rossum, M. (2020) From bondage to precariousness? New perspectives on labor and social history, *Journal of Social History*, 54(2): 644–62.

Dean, J. (2012) *The Communist Horizon*. London: Verso.

Debt Collective (2020) *Can't Pay, Won't Pay: The Case for Economic Disobedience and Debt Abolition*. Chicago: Haymarket Books.

Deganis, I., Tagashira, M., and Yang, W. (2021) Digitally enabled new forms of work and policy implications for labour regulation frameworks and social protection systems, *United Nations Policy Brief* no. 113.

Dekel-Chen, J., Gaunt, D., Meir, N. M., and Bartal, I., eds (2010) *Anti-Jewish Violence: Rethinking the Pogrom in East European History*. Bloomington: Indiana University Press.

Dekkers, R., ed. (2009) *Dispersed Manufacturing Networks: Challenges for Research and Practice*. London: Springer.

Delphy, C. (2016) *Close to Home: A Materialist Analysis of Women's Oppression*. London: Verso.

Dengel, A. (2018) Virtuality literacy: on the representation of perception, *Proceedings of the International Conference on Computational Thinking Education*, pp. 187–8.

Di Giminiani, P. (2018) *Sentient Lands: Indigeneity, Property, and Political Imagination in Neoliberal Chile*. Tucson: University of Arizona Press.

Dickerson, A. M. (2020) Systemic racism and housing, *Emory Law Journal*, 70, https://scholarlycommons.law.emory.edu/elj/vol70/iss7/5.

Diken, B., and Laustsen, C. B. (2005) *The Culture of Exception: Sociology Facing the Camp*. New York: Routledge.

Donovan, S. A., and Bradley, D. H. (2019) *Real Wage Trends, 1979 to 2018*. Washington, DC: Congressional Research Service.

Dorries, H., Hugill, D., and Tomiak, J. (2022) Racial capitalism and the production of settler colonial cities, *Geoforum*, 132: 263–70.

Doshi, S. (2017) Embodied urban political ecology: five propositions, *Area*, 49(1): 125–8.

Drahokoupil, J., and Fabo, B. (2016) *The Platform Economy and the Disruption of the Employment Relationship*, ETUI Research Paper: Policy Brief no. 5.

Dubal, V. (2020) The time politics of home-based digital piecework, *Center for Ethics Journal*, 2020: C4eJ 50.

Dunbar-Ortiz, R. (2014) *An Indigenous Peoples' History of the United States*. Boston: Beacon Press.

Edgell, P., Ammons, S. K., and Dahlin, E. C. (2012) Making ends meet: insufficiency and work–family coordination in the new economy, *Journal of Family Issues*, 33(8): 999–1026.

Ekanem, I. (2013) Influences on the behaviour of Black and minority ethnic (BME) communities towards debt and bankruptcy, *International Journal of Consumer Studies*, 37(2): 199–205.

El-Enany, N. (2020) (B)ordering Britain: law, race and empire, in El-Enany, *(B)ordering Britain*. Manchester: Manchester University Press.

Engel, J. (2019) An addiction to capitalism: a rhetorical criticism of mainstream environmentalism, *IdeaFest: Interdisciplinary Journal of Creative Works and Research from Humboldt State University*, 3(1): https://digitalcommons.humboldt.edu/ideafest/vol3/iss1/12.

Englert, S. P. (2022) *Settler Colonialism: An Introduction*. London: Pluto Press.

Escudero, J. C. (1994) The hungry body politic: structural adjustment in Latin America, *Capitalism Nature Socialism*, 5(2): 17–22.

Eurofound (2018) *Employment and Working Conditions of Selected Types of Platform Work*. Luxembourg: Publications Office of the European Union.

Fanon, F. ([1961] 2001) *The Wretched of the Earth*. Harmondsworth: Penguin.

Fanon, F. ([1952] 2021) *Black Skin, White Masks*. Harmondsworth: Penguin.

Featherstone, M. (1990) Perspectives on consumer culture, *Sociology*, 24(1): 5–22.

Federici, S. (1975) *Wages against Housework*. Bristol: Falling Wall Press, pp. 187–94.

—— (2020) *Revolution at Point Zero: Housework, Reproduction, and Feminist Struggle*. Oakland, CA: PM Press.

Federici, S., and Jones, C. (2020) Counterplanning in the crisis of social reproduction, *South Atlantic Quarterly*, 119(1): 153–65.

Fejzula, S. (2019) The anti-Roma Europe: modern ways of disciplining the Roma body in urban spaces, *Revista direito e práxis*, 10: 2097–116.

Feraboli, O., and Morelli, C. (2018) *Post-Crash Economics: Plurality and Heterodox Ideas in Teaching and Research*. London: Palgrave Macmillan.

Ferguson, S. (2016) Intersectionality and social-reproduction feminisms: toward an integrative ontology, *Historical Materialism*, 24(2): 38–60.

REFERENCES 183

—— (2019) *Women and Work: Feminism, Labour and Social Reproduction.* London: Pluto Press.

Fernández Bessa, C., and Brandariz García, J. A. (2018) 'Profiles' of deportability: analyzing Spanish migration control policies from a neocolonial perspective, in K. Carrington, R. Hogg, J. Scott and M. Sozzo, eds, *The Palgrave Handbook of Criminology and the Global South.* Cham: Springer, pp. 775–95.

Ferretti, F., and Vandone, D. (2019) *Personal Debt in Europe: The EU Financial Market and Consumer Insolvency.* Cambridge: Cambridge University Press.

Field, M. G., and Twigg, J. L., eds (2000) *Russia's Torn Safety Nets: Health and Social Welfare during the Transition.* New York: St Martin's Press.

Finnsdottir, M., and Hallgrimsdottir, H. K. (2019) Welfare state chauvinists? Gender, citizenship, and anti-democratic politics in the welfare state paradise, *Frontiers in Sociology,* 3, https://doi.org/10.3389/fsoc.2018.00046.

Fiorentini, R. (2015) Neoliberal policies, income distribution inequality and the financial crisis, *Forum for Social Economics,* 44(2): 115–32.

Fisher, M. (2009) *Capitalist Realism: Is There No Alternative?* Ropley, Hampshire: O Books.

Fisher, P., and Nandi, A. (2015) *Poverty across Ethnic Groups through Recession and Austerity.* York: Joseph Rowntree Foundation.

Flecker, J., ed. (2016) *Space, Place and Global Digital Work.* London: Palgrave Macmillan.

Forchtner, B., ed. (2019) *The Far Right and the Environment: Politics, Discourse and Communication.* Abingdon: Routledge.

Ford, A. (2019) The self-sufficient citizen: ecological habitus and changing environmental practices, *Sociological Perspectives,* 62(5): 627–45.

Forkert, K., Oliveri, F., Bhattacharyya, G., and Graham, J. (2020) *How Media and Conflicts Make Migrants.* Manchester: Manchester University Press.

Foster, H. (1983) *The Anti-Aesthetic: Essays on Postmodern Culture.* Winnipeg: Bay Press.

Foster, J. B., and Suwandi, I. (2020) COVID-19 and catastrophe capitalism: commodity chains and ecological-epidemiological-economic crises, in A. Callinicos, S. Kouvelakis, and L. Pradella, eds, *Routledge Handbook of Marxism and Post-Marxism.* New York: Routledge, pp. 545–59.

Fountain, J. E. (2022) The moon, the ghetto and artificial intelligence: reducing systemic racism in computational algorithms, *Government Information Quarterly,* 39(2): https://doi.org/10.1016/j.giq.2021.101645.

Fraser, N. (1994) After the family wage: gender equity and the welfare state, *Political Theory,* 22(4): 591–618.

—— (2016) Expropriation and exploitation in racialized capitalism: a reply to Michael Dawson, *Critical Historical Studies*, 3(1): 163–78.

—— (2022) *Cannibal Capitalism: How our System is Devouring Democracy, Care, and the Planet – and What We Can Do About It.* London: Verso.

Freeman, C. (2010) Respectability and flexibility in the neoliberal service economy, in D. Howcroft and H. Richardson, eds, *Work and Life in the Global Economy*. London: Palgrave Macmillan, pp. 33–51.

Frenken, K., and Fuenfschilling, L. (2021) The rise of online platforms and the triumph of the corporation, *Sociologica*, 14(3): 101–13.

Friedman, T. L. (2000) *The Lexus and the Olive Tree: Understanding Globalization*. New York: Farrar, Straus & Giroux.

Fröbel, F., Heinrichs, J., and Kreye, O. (1978) The new international division of labour, *Social Science Information*, 17(1): 123–42.

Fudge, J. (2017) The future of the standard employment relationship: labour law, new institutional economics and old power resource theory, *Journal of Industrial Relations*, 59(3): 374–92.

Fumagalli, A., Lucarelli, S., Musolino, E., and Rocchi, G. (2018) Digital labour in the platform economy: the case of Facebook, *Sustainability*, 10(6): 1757–73.

Gago, V., and Mezzadra, S. (2017) A critique of the extractive operations of capital: toward an expanded concept of extractivism, *Rethinking Marxism*, 29(4): 574–91.

Gahman, L., and Hjalmarson, E. (2019) Border imperialism, racial capitalism, and geographies of deracination, *ACME: An International Journal for Critical Geographies*, 18(1): 107–29.

Gallagher, J., and Hartley, D. (2017) Household finance after a natural disaster: the case of Hurricane Katrina, *American Economic Journal: Economic Policy*, 9(3): 199–228.

Ganguly, S. (2018) Socio-spatial stigma and segregation, *Economic & Political Weekly*, 53(50).

García Hernández, C. C. (2018) Deconstructing crimmigration, *University of California, Davis, Law Review*, 52: 197–253.

Garner, S. (2011) Reflections on the 'wages of Whiteness' in contemporary Britain, in K. Hylton et al., eds, *Atlantic Crossings: International Dialogues on Critical Race Theory*. Birmingham: University of Birmingham Higher Education Academic Network.

Gebrial, D. (2022) Racial platform capitalism: empire, migration and the making of Uber in London, *Environment and Planning A: Economy and Space*, https://doi.org/10.1177/0308518X221115439.

Geddes, A., Espinoza, M. V., Abdou, L. H., and Brumat, L. (2019)

The Dynamics of Regional Migration Governance. Cheltenham: Edward Elgar.

Gilmore, R. W. (1999) Globalisation and US prison growth: from military Keynesianism to post-Keynesian militarism, *Race & Class*, 40(2/3): 171–88.

—— (2007) *Golden Gulag: Prisons, Surplus, Crisis, and Opposition in Globalizing California*. Berkeley: University of California Press.

—— (2022) *Abolition Geography: Essays Towards Liberation*. London: Verso.

Gingrich, L. G., and Köngeter, S., eds (2017) *Transnational Social Policy: Social Welfare in a World on the Move*. Abingdon: Routledge.

Giroux, S. S. (2010) Sade's revenge: racial neoliberalism and the sovereignty of negation, *Patterns of Prejudice*, 44(1): 1–26.

Glassman, J. (2006) Primitive accumulation, accumulation by dispossession, accumulation by 'extra-economic' means, *Progress in Human Geography*, 30(5): 608–25.

Glenn, E. N. (1992) From servitude to service work: historical continuities in the racial division of paid reproductive labor, *Signs: Journal of Women in Culture and Society*, 18(1): 1–43.

—— (2015) Settler colonialism as structure: a framework for comparative studies of US race and gender formation, *Sociology of Race and Ethnicity*, 1(1): 52–72.

Godefroid, R. (2021) Climate migration as a challenge of global governance, https://blogs.fasos.maastrichtuniversity.nl/EUS2516/climatechange/2021 /11/15/migration-crisis-as-a-challenge-of-global-governance/.

Godreau, I., and Bonilla, Y. (2021) Nonsovereign racecraft: how colonialism, debt, and disaster are transforming Puerto Rican racial subjectivities, *American Anthropologist*, 123(3): 509–25.

Golash-Boza, T. (2016) The parallels between mass incarceration and mass deportation: an intersectional analysis of state repression, *Journal of World-Systems Research*, 22(2): 484–509.

Goldberg, D. T. (1992) The semantics of race, *Ethnic and Racial Studies*, 15(4): 543–69.

—— (2001) *The Racial State*. Oxford: Wiley-Blackwell.

—— (2008) *The Threat of Race: Reflections on Racial Neoliberalism*. Oxford: Wiley-Blackwell.

—— (2010) Call and response, *Patterns of Prejudice*, 44(1): 89–106.

Gotanda, N. (2011) Beyond Supreme Court anti-discrimination: an essay on racial subordinations, racial pleasures and commodified race, *Columbia Journal of Race & Law*, 1(3): https://doi.org/10.7916/cjrl.v1i3.2260.

Gould, R. (2010) *Public Discourses on Integration: Anti-Migrant and Anti-Minority*

Rhetoric in Old and New EU Member States. Brussels: Europe for Citizens Programme of the European Union.

Graham, C., and Pinto, S. (2021) The geography of desperation in America: labor force participation, mobility, place, and well-being, *Social Science & Medicine*, 270: https://doi.org/10.1016/j.socscimed.2020.113612.

Graham, M., and Anwar, M. (2019) The global gig economy: towards a planetary labour market?, *First Monday*, 24(4): https://doi.org/10.5210/fm.v24 i4.9913.

Graham, M., Woodcock, J., Heeks, R., Mungai, P., Van Belle, J. P., du Toit, D., Fredman, S., Osiki, A., van der Spuy, A., and Silberman, S. M. (2020) The Fairwork Foundation: strategies for improving platform work in a global context, *Geoforum*, 112: 100–3.

Graham, S., ed. (2009) *Disrupted Cities: When Infrastructure Fails*. Abingdon: Routledge.

Green, A. E., and Livanos, I. (2015) Involuntary non-standard employment and the economic crisis: regional insights from the UK, *Regional Studies*, 49(7): 1223–35.

—— (2017) Involuntary non-standard employment in Europe, *European Urban and Regional Studies*, 24(2): 175–92.

Green, W. N., and Estes, J. (2019) Precarious debt: microfinance subjects and intergenerational dependency in Cambodia, *Antipode*, 51(1): 129–47.

Greenberg, M., and Lewis, P., eds (2017) *The City is the Factory: New Solidarities and Spatial Strategies in an Urban Age*. Ithaca, NY: Cornell University Press.

Gudynas, E. (2021) *Extractivisms: Politics, Economy and Ecology*. Black Point, Nova Scotia: Fernwood.

Guérin, I., and Venkatasubramanian, G. (2022) The socio-economy of debt: revisiting debt bondage in times of financialization, *Geoforum*, 137: 174–84.

Guo, S. (2015) The colour of skill: contesting a racialised regime of skill from the experience of recent immigrants in Canada, *Studies in Continuing Education*, 37(3): 236–50.

Gurumurthy, A., Zainab, K., and Sanjay, S. (2021) The macro frames of microwork: a study of Indian women workers on AMT in the post-pandemic moment, http://dx.doi.org/10.2139/ssrn.3872428.

Gutman, H. G., and Sims, S. A. (1978) The Black family in slavery and freedom 1750–1925, *Journal of Black Psychology*, 4(1/2): 161–8.

Hall, D. (2013) Primitive accumulation, accumulation by dispossession and the global land grab, *Third World Quarterly*, 34(9): 1582–604.

Hall, S., and Jacques, M. (1983) *The Politics of Thatcherism*. London: Lawrence & Wishart.

Halliday, F. (1990) The ends of cold war, *New Left Review*, 180: 5–66.

Han, B. C. (2021) *Capitalism and the Death Drive*. Cambridge: Polity.

Hansen, R., Koehler, J., and Money, J., eds (2011) *Migration, Nation States, and International Cooperation*. London: Routledge.

Hanson, R. (1984) *Perspectives on Urban Infrastructure*. Washington, DC: National Academy Press.

Haraway, D. J. (2016) *Staying with the Trouble: Making Kin in the Chthulucene*. Durham, NC: Duke University Press.

Harney, S., and Moten, F. (2013) *The Undercommons: Fugitive Planning and Black Study*. New York: Minor Compositions; www.minorcompositions.info/wp-content/uploads/2013/04/undercommons-web.pdf.

Harris, C. I. (1993) Whiteness as property, *Harvard Law Review*, 106(8): 1707–91.

Harris, J. (2019) Conversations with Stuart Hall: disorganised capitalism, *Soundings*, no. 71: 128–33.

Hartman, G. (2022) Supply chain workers' inquiries: class struggle along value chains, *New Global Studies*, 16(1): 113–39.

Hartman, S. (2016) The belly of the world: a note on Black women's labors, *Souls*, 18(1): 166–73.

Harvey, D. (1982) *The Limits of Capital*. London: Verso.

—— (1989) *The Condition of Postmodernity*. Oxford: Blackwell.

—— (2002) *Spaces of Capital: Towards a Critical Geography*. London: Routledge.

—— (2003) *The New Imperialism*. Oxford: Oxford University Press.

—— (2007) *A Brief History of Neoliberalism*. Oxford: Oxford University Press.

Hasian, M. A., and Paliewicz, N. S. (2020) *Racial Terrorism: A Rhetorical Investigation of Lynching*. Jackson: University Press of Mississippi.

Havik, P. J., Pinto Janeiro, H., Aires Oliveira, P., and Pimentel, I. (2019) Empires and colonial incarceration in the twentieth century, *Journal of Imperial and Commonwealth History*, 47(2): 201–12.

Hays, C. (2018) A global view of household debt, https://connorhays.com/papers/CH-2018-A-Global-View-of-Household-Debt.pdf.

Headrick, D. (1981) *Tools of Empire: Technology and European Imperialism in the Nineteenth Century*. New York: Oxford University Press.

Heller, C., and Pécoud, A. (2020) Counting migrants' deaths at the border: from civil society counterstatistics to (inter)governmental recuperation, *American Behavioral Scientist*, 64(4): 480–500.

Hester, H., and Srnicek, N. (2017) The crisis of social reproduction and the end of work, in *The Age of Perplexity: Rethinking the World We Knew*. Madrid: BBVA, pp. 372–89.

Hickel, J. (2016) The true extent of global poverty and hunger: questioning the good news narrative of the Millennium Development Goals, *Third World Quarterly*, 37(5): 749–67.

High, S. (2020) Deindustrialization and its consequences, in M. Fazio, C. Launius, and T. Strangleman, eds, *Routledge International Handbook of Working-Class Studies*. Abingdon: Routledge, pp. 169–79.

Hirsch, A. L., and Doig, C. (2018) Outsourcing control: the international organization for migration in Indonesia, *International Journal of Human Rights*, 22(5): 681–708.

Hirsch, S. (2020) *In the Shadow of Enoch Powell: Race, Locality and Resistance*. Manchester: Manchester University Press.

Hirst, P., and Thompson, G. (1995) Globalization and the future of the nation state, *Economy and Society*, 24(3): 408–42.

—— (2011) The future of globalisation, in J. Michie, ed., *The Handbook of Globalisation*. 2nd edn, Cheltenham: Edward Elgar.

Hoang, L. A. (2020) Debt and (un)freedoms: the case of transnational labour migration from Vietnam, *Geoforum*, 116: 33–41.

Hollifield, J. F. (1992) *Immigrants, Markets, and States: The Political Economy of Postwar Europe*. Cambridge, MA: Harvard University Press.

Holloway, L. X. (1974) Prison abolition or destruction is a must, *Mississippi Law Journal*, 45: 757.

Hönke, J. (2013) *Transnational Companies and Security Governance: Hybrid Practices in a Postcolonial World*. Abingdon: Routledge.

hooks, b. (1998) *Killing Rage, Ending Racism*. New York: Henry Holt.

—— (1999) *All about Love*. New York: Harper.

—— (2004) *The Will to Change: Men, Masculinity and Love*. New York: Washington Square Press.

Horsti, K. (2012) Humanitarian discourse legitimating migration control: FRONTEX public communication, in M. Messer, R. Schroeder and R. Wodak, eds, *Migrations: Interdisciplinary Perspectives*. Vienna: Springer, pp. 297–308.

Hovden, J. F., and Mjelde, H. (2019) Increasingly controversial, cultural, and political: the immigration debate in Scandinavian newspapers 1970–2016, *Javnost – The Public*, 26(2): 138–57.

Hu, C., Kumar, S., Huang, J., and Ratnavelu, K. (2021) The expression of the true self in the online world: a literature review, *Behaviour & Information Technology*, 40(3): 271–81.

Hurston, Z. N. (1979) *I Love Myself when I am Laughing . . . and Then Again when I am Looking Mean and Impressive*. New York: Feminist Press.

ICPR (Institute for Crime & Justice Policy Research) (2021) Prison populations continue to rise in many parts of the world, https://icpr.org.uk/news

-events/2021/prison-populations-continue-rise-many-parts-world-new-re port-published-institute.

ILO (International Labour Organization) (2018) *World Employment and Social Outlook: Trends 2018*. Geneva: ILO.

—— (2022) *World Employment and Social Outlook: Trends 2022*. Geneva: ILO.

Inwood, J. (2019) White supremacy, white counter-revolutionary politics, and the rise of Donald Trump, *Environment and Planning C: Politics and Space*, 37(4): 579–96.

Issar, S. (2021) Listening to Black Lives Matter: racial capitalism and the critique of neoliberalism, *Contemporary Political Theory*, 20: 48–71.

IWGB (Independent Workers' Union of Great Britain) (2022) Statement on the recent police raids targeted at couriers in Dalston, 16 May, https://iwgb .org.uk/en/post/dalston-raid/.

Jacobs, R. N. (2000) *Race, Media, and the Crisis of Civil Society: From Watts to Rodney King*. Cambridge: Cambridge University Press.

Jančošekovà, V. (2017) Regional cooperation in Central and Eastern Europe and its implications for the EU, *European View*, 16(2): 231–8.

Jati, I., and Sunderland, E. (2018) Playing with words: the securitization construction of 'refugee' in ASEAN politics, *Jurnal Hubungan Internasional*, 6(2): 233–40.

Jayaweera, H., and Anderson, B. (2008) *Migrant Workers and Vulnerable Employment: A Review of Existing Data*. Oxford: Centre on Migration, Policy and Society.

Jean, Y. S., and Feagin, J. R. (1998) The family costs of white racism: the case of African American families, *Journal of Comparative Family Studies*, 29(2): 297–312.

Jefferys, S. (2007) Why do unions find fighting workplace racism difficult?, *Transfer: European Review of Labour and Research*, 13(3): 377–95.

—— (2019) Labour market, work and employment segregation by race, in G. Gall, ed., *Handbook of the Politics of Labour, Work and Employment*. Cheltenham: Edward Elgar, pp. 375–97.

Johnston, A., Fuller, G. W., and Regan, A. (2021) It takes two to tango: mortgage markets, labor markets and rising household debt in Europe, *Review of International Political Economy*, 28(4): 843–73.

Jonas, A. E. (1996) Local labour control regimes: uneven development and the social regulation of production, *Regional Studies*, 30(4): 323–38.

Jones, P. (2021) *Work without the Worker: Labour in the Age of Platform Capitalism*. London: Verso.

Joshi, P., Walters, A. N., Noelke, C., and Acevedo-Garcia, D. (20220 Families' job characteristics and economic self-sufficiency: differences by income, race-ethnicity, and nativity, *RSF: The Russell Sage Foundation Journal of the Social Sciences*, 8(5): 67–95.

Kalleberg, A. L., and Vallas, S. P., eds (2017) *Precarious Work*. Bingley: Emerald.

Kalpokas, I. (2019) *Algorithmic Governance: Politics and Law in the Post-Human Era*. Cham: Palgrave Macmillan.

—— (2021) *Malleable, Digital, and Posthuman: A Permanently Beta Life*. Bingley: Emerald.

Karger, H. J. (2005) *Shortchanged: Life and Debt in the Fringe Economy*. Oakland, CA: Berrett-Koehler.

Katsikana, M. (2021) Gender in resistance: emotion, affective labour, and social reproduction in Athens, in L. Peake, E. Koleth, G. S. Tanyildiz, R. N. Reddy and d. patrick, eds, *A Feminist Urban Theory for Our Time: Rethinking Social Reproduction and the Urban*. Chichester: Wiley, pp. 92–114.

Katz, C. (2001) Vagabond capitalism and the necessity of social reproduction, *Antipode*, 33(4): 709–28.

—— (2008) Bad elements: Katrina and the scoured landscape of social reproduction, *Gender, Place and Culture*, 15(1): 15–29.

Keeble, M., Adams, J., Sacks, G., Vanderlee, L., White, C. M., Hammond, D., and Burgoine, T. (2020) Use of online food delivery services to order food prepared away-from-home and associated sociodemographic characteristics: a cross-sectional, multi-country analysis, *International Journal of Environmental Research and Public Health*, 17(14): https://doi.org/10.3390 /ijerph17145190.

Kenney, M., and Zysman, J. (2020) The platform economy: restructuring the space of capitalist accumulation, *Cambridge Journal of Regions, Economy and Society*, 13(1): 55–76.

Kenney, M., Rouvinen, P., Seppälä, T., and Zysman, J. (2019) Platforms and industrial change, *Industry and Innovation*, 26(8): 871–9.

Kiely, R., and Marfleet, P., eds. (1998) *Globalisation and the Third World*. London: Routledge.

King, M. (2017) Aggrieved whiteness: white identity politics and modern American racial formation, *Abolition Journal*, 1(1): https://abolitionjournal .org/tag/aggrieved-whiteness/.

Kleinman, M. (2003) The economic impact of labour migration, *Political Quarterly*, 74: 59–74.

Klesse, C. (2014) Polyamory: intimate practice, identity or sexual orientation?, *Sexualities*, 17(1/2): 81–99.

Kmec, J. A. (2003) Minority job concentration and wages, *Social Problems*, 50(1): 38–59.

Knauft, B. M. (2007) Provincializing America: imperialism, capitalism, and counterhegemony in the twenty-first century, *Current Anthropology*, 48(6): 781–805.

Ko, M. N., Cheek, G. P., Shehab, M., and Sandhu, R. (2010) Social-networks connect services, *Computer*, 43(8): 37–43.

Kofman, E., and Sales, R. (1992) Towards Fortress Europe?, *Women's Studies International Forum*, 15(1): 29–39.

Konishi, S. (2019) First Nations scholars, settler colonial studies, and Indigenous history, *Australian Historical Studies*, 50(3): 285–304.

Kose, M. A., Nagle, P., Ohnsorge, F., and Sugawara, N. (2021) *Global Waves of Debt: Causes and Consequences*. Washington, DC: World Bank.

Kramek, J. E. (2000) Bilateral maritime counter-drug and immigrant interdiction agreements: is this the world of the future?, *University of Miami Inter-American Law Review*, 31(1): 121–61.

Krzywdzinski, M., and Gerber, C. (2020) *Varieties of Platform Work. Platforms and Social Inequality in Germany and the United States*, https://doi.org/10.34 669/wi.ws/7.

Kubin, E., and von Sikorski, C. (2021) The role of (social) media in political polarization: a systematic review, *Annals of the International Communication Association*, 45(3): 188–206.

Kuek, S. C., Paradi-Guilford, C., Fayomi, T., Imaizumi, S., Ipeirotis, P., Pina, P., and Singh, M. (2015) *The Global Opportunity in Online Outsourcing*. Washington, DC: World Bank.

Kundnani, A. (2021) The racial constitution of neoliberalism, *Race & Class*, 63(1): 51–69.

Kwan, H. (2022) Women's solidarity, communicative space, the gig economy's social reproduction and labour process: the case of female platform drivers in China, *Critical Sociology*, 48(7/8): 1221–36.

Langley, P., and Leyshon, A. (2017) Platform capitalism: the intermediation and capitalization of digital economic circulation, *Finance and Society*, 3(1): 11–31.

Larson, A., Gillies, M., Howard, P. J., and Coffin, J. (2007) It's enough to make you sick: the impact of racism on the health of Aboriginal Australians, *Australian and New Zealand Journal of Public Health*, 31(4): 322–9.

Lazar, S., and Sanchez, A. (2019) Understanding labour politics in an age of precarity, *Dialectical Anthropology*, 43(1): 3–14.

Lazzarato, M. (2012) *The Making of the Indebted Man*. Los Angeles: Semiotext(e).

—— (2021) *Capital Hates Everyone. Fascism or Revolution*. South Pasadena, CA: Semiotext(e).

LeBaron, G. (2014) Reconceptualizing debt bondage: debt as a class-based form of labor discipline, *Critical Sociology*, 40(5): 763–80.

LeBaron, G., and Roberts, A. (2010) Toward a feminist political economy of capitalism and carcerality, *Signs: Journal of Women in Culture and Society*, 36(1): 19–44.

Lee, C., and Ostergard, R. L. (2017) Measuring discrimination against LGBTQ people: a cross-national analysis, *Human Rights Quarterly*, 39(1): 37–72.

Lehdonvirta, V. (2016) Algorithms that divide and unite: delocalisation, identity and collective action in 'microwork', in J. Flecker, ed., *Space, Place and Global Digital Work*. London: Palgrave Macmillan, pp. 53–80.

—— (2018) Flexibility in the gig economy: managing time on three online piecework platforms, *New Technology, Work and Employment*, 33(1): 13–29.

Leroy, J., and Jenkins, D., eds (2021) *Histories of Racial Capitalism*. New York: Columbia University Press.

Lewis, S. (2022) *Abolish the Family: A Manifesto for Care and Liberation*. London: Verso.

Leyshon, A., and Thrift, N. (1995) Geographies of financial exclusion: financial abandonment in Britain and the United States, *Transactions of the Institute of British Geographers*, 20(3): 312–41.

Liebman, A., Rhiney, K., and Wallace, R. (2020) To die a thousand deaths: COVID-19, racial capitalism, and anti-Black violence, *Human Geography*, 13(3): 331–5.

Linkon, S. L. (2018) *The Half-Life of Deindustrialization: Working-Class Writing about Economic Restructuring*. Ann Arbor: University of Michigan Press.

Lipietz, A. (1985) The world crisis: the globalisation of the general crisis of Fordism, *IDS Bulletin*, 16(2): 6–11.

Lofquist, D. (2013) *Multigenerational Households*, working paper given at the Annual Meeting of the American Sociological Association, New York.

Loftus, A., March, H., and Purcell, T. F. (2019) The political economy of water infrastructure: an introduction to financialization, *Wiley Interdisciplinary Reviews: Water*, 6(1): https://doi.org/10.1002/wat2.1326.

Lorde, A. (1984) *Sister Outsider: Essays and Speeches by Audre Lorde*. Berkeley, CA: Crossing Press.

Lori, N., and Schilde, K. (2021) A political economy of global security approach to migration and border control, *Journal of Global Security Studies*, 6(1): https://doi.org/10.1093/jogss/ogaa011.

Lu, J. H., and Steele, C. K. (2019) 'Joy is resistance': cross-platform resilience and (re)invention of Black oral culture online, *Information, Communication & Society*, 22(6): 823–37.

Lund-Thomsen, P., Nadvi, K., Chan, A., Khara, N., and Xue, H. (2012) Labour in global value chains: work conditions in football manufacturing in China, India and Pakistan, *Development and Change*, 43(6): 1211–37.

MacDonald, M. (1991) Post-Fordism and the flexibility debate, *Studies in Political Economy*, 36(1): 177–201.

McDowell, L., and Massey, D. (1984) A woman's place, in D. Massey and J. Allen, eds, *Geography Matters! A Reader*. Cambridge: Cambridge University Press.

Macharia, K. (2019) *Frottage: Frictions of Intimacy across the Black Diaspora*. New York: New York University Press.

McKenzie, H. A., Varcoe, C., Browne, A. J., and Day, L. (2016) Disrupting the continuities among residential schools, the sixties scoop, and child welfare: an analysis of colonial and neocolonial discourses, *International Indigenous Policy Journal*, 7(2).

McKinnon, K., Dombroski, K., and Morrow, O. (2018) The diverse economy: feminism, capitalocentrism and postcapitalist futures, in J. Elias and A. Roberts, eds, *Handbook on the International Political Economy of Gender*. Cheltenham: Edward Elgar, pp. 335–50.

McLeod, A. M. (2010) Exporting U.S. criminal justice, *Yale Law and Policy Review*, 29: 83–164.

McMahon, S., and Sigona, N. (2021) Death and migration: migrant journeys and the governance of migration during Europe's 'migration crisis', *International Migration Review*, 55(2): 605–28.

McMillan Cottom, T. (2020) Where platform capitalism and racial capitalism meet: the sociology of race and racism in the digital society, *Sociology of Race and Ethnicity*, 6(4): 441–9.

Madianou, M. (2019) Technocolonialism: digital innovation and data practices in the humanitarian response to refugee crises, *Social Media + Society*, 5(3): https://doi.org/10.1177/2056305119863146.

Magnet, S., and Orr, C. E. (2022) Feminist loneliness studies: an introduction, *Feminist Theory*, 23(1): 3–22.

Makhulu, A. M. (2016) A brief history of the social wage: welfare before and after racial Fordism, *South Atlantic Quarterly*, 115(1): 113–24.

Malgieri, G., and Custers, B. (2018) Pricing privacy – the right to know the value of your personal data, *Computer Law & Security Review*, 34(2): 289–303.

Mallett, C. A. (2015) *The School-to-Prison Pipeline: A Comprehensive Assessment*. New York: Springer.

Malm, A. (2021) *White Skin, Black Fuel: On the Danger of Fossil Fascism*. London: Verso.

Mann, M. (1997) Has globalization ended the rise and rise of the nation-state?, *Review of International Political Economy*, 4(3): 472–96.

—— (2004) The first failed empire of the 21st century, *Review of International Studies*, 30(4): 631–53.

Martin, J. D. (2004) *Divided Mastery: Slave Hiring in the American South*. Cambridge, MA: Harvard University Press.

Martin, N. (2010) The crisis of social reproduction among migrant workers: interrogating the role of migrant civil society, *Antipode*, 42(1): 127–51.

Mason, T., and Mason, T. W. (1995) *Nazism, Fascism and the Working Class*. Cambridge: Cambridge University Press.

Massey, D. (2007) *World City*. Cambridge: Polity.

Mastanduno, M. (1999) Economic statecraft, interdependence, and national security: agendas for research, *Security Studies*, 9(1/2): 288–316.

Mathews, G., Ribeiro, G. L., and Vega, C. A., eds (2012) *Globalization from Below: The World's Other Economy*. Abingdon: Routledge.

Mayblin, L. (2019) *Impoverishment and Asylum: Social Policy as Slow Violence*. Abingdon: Routledge.

Mbembe, A. (2019) *Necropolitics*. Durham, NC: Duke University Press.

Means, B., and Seiner, J. A. (2015) Navigating the Uber economy, *University of California, Davis, Law Review*, 49: 1511–46.

Melamed, J. (2015) Racial capitalism, *Critical Ethnic Studies*, 1(1): 76–85.

Melgaço, L., and Coelho, L. X. P. (2022) Race and space in the postcolony: a relational study on urban planning under racial capitalism in Brazil and South Africa, *City & Community*, 21(3): 214–37.

Melossi, D. (1981) The penal question in capital, in T. Platt and P. Takagi, eds, *Crime and Social Justice*. London: Palgrave, pp. 187–204.

Melossi, D., and Pavarini, M. (2018) *The Prison and the Factory: Origins of the Penitentiary System*. 40th anniversary edn, Basingstoke: Palgrave Macmillan.

Memmi, A. ([1957] 2013) *The Colonizer and the Colonized*. London: Routledge.

Mendonca, A., D'Cruz, P., and Noronha, E. (2022) Identity work at the intersection of dirty work, caste, and precarity: how Indian cleaners negotiate stigma, *Organization*, https://doi.org/10.1177/13505084221080540.

Menz, G. (2011) Stopping, shaping and moulding Europe: two-level games, non-state actors and the Europeanization of migration policies, *Journal of Common Market Studies*, 49(2): 437–62.

Mercille, J., and Murphy, E. (2017) What is privatization? A political economy framework, *Environment and Planning A*, 49(5): 1040–59.

Mezzadra, S., and Neilson, B. (2019) *The Politics of Operations: Excavating Contemporary Capitalism*. Durham, NC: Duke University Press.

Mezzadri, A. (2019) On the value of social reproduction: informal labour, the majority world and the need for inclusive theories and politics, *Radical Philosophy*, 2(4): 33–41.

Mezzadri, A., and Majumder, S. (2022) Towards a feminist political economy of time: labour circulation, social reproduction and the 'afterlife' of cheap labour, *Review of International Political Economy*, 29(6): 1804–26.

MIDEQ (Migration for Development & Equality (n.d.) Migration corridors, www.mideq.org/en/migration-corridors/.

Mies, M. (1986) *Patriarchy and Accumulation on a World Scale: Women in the International Division of Labour*. London: Zed Press.

Miller, T. (2019) *Empire of Borders: The Expansion of the US Border around the World*. London: Verso.

Minca, C. (2015) Geographies of the camp, *Political Geography*, 49: 74–83.

Minchin, T. J. (2022) A defining battle: the fight for $15 campaign and labor advocacy in the U.S., *Labor History*, 63(1): 37–54.

Mirković, D. (1996) Ethnic conflict and genocide: reflections on ethnic cleansing in the former Yugoslavia, *Annals of the American Academy of Political and Social Science*, 548(1): 191–9.

Mitchell, A., and Chaudhury, A. (2020) Worlding beyond 'the' 'end' of 'the world': white apocalyptic visions and BIPOC futurisms, *International Relations*, 34(3): 309–32.

Mitchell, T. (2014) Introduction: life of infrastructure, *Comparative Studies of South Asia, Africa and the Middle East*, 34(3): 437–9.

Mittelman, J. H. (1995) Rethinking the international division of labour in the context of globalisation, *Third World Quarterly*, 16(2): 273–96.

Mojzes, P. (2011) *Balkan Genocides: Holocaust and Ethnic Cleansing in the Twentieth Century*. Lanham, MD: Rowman & Littlefield.

Molyneux, M. (1979) Beyond the domestic labour debate, *New Left Review*, 1(116).

Mondon, A., and Winter, A. (2019) Whiteness, populism and the racialisation of the working class in the United Kingdom and the United States, *Identities*, 26(5): 510–28.

—— (2020) *Reactionary Democracy: How Racism and the Populist Far Right Became Mainstream*. London: Verso.

Montgomerie, J. (2018) Curbing the debt economy, in *New Thinking for the British Economy*. London: openDemocracy.

Moore, J. W. (2015) *Capitalism and the Web of Life: Ecology and the Accumulation of Capital*. London: Verso.

—— ed. (2016) *Anthropocene or Capitalocene? Nature, History, and the Crisis of Capitalism*. Oakland, CA: PM Press.

Moore, P. V. (2018) *The Threat of Physical and Psychosocial Violence and Harassment in Digitalized Work*. Geneva: International Labour Office, p. 54.

Morris, R. (2000) Gypsies, travellers and the media: press regulation and racism in the UK, *Tolley's Communications Law*, 5(6): 213–19.

Moses, A. D. (2019) 'White genocide' and the ethics of public analysis, *Journal of Genocide Research*, 21(2): 201–13.

Mothobi, O., Schoentgen, A., and Gillwald, A. (2017) *What is the State of Microwork in Africa? A View from Seven Countries*. Policy Paper no. 2, Research ICT Africa.

Mourão Permoser, J. (2017) Redefining membership: restrictive rights and categorisation in European Union migration policy, *Journal of Ethnic and Migration Studies*, 43(15): 2536–55.

Mueller, G. (2021) *Breaking Things at Work: The Luddites Are Right about Why You Hate Your Job*. London: Verso.

Mukherjee, R. (2020) Mobile witnessing on WhatsApp: vigilante virality and the anatomy of mob lynching, *South Asian Popular Culture*, 18(1): 79–101.

Munich Re Group (2004) *Megacities – Megarisks: Trends and Challenges for Insurance and Risk Management*, http://lib.riskreductionafrica.org/bitstream/handle/123456789/331/5964%20-%20Megacities-Megarisks.%20Trends%20and%20challenges%20for%20insurance%20and%20risk%20management.pdf?sequence=1.

Myers, A., and Moshenska, G., eds (2011) *Archaeologies of Internment*. New York: Springer.

Naimark, N. M. (2002) *Fires of Hatred: Ethnic Cleansing in Twentieth-Century Europe*. Cambridge, MA: Harvard University Press.

Nair, S. (2021) Sovereignty, security and the exception, in G. Delanty and S. P. Turner, eds, *Routledge International Handbook of Contemporary Social and Political Theory*. London: Routledge, pp. 409–20.

Nazroo, J. Y., Bhui, K. S., and Rhodes, J. (2020) Where next for understanding race/ethnic inequalities in severe mental illness? Structural, interpersonal and institutional racism, *Sociology of Health & Illness*, 42(2): 262–76.

Neubeck, K. J., and Cazenave, N. A. (2001) *Welfare Racism: Playing the Race Card against America's Poor*. New York: Routledge.

Ngai, P., and Chan, J. (2012) Global capital, the state, and Chinese workers: the Foxconn experience, *Modern China*, 38(4): 383–410.

Nguyen, V. T. (2018) Asian-Americans need more movies, even mediocre ones, *New York Times*, 21 August, www.nytimes.com/2018/08/21/opinion/crazy-rich-asians-movie.html.

Nichols, R. (2017) The colonialism of incarceration, in J. Nichols and A. Swiffen, eds, *Legal Violence and the Limits of the Law*. New York: Routledge, pp. 49–67.

—— (2020) *Theft is Property! Dispossession and Critical Theory*. Durham, NC: Duke University Press.

Nirmala, M. M., and Seethamma, K. K. (2018) The role of public distribution system in ensuring food security: a study on Indira Canteen in Bangalore City, *Aayushi International Interdisciplinary Research Journal*, 5(3): 180–6.

Noble, S. U. (2018) *Algorithms of Oppression: How Search Engines Reinforce Racism*. New York: New York University Press.

Nyong'o, T. (2018) *Afro-Fabulations: The Queer Drama of Black Life*. New York: New York University Press.

O'Connell Davidson, J. (2013) Troubling freedom: migration, debt, and modern slavery, *Migration Studies*, 1(2): 176–95.

Oddie, M. (2022) 'Playing' with race: BDSM, race play, and whiteness in kink, *Panic at the Discourse: An Interdisciplinary Journal*, 2(1): 86–95.

OHCHR (2022) OHCHR Assessment of Human Rights Concerns in the Xinjiang Uyghur Autonomous Region, People's Republic of China, www .ohchr.org/en/documents/country-reports/ohchr-assessment-human-righ ts-concerns-xinjiang-uyghur-autonomous-region.

Olvera, J. (2017) Managing the 'dirty work' of illegality, *Sociology of Race and Ethnicity*, 3(2): 253–67.

Ore, E. J. (2019) *Lynching: Violence, Rhetoric, and American Identity*. Jackson: University Press of Mississippi.

Ortiz, S. M. (2021) Racists without racism? From colourblind to entitlement racism online, *Ethnic and Racial Studies*, 44(14): 2637–57.

Ozduzen, O., Korkut, U., and Ozduzen, C. (2021) 'Refugees are not welcome': digital racism, online place-making and the evolving categorization of Syrians in Turkey, *New Media & Society*, 23(11): 3349–69.

Panitch, L. (1994) Globalisation and the state, *Socialist Register*, 30: 60–93.

Paret, M., and Gleeson, S. (2016) Precarity and agency through a migration lens, *Citizenship Studies*, 20(3/4): 277–94.

Parker, N., and Adler-Nissen, R. (2012) Picking and choosing the 'sovereign' border: a theory of changing state bordering practices, *Geopolitics*, 17(4): 773–96.

Pasquale, F. (2016) Two narratives of platform capitalism, *Yale Law & Policy Review*, 35(1): 309–19.

Pastore, F. (2019) From source to corridor: changing geopolitical narratives about migration and EU–Western Balkans relations, *Journal of Balkan and Near Eastern Studies*, 21(1): 11–26.

Patel, R., and Moore, J. W. (2017) *A History of the World in Seven Cheap Things: A Guide to Capitalism, Nature, and the Future of the Planet*. Berkeley: University of California Press.

Paulose, R. M. (2022) Death by a thousand cuts? Green tech, traditional knowledge, and genocide, *Genocide Studies and Prevention: An International Journal*, 16(1): 40–59.

Penal Reform International (2021) *Global Prison Trends 2021*. London: Penal Reform International.

Perlman, J. (2010) *Favela: Four Decades of Living on the Edge in Rio de Janeiro*. Oxford: Oxford University Press.

Però, D. (2020) Indie unions, organizing and labour renewal: learning from precarious migrant workers, *Work, Employment and Society*, 34(5): 900–18.

Perocco, F. (2022) Racism in and for the welfare state, in F. Perocco, ed., *Racism in and for the Welfare State: Marx, Engels, and Marxisms*. London: Palgrave Macmillan.

Pierce, J., Lawhon, M., and McCreary, T. (2019) From precarious work to obsolete labour? Implications of technological disemployment for geographical scholarship, *Geografiska Annaler: Series B, Human Geography*, 101(2): 84–101.

Pillai, S., and Williams, G. (2017) Twenty-first century banishment: citizenship stripping in common law nations, *International & Comparative Law Quarterly*, 66(3): 521–55.

Piracha, A., Sharples, R., Forrest, J., and Dunn, K. (2019) Racism in the sharing economy: regulatory challenges in a neo-liberal cyber world, *Geoforum*, 98: 144–52.

Plantin, J. C., Lagoze, C., Edwards, P. N., and Sandvig, C. (2018) Infrastructure studies meet platform studies in the age of Google and Facebook, *New Media & Society*, 20(1): 293–310.

Posch, L., Bleier, A., Flöck, F., et al. (2018) Characterizing the global crowd workforce: a cross-country comparison of crowdworker demographics, *arXiv*, https://doi.org/10.48550/arXiv.1812.05948.

Potocka-Sionek, N. (2022) Crowdwork and global supply chains: regulating digital piecework, in V. De Stefano, I. Durri, C. Stylogiannis and M. Wouters, eds, *A Research Agenda for the Gig Economy and Society*. Cheltenham: Edward Elgar, pp. 215–34.

Powell, J., and Rogers, C. (2013) *Where Credit is Due: Bringing Equity to Credit and Housing after the Market Meltdown*. Lanham, MD: University Press of America.

Preciado, P. B. (2023) Pharmaco-pornographic regime: sex, gender, and subjectivity in the age of punk capitalism, in S. Stryker and D. M. Blackston, eds, *The Transgender Studies Reader Remix*. New York: Routledge, pp. 404–13.

Pretrial Rights International (n.d.) Republic of India, https://pretrialrights.org/india/.

Pulido, L. (2017) Geographies of race and ethnicity II: environmental racism, racial capitalism and state-sanctioned violence, *Progress in Human Geography*, 41(4): 524–33.

REFERENCES 199

Pulignano, V. (2019) Work and employment under the gig economy, *Partecipazione e conflitto*, 12(3): 629–39.

Rahman, G., and Sohag, K. H. (2011) Urbanization *and* climate refugees: a study on some selected victims of Dhaka metropolitan area, *Environmental Justice*, 4(3): 163–70.

Ram, U., and Kumar, P. (2021) Incarcerated population in India: how many are dying? How are they dying?, *International Journal of Prisoner Health*, 17(2): 171–86.

Rancière, J. (2012) *Proletarian Nights: The Workers' Dream in Nineteenth-Century France*. London: Verso.

Rasmussen, M. B. (2021) *Late Capitalist Fascism*. Cambridge: Polity.

Ravenelle, A. J. (2019) *Hustle and Gig: Struggling and Surviving in the Sharing Economy*. Berkeley: University of California Press.

Recchi, E. (2015) *Mobile Europe: The Theory and Practice of Free Movement in the EU*. Basingstoke: Palgrave Macmillan.

Reynoso, J. S. (2021) The racist within, *Psychoanalytic Quarterly*, 90(1): 49–76.

Rice, J. L., Long, J., and Levenda, A. (2022) Against climate apartheid: confronting the persistent legacies of expendability for climate justice, *Environment and Planning E: Nature and Space*, 5(2): 625–45.

Richards, C., Bouman, W. P., and Barker, M. (2017) *Non-Binary Genders*. London: Palgrave Macmillan.

Ritzer, G., and Jurgenson, N. (2010) Prosumption: the nature of capitalism in the age of the digital 'prosumer', *Journal of Consumer Culture*, 10(1): 13–36.

Roberts, A. (2016) Household debt and the financialization of social reproduction: theorizing the UK housing and hunger crises, in S. Soederberg, ed., *Risking Capitalism*. Bingley: Emerald, pp. 135–64.

Roberts, A., and Soederberg, S. (2014) Politicizing debt and denaturalizing the 'new normal', *Critical Sociology*, 40(5): 657–68.

Roberts, D. (1999) *Killing the Black Body: Race, Reproduction and the Meaning of Liberty*. New York: Vintage.

Roberts, J. (2021) *Capitalism and the Limits of Desire*. London: Bloomsbury.

Robinson, C. J. (1983) *Black Marxism: The Making of the Black Radical Tradition*. Chapel Hill: University of North Carolina Press.

Robinson, W. I. (2018) The next economic crisis: digital capitalism and global police state, *Race & Class*, 60(1): 77–92.

—— (2020) *The Global Police State*. London: Pluto Press.

Roediger, D. (1991) *The Wages of Whiteness: Race and the Making of the American Working Class*. London: Verso.

Rogers, B. (2015) The social costs of Uber, *University of Chicago Law Review*, 82: 85–102.

Rosenblat, A., Levy, K. E., Barocas, S., and Hwang, T. (2017) Discriminating tastes: Uber's customer ratings as vehicles for workplace discrimination, *Policy & Internet*, 9(3): 256–79.

Rottinghaus, B., and Baldwin, G. (2007) Voting behind bars: explaining variation in international enfranchisement practices, *Electoral Studies*, 26(3): 688–98.

Roy, A. (2022) *Citizenship Regimes, Law, and Belonging: The CAA and the NRC*. Oxford: Oxford University Press.

Rugh, J. S., and Massey, D. S. (2010) Racial segregation and the American foreclosure crisis, *American Sociological Review*, 75(5): 629–51.

Ryan, M., and Ward, T. (2014) Prison abolition in the UK: they dare not speak its name?, *Social Justice*, 41(3): 107–19.

Sadowski, J. (2020) *Too Smart: How Digital Capitalism is Extracting Data, Controlling Our Lives, and Taking Over the World*. Cambridge, MA: MIT Press.

Saed (2012) Prison abolition as an ecosocialist struggle, *Capitalism Nature Socialism*, 23(1): 1–5.

Sajjad, H., and Chauhan, C. (2012) Agrarian distress and indebtedness in rural India: emerging perspectives and challenges ahead, *Journal of Geography and Regional Planning*, 5(15): 397–408.

Sanders, T. (2008) Selling sex in the shadow economy, *International Journal of Social Economics*, 35(10): 704–16.

Sannon, S., Sun, B., and Cosley, D. (2022) Privacy, surveillance, and power in the gig economy, *Proceedings of the 2022 CHI Conference on Human Factors in Computing Systems*, pp. 1–15.

Sanyal, K. (2014) *Rethinking Capitalist Development: Primitive Accumulation, Governmentality and Post-Colonial Capitalism*. New Delhi: Routledge.

Sassen, S. (1996) Beyond sovereignty: immigration policy making today, *Social Justice*, 23(3): 9–20.

—— (2013a) Expelled: humans in capitalism's deepening crisis, *Journal of World-Systems Research*, 19(2): 198–201.

—— (2013b) *The Global City: New York, London, Tokyo*. Princeton, NJ: Princeton University Press.

Sayer, A. (1986) New developments in manufacturing: the just-in-time system, *Capital & Class*, 10(3): 43–72.

Scheiber, N. (2017) How Uber uses psychological tricks to push its drivers' buttons, in K. Martin, ed., *Ethics of Data and Analytics*. Boca Raton, FL: Auerbach, pp. 362–71.

Schindlmayr, T. (2003) Sovereignty, legal regimes, and international migration, *International Migration*, 41(2): 109–23.

Schor, J. B., Attwood-Charles, W., Cansoy, M., Ladegaard, I., and Wengronowitz, R. (2020) Dependence and precarity in the platform economy, *Theory and Society*, 49: 833–61.

Schultz, S. K., and McShane, C. (1978) To engineer the metropolis: sewers, sanitation, and city planning in late-nineteenth-century America, *Journal of American History*, 65(2): 389–411.

Schulze Heuling, L., and Filk, C., eds (2021) *Algorithmic and Aesthetic Literacy: Emerging Transdisciplinary Explorations for the Digital Age*. Opladen: Barbara Budrich.

Schwarz, A. (2021) In-work poverty in the EU: a gendered decomposition analysis, *Momentum Kongress*.

Scully, B. (2016) Precarity north and south: a southern critique of Guy Standing, *Global Labour Journal*, 7(2): 160–73.

Seamster, L. (2019) Black debt, white debt, *Contexts*, 18(1): 30–5.

Sedacca, N. (2022) Domestic work and the gig economy, in V. De Stefano, I. Durri, C. Stylogiannis, and M. Wouters, eds, *A Research Agenda for the Gig Economy and Society*. Cheltenham: Edward Elgar, pp. 149–66.

Selwyn, B. (2019) Poverty chains and global capitalism, *Competition & Change*, 23(1): 71–97.

Sen, S. (2012) *Disciplined Natives: Race, Freedom and Confinement in Colonial India*. Delhi: Primus Books.

Sevilla-Buitrago, A. (2015) Capitalist formations of enclosure: space and the extinction of the commons, *Antipode*, 47(4): 999–1020.

Shaw, R. (2010) Neoliberal subjectivities and the development of the night-time economy in British cities, *Geography Compass*, 4(7): 893–903.

Shelley, T. (2007) *Exploited: Migrant Labour in the New Global Economy*. London: Zed Books.

Shire, K. (2020) The social order of transnational migration markets, *Global Networks*, 20(3): 434–53.

Short, D. (2016) *Redefining Genocide: Settler Colonialism, Social Death and Ecocide*. London: Bloomsbury.

Sigal, P., Tortorici, Z., and Whitehead, N. L., eds (2019) *Ethnopornography: Sexuality, Colonialism, and Archival Knowledge*. Durham, NC: Duke University Press.

Sigona, N. (2015) Campzenship: reimagining the camp as a social and political space, *Citizenship Studies*, 19(1): 1–15.

Simpson, R., and Simpson, A. (2018) 'Embodying' dirty work: a review of the literature, *Sociology Compass*, 12(6): https://doi.org/10.1111/soc4.12581.

Simpson, R., Slutskaya, N., Lewis, P., and Höpfl, H. (2012) *Dirty Work. Identity Studies in the Social Sciences*. London: Palgrave Macmillan.

Smith, L. T. (2021) *Decolonizing Methodologies: Research and Indigenous Peoples*. London: Bloomsbury.

Snider, L. (2018) Enabling exploitation: law in the gig economy, *Critical Criminology*, 26: 563–77.

Soederberg, S. (2018) Debtfarism, predatory lending and imaginary social orders: the case of the US payday lending industry, in *Revisiting Crimes of the Powerful*. Abingdon: Routledge, pp. 257–69.

Sokolski, H. D., ed. (2004) *Getting MAD: A Nuclear Mutual Assured Destruction, its Origins and Practice*. Carlisle, PA: US Army War College Press.

Sowels, N. (2019) Changes in official poverty and inequality rates in the anglophone world in the age of neoliberalism, *Angles: New Perspectives on the Anglophone World*, 8, https://doi.org/10.4000/angles.560.

Spaan, E., and van Naerssen, T. (2017) Migration decision-making and migration industry in the Indonesia–Malaysia corridor, *Journal of Ethnic and Migration Studies*, 44(4): 680–95.

Spiekermann, S., and Korunovska, J. (2017) Towards a value theory for personal data, *Journal of Information Technology*, 32(1): 62–84.

Spillers, H. J. (2003) *Black, White, and in Color: Essays on American Literature and Culture*. Chicago: University of Chicago Press.

Srnicek, N. (2016) *Platform Capitalism*. Cambridge: Polity.

Standing, G. (2011) *The Precariat: The New Dangerous Class*. London: Bloomsbury Academic.

Stankovic, A. (2021) On collaboration and cooperation: transnational governance as a framework for migration control, in J. L. Diab, ed., *Dignity in Movement: Borders, Bodies and Rights*. E-International Relations, pp. 257–81; www.academia.edu/44459371/Dignity_in_Movement_Borders_Bodies_and_Rights.

Stansfield, R., and Stone, B. (2018) Threat perceptions of migrants in Britain and support for policy, *Sociological Perspectives*, 61(4): 592–609.

Staring, R., and van Swaaningen, R. (2021) Borders, mobilities, and governance in transnational perspective, in H. N. Pontell, ed., *Oxford Research Encyclopedia of Criminology and Criminal Justice*.

Steinberg, M. (2022) From automobile capitalism to platform capitalism: Toyotism as a prehistory of digital platforms, *Organization Studies*, 43(7): 1069–90.

Steinhoff, J. (2022) Toward a political economy of synthetic data: a data-intensive capitalism that is not a surveillance capitalism?, *New Media & Society*, https://doi.org/10.1177/14614448221099217.

Stewart, A., Stanford, J., and Hardy, T. (2018) *The Wages Crisis in Australia*. Adelaide: University of Adelaide Press.

Stewart, C. F. (1997) *Joy Songs, Trumpet Blasts, and Hallelujah Shouts! Sermons in the African-American Preaching Tradition*. Lima, OH: CSS.

Stiegler, B. (2011) Pharmacology of desire: drive-based capitalism and libidinal dis-economy, *New Formations*, 72(72): 150–61.

Stoll, D. (2010) From wage migration to debt migration? Easy credit, failure in El Norte, and foreclosure in a bubble economy of the Western Guatemalan Highlands, *Latin American Perspectives*, 37(1): 123–42.

Stone, K. V. W. (2013) The decline in the standard employment contract: a review of the evidence, in K. V. W. Stone and H. Arthurs, eds, *Rethinking Workplace Regulation: Beyond the Standard Contract of Employment*. New York: Russell Sage Foundation, pp. 366–404.

Stumpf, J. (2006) The crimmigration crisis: immigrants, crime, and sovereign power, *American University Law Review*, 56: 367–419.

Su, C., and Flew, T. (2021) The rise of Baidu, Alibaba and Tencent (BAT) and their role in China's Belt and Road Initiative (BRI), *Global Media and Communication*, 17(1): 67–86.

Sudbury, J. (2002) Celling Black bodies: Black women in the global prison industrial complex, *Feminist Review*, 70(1): 57–74.

Suwandi, I., and Foster, J. B. (2016) Multinational corporations and the globalization of monopoly capital: from the 1960s to the present, *Monthly Review*, 68(3): 114–31.

Svampa, M. (2019) *Neo-Extractivism in Latin America: Socio-Environmental Conflicts, the Territorial Turn, and New Political Narratives*. Cambridge: Cambridge University Press.

Swyngedouw, E. (2005) Dispossessing H_2O: the contested terrain of water privatization, *Capitalism Nature Socialism*, 16(1): 81–98.

Talani, L. S., Clarkson, A., and Pardo, R. P. (2013) *Dirty Cities*. London: Palgrave Macmillan.

Tang, C. S., and Veelenturf, L. P. (2019) The strategic role of logistics in the industry 4.0 era, *Transportation Research Part E: Logistics and Transportation Review*, 129: 1–11.

Tarulevicz, N. (2018) Hawkerpreneurs: hawkers, entrepreneurship, and reinventing street food in Singapore, *Revista de administração de empresas*, 58: 291–302.

Taylor-Gooby, P., ed. (2004) *New Risks, New Welfare: The Transformation of the European Welfare State*. Oxford: Oxford University Press.

Terranova, T. (2013) Debt and autonomy: Maurizio Lazzarato and the constituent powers of the social, http://thenewreader.org/Issues/1/DebtAnd Autonomy.

Thiede, B. C., and Monnat, S. M. (2016) The Great Recession and America's geography of unemployment, *Demographic Research*, 35: 891–928.

Thieme, T. A. (2018) The hustle economy: informality, uncertainty and the geographies of getting by, *Progress in Human Geography*, 42(4): 529–48.

Thompson, E. P. (1990) The ends of cold war, *New Left Review*, 182: 139–46.

Ticona, J., and Mateescu, A. (2018) Trusted strangers: carework platforms' cultural entrepreneurship in the on-demand economy, *New Media & Society*, 20(11): 4384–404.

Tilly, C. (1979) *Proletarianization: Theory and Research*, University of Michigan, CRSO Working Paper no. 202.

Titley, G. (2019) *Racism and the Media*. London: Sage.

—— (2020) *Is Free Speech Racist?* Cambridge: Polity.

Tittel-Mosser, F. (2018) Reversed conditionality in EU external migration policy: the case of Morocco, *Journal of Contemporary European Research*, 14(4): 349–63.

Tomaskovic-Devey, D. (1993) *Gender & Racial Inequality at Work: The Sources & Consequences of Job Segregation*. Ithaca, NY: Cornell University Press.

Trafford, J. (2020) *The Empire at Home: Internal Colonies and the End of Britain*. London: Pluto Press.

Transnational Social Strike Platform (2019) *Strike the Giant: Transnational Organisation against Amazon*, www.transnational-strike.info/app/uploads/20 19/11/Strike-the-Giant_TSS-Journal.pdf.

Traverso, E. (2019) *The New Faces of Fascism: Populism and the Far Right*. London: Verso.

Trimarchi, M., and Gleim, S. (2020) One Billion People May Become Climate Refugees By 2050, EcoWatch, 24 September, www.ecowatch.com/climate -refugee-2050-2647788456.html.

Trujillo, S. V. (2020) *Land Uprising: Native Story Power and the Insurgent Horizons of Latinx Indigeneity*. Tucson: University of Arizona Press.

Tuana, N. (2019) Climate apartheid: the forgetting of race in the Anthropocene, *Critical Philosophy of Race*, 7(1): 1–31.

Tucker, R. W. (2019) *Immigration and US Foreign Policy*. New York: Routledge.

Tunio, Z. (2022) In Pakistan, 33 million people have been displaced by climate-intensified floods, *Inside Climate News*, 16 September, https://insi declimatenews.org/news/16092022/pakistan-flood-displacement/.

Turnbull, P. (2006) The war on Europe's waterfront: repertoires of power in the port transport industry, *British Journal of Industrial Relations*, 44(2): 305–26.

Turner, B. S. (1988) Individualism, capitalism and the dominant culture: a note on the debate, *Australian and New Zealand Journal of Sociology*, 24(1): 47–64.

Tzifakis, N. (2012) *Contracting Out to Private Military and Security Companies*. Brussels: Centre for European Studies.

UNHCR (2016) Legal considerations on the return of asylum-seekers and refugees from Greece to Turkey, https://reliefweb.int/report/greece/legal-considerations-return-asylum-seekers-and-refugees-greece-turkey-part-eu-turkey.

—— (2022) Figures at a glance, www.unhcr.org/uk/figures-at-a-glance.html.

Urbina, I. (2021) The secretive prisons that keep migrants out of Europe, *New Yorker*, 28 November, www.newyorker.com/magazine/2021/12/06/the-secretive-libyan-prisons-that-keep-migrants-out-of-europe.

Vallas, S., and Schor, J. B. (2020) What do platforms do? Understanding the gig economy, *Annual Review of Sociology*, 46: 273–94.

van der Linden, M., ed. (2008) *Workers of the World: Essays toward a Global Labor History*. Leiden: Brill.

van der Woude, M., Barker, V., and van der Leun, J. (2017) Crimmigration in Europe, *European Journal of Criminology*, 14(1): 3–6.

van Doorn, N. (2017) Platform labor: on the gendered and racialized exploitation of low-income service work in the 'on-demand' economy, *Information, Communication and Society*, 20(6): 898–914.

van Doorn, N., and Badger, A. (2020) Platform capitalism's hidden abode: producing data assets in the gig economy, *Antipode*, 52(5): 1475–95.

van Doorn, N., Ferrari, F., and Graham, M. (2020) Migration and migrant labour in the gig economy: an intervention, *Work, Employment and Society*, http://dx.doi.org/10.2139/ssrn.3622589.

van Reekum, R. (2016) The Mediterranean: migration corridor, border spectacle, ethical landscape, *Mediterranean Politics*, 21(2): 336–41.

Vandaele, K. (2018) *Will Trade Unions Survive in the Platform Economy? Emerging Patterns of Platform Workers' Collective Voice and Representation in Europe*. ETUI Working Paper 2018.05.

Vasudevan, P., and Smith, S. (2020) The domestic geopolitics of racial capitalism, *Environment and Planning C: Politics and Space*, 38(7/8): 1160–79.

Veltmeyer, H., and Petras, J. (2014) *The New Extractivism: A Post-Neoliberal Development Model or Imperialism of the Twenty-First Century?* London: Zed Press.

Vergès, F. (2019) Capitalocene, waste, race, and gender, *e-flux journal*, no. 100.

—— (2021) *A Decolonial Feminism*. London: Pluto Press.

Vertovec, S. (2020) Global migration and the 'Great Reshaping', *Max Planck Research*, 3: 20–5.

Vij, R. (2019) The global subject of precarity, *Globalizations*, 16(4): 506–24.

Virdee, S., and Grint, K. (1994) Black self-organization in trade unions, *Sociological Review*, 42(2): 202–26.

Vogel, L. (2013) *Marxism and the Oppression of Women: Toward a Unitary Theory*. 2nd edn, Leiden: Brill.

Wacquant, L. (2008) *Urban Outcasts: A Comparative Sociology of Advanced Marginality*. Cambridge: Polity.

—— (2009) *Punishing the Poor: The Neoliberal Government of Social Insecurity*. Durham, NC: Duke University Press.

Walia, H. (2014) *Undoing Border Imperialism*. Chico, CA: Ak Press.

—— (2021) *Border and Rule: Global Migration, Capitalism, and the Rise of Racist Nationalism*. Chicago: Haymarket Books.

Wallerstein, I. (1984) *The Politics of the World-Economy: The States, the Movements and the Civilizations*. Cambridge: Cambridge University Press.

Wang, J. (2018) *Carceral Capitalism*. South Pasadena, CA: Semiotext(e).

Ward, K., and Dawdy, S. L. (2006) *Discipline and the Other Body: Correction, Corporeality, Colonialism*. Durham, NC: Duke University Press.

Ware, N. ([1924] 1964) *The Industrial Worker, 1840–1860*. New York: Quadrangle Books.

Wark, M. (2019) *Capital is Dead*. London: Verso.

Warren, E. (2004) The economics of race: when making it to the middle is not enough, *Washington and Lee Law Review*, 61(4): https://scholarlycommons.law.wlu.edu/wlulr/vol61/iss4/10.

Webb, A., McQuaid, R., and Rand, S. (2020) Employment in the informal economy: implications of the COVID-19 pandemic, *International Journal of Sociology and Social Policy*, 40(9/10): 1005–19.

Weeks, K. (2021) Abolition of the family: the most infamous feminist proposal, *Feminist Theory*, doi:10.1177/14647001211015841.

Weiner, M. (1996) Ethics, national sovereignty and the control of immigration, *International Migration Review*, 30(1): 171–97.

West, S. M. (2019) Data capitalism: redefining the logics of surveillance and privacy, *Business & Society*, 58(1): 20–41.

Widick, B. J. (1989) *Detroit: City of Race and Class Violence*. Detroit: Wayne State University Press.

Wiegman, R. (1993) The anatomy of lynching, *Journal of the History of Sexuality*, 3(3): 445–67.

Williams, C. C., and Horodnic, I. A. (2019) *Dependent Self-Employment: Theory, Practice and Policy*. Cheltenham: Edward Elgar.

Williamson, B., Gulson, K. N., Perrotta, C., and Witzenberger, K. (2022) Amazon and the new global connective architectures of education governance, *Harvard Educational Review*, 92(2): 231–56.

Wimmer, A., and Glick Schiller, N. (2002) Methodological nationalism and beyond: nation-state building, migration and the social sciences, *Global Networks*, 2(4): 301–34.

Wolf-Meyer, M. J. (2019) *Theory for the World to Come: Speculative Fiction and Apocalyptic Anthropology*. Minneapolis: University of Minnesota Press.

Wood, S. (1993) The Japanization of Fordism, *Economic and Industrial Democracy*, 14(4): 535–55.

Woodcock, J., and Graham, M. (2019) *The Gig Economy: A Critical Introduction*. Cambridge: Polity.

Woodcock, J., and Johnson, M. R. (2018) Gamification: what it is, and how to fight it, *Sociological Review*, 66(3): 542–58.

World Prisons Brief (2018) www.prisonstudies.org/country/china.

World Prisons Brief (2021) www.prisonstudies.org/country/india.

Wrench, J., Rea, A., and Ouali, N., eds (2016) *Migrants, Ethnic Minorities and the Labour Market: Integration and Exclusion in Europe*. Berlin: Springer.

Ye, J., van der Ploeg, J. D., Schneider, S., and Shanin, T. (2020) The incursions of extractivism: moving from dispersed places to global capitalism, *Journal of Peasant Studies*, 47(1): 155–83.

Yuval-Davis, N., Wemyss, G., and Cassidy, K. (2018) Everyday bordering, belonging and the reorientation of British immigration legislation, *Sociology*, 52(2): 228–44.

—— (2019) *Bordering*. Cambridge: Polity.

Zatz, N. D. (2020) Get to work or go to jail: state violence and the racialized production of precarious work, *Law & Social Inquiry*, 45(2): 304–38.

Zechner, M., and Hansen, B. R. (2015) Building power in a crisis of social reproduction, *Roar Magazine*, 1: 132–51.

Zimmerer, J., ed. (2017) *Climate Change and Genocide: Environmental Violence in the 21st Century*. Abingdon: Routledge.

Zuboff, S. (2019) *The Age of Surveillance Capitalism: The Fight for a Human Future at the New Frontier of Power*. London: Profile Books.

Index

accumulation
   by dispossession 11–12, 13–16
   by repression 109–11
   through population displacement
     100–1
'aggravated felony' 94
Alexander, N. 6
Amazon 74, 123–4, 129, 139–40
Andrew, J. 92, 95
ASEAN 82, 96
Asia: factory–canteen–dormitory
   cultures 47
atomization
   raciality as compensation for 128
   vs racialized division 159–61
Australia: border controls 94–6
authoritarianism 110–11

Bada, X. 91–2
Berlant, L. 145, 147
Bhattacharyya, D. 9, 39, 142, 151, 161
borders/cooperative bordering 78
   accumulation through population
     displacement 100–1
   and 'age of migration' framework
     80–3
   cheaper labour 84–5

   and climate crisis 96–9
   migrant corridor and other fictional
     non-territories 89–93
   modes of 93–6
   new practices 78–80
   reframing of 'international division of
     labour' 85–8
   targeting the vulnerable 89
   and underprotection of migrant
     populations 83–4
   and understanding racial capitalism
     101–4
Bowling, B. 93, 94
Brexit 79

capital–labour relations 20
capitalist reproduction
   and social reproduction 155–6
   vs reproduction of life 145–6
capitalist state, changing role and
   activity of 23
capitalist subjectification, pleasures of
   147–8
carcerality *see* prisons and carcerality
Cavallero, L. 53, 54
Chagnon, C. W. 19
China: carceral system 113

INDEX

class struggle 25–6, 29–30, 40
cleaning and care work 71
climate change/catastrophe 19, 28, 29–30
  and datafication 142
  and global migration 80, 96–9, 103–4
  and infrastructure 146
collectivity 128, 160–1
  disrupting solidarity 20–4
  see also raciality
colonial perspective
  community and family 50–1
  and Indigenous perspective 17–20, 112
  platform capitalism 122–3
  prisons and carcerality 105, 107, 111, 112, 113–14
  see also neocolonialism
colonization of the lifeworld 49, 154
consumer markets 49
consumers
  datafication 127–8
  of platform services 138
cooperative bordering *see* borders/cooperative bordering
Covid-19 pandemic 33, 85, 106
'crimmigration' 93–4
cultural articulation of racialized identities 153–4

data and datafication 125–8, 136–8, 142
de Rivera, J. 125
debt/indebtedness
  changes in our time 75–7
  as everyday life 52–6
  history, varieties and structures of 56–60
  as new moment of capitalism 66–9
  and non-waged sphere 60–3
  and platform capitalism 64, 73–5, 117, 118
  precarity, vagabondage and 63–6
  shitty work 69–73
  and social reproduction 38–43
dehumanization 21, 22, 61, 154–5
differential status/differentiating populations 20–1

and digital capitalism 124–6
and migration 100–1
and working conditions 69–73
see also racialized division
digital capitalism
  colonizing the lifeworld 154
  and differentiation of populations 124–6
  and self 151, 163
digital work
  and digital labour distinction 134–5
  and office-based tasks 70–1
disciplining labour 107
dispossession
  accumulation by 11–12, 13–16
  histories of 58–9, 61, 62–3, 77
  violence of 12, 49–51
  see also colonial perspective
'domestic labour' *see* housewifization

economics
  and debt 58–9, 67
  heterodox and postcapitalist 166–7
  and social reproduction 34–8
  and surplus populations 27–9
Eden, D. 92, 95
emotional labour 156
employment rights/protection, lack of 41, 63, 97, 129–30, 149–50
European Union (EU) 79, 82–3, 96
exploitation 60, 61
  exchange and 6–7
expropriation
  concept of 6–7
  see also dispossession
extractivism
  Indigenous and colonial perspective 17–20
  neo-extractivism 19
  penality and decentring of wage 113–14
  see also debt/indebtedness; value extraction

family
  changing model 43–4
  without privilege of 49–51

family wage model, changing 40, 45–6
Feldman, A. E. 91–2
feminist perspectives 35, 54
financial crash (2008) 75–6
fine-based regime 53–4, 113, 114
forced displacement 114–16
foreign policy and/or trade policy:
    migration control 82–3, 96
Fumagalli, A. 134

Gago, V. 19, 20, 53, 54
gender
    and family model 43
    housewifization 16–17, 38
    and platform capitalism 133–4
gig economy 26
global colour line 100–1, 112
Global Division of Labour (GDL) 86–7
global migration *see* borders/cooperative
    bordering
global movement against borders 102
global police state 109–10
global racial capitalism, remaking of
    13–16
globalization and borders 85–8
Gotanda, N. 156–8

Hansen, R. 79
Harvey, D. 12, 13, 14–15, 17
home–work life 43–4
housewifization 16–17, 38
'human security' and migration control
    82, 93–4
humanitarianism and migration control
    95–6, 112–13

immigration *see* borders/cooperative
    bordering
indebtedness *see* debt/indebtedness
India: carceral system 112–13
Indigenous and colonial perspectives
    17–20, 112
industrialization and new forms of
    employment 117–20
informal work 40, 57
infrastructure
    and climate change/catastrophe 146

and platform capitalism 122–4,
    161–2
and urbanization/mega-cities 145–6
institutional power 47–8
institutions, carceral machinery across
    107–9, 111
interdependence between life-forms 48
'international division of labour',
    reframing of 85–8
International Labour Organization
    (ILO)
    global employment trends (2018) 33
    wage inequalities 85
International Organization for
    Migration (IOM) 95–6
Iraq: US-led invasion (2003) 14–15

jokes and will to survive 154–6, 165–6

labour markets
    changing 131–6
    lack of employment rights/protection
        41, 63, 97, 129–30, 149–50
    and migration 26, 84–5, 97, 98–9
labour organizations 143
Lazzarato, M. 54–7, 58, 60
local government: fine-based regime
    53–4, 113, 114
logistics and platform capitalism 122–4,
    139–45
love 51, 149, 159

Macharia, K. 158
McMillan Cottom, T. 42–3
manufacturing, changes in 118–19,
    126–7
Marx/Marxist perspective 4–6, 12, 14,
    36–7, 48, 60, 115, 117–18, 156
massification
    and platform capitalism 73–5, 140,
        161–2
    shift from 22
mega-cities *see* urbanization/mega-cities
Memmi, A. 50
Mezzadra, S. 19, 20, 53
MIDEQ 90–1
Mies, M. 16, 17, 38

INDEX

migration *see* borders/cooperative
  bordering
Miller, T. 100, 101
Mittleman, J. H. 86–7

neocolonialism/'new imperialism' 13,
  14–15
  border controls 84
  and neo-extractivism 19
  new moment of capitalism 66–9
Nichols, R. 18
Noble, S. U. 136–7
non-wagedness
  and debt/indebtedness 60–3
  and value extraction 7
non-workers 65–6

outsourcing border controls 91, 94–5

partner nations and migration control
  83
performing racialized self 132–3
piecework 44, 129, 134–5
Pierce, J. 64–5
platform capitalism 121–2
  capital reproduction vs reproduction
    of life 145–6
  capitalist and anticapitalist subjects
    138–9
  data and datafication 125–8, 136–8,
    142
  and differentiation of populations
    124–6
  and indebtedness 64–5, 73–5, 117,
    118
  logistics 122–4, 139–45
  migrant labour 26
  raciality as compensation for
    atomization 128
  racist representations of digital
    capitalism 136–8
  remaking waged work and
    segregating labour market 128–30
  and social reproduction 42–3
  and understanding racial capitalism
    122–4
  varieties of racism 131–6

pleasures
  jokes and will to survive 154–6, 165–6
  racial 156–9
  response to violence 153–4, 157–8
  seductive sensation of racialized self
    162–4
  of subjectification 147–9
political repression 109–11
positioning of racial capitalism 152–3
postcapitalist economics 166–7
precarity
  extension of 72–3
  platform labour 135
  and underprotected work 41–2
  vagabondage and debt 63–6
'predatory inclusion' 42–3
predictive data 137–8
primitive accumulation 11–12
prison labour 107, 117
prisons and carcerality 105–6
  detention of migrants, Australia 94–5
  and extractivism 113–14
  global perspective 106–13
  and indebtedness 53–4, 59, 76
  old and new 117–20
  vagabondage 114–16
proletarianization
  and accumulation by dispossession
    11–12, 15, 25–6
  deproletarianization and
    reproletarianization 69, 161
  displacement of wagedness 33
  and indebtedness 57, 66, 73, 76
  resistance to 105, 117–18, 138
property, dispossession of 17–18, 112

racial capitalism
  components 10–11
  formulation and conceptualization 4–7
  framework 2–4, 7
  puzzles 1–2, 27
  term/phrase 1, 2, 9, 10, 23, 168
racial profiling 137
raciality
  as class struggle 25–6
  as compensation for atomization 137
  see also collectivity

racialized division
  labour market 133–6
  vs atomization 159–61
  see also differential status/
    differentiating populations
racialized hierarchy 23–4, 61, 130
  see also subordination of racialized
    groups
racialized identity 149–54
  cultural articulation of 153–4
racialized self
  love 149
  performing 132–3
  seductive sensation of 162–4
racialized subjectification, pleasures of
  148–9
ratings system and platform capitalism
  133
remaking of capital 161–2, 167–70
reproductive labour 36–7
Robinson, C. 4–6
Robinson, W. 109–10
Rogers, B. 132–3

Schengen Agreement, EU 79
school-to-prison pipeline 109
Schor, J. B. 135, 136
self
  and digital capitalism 151, 163
  see also racialized self
services sector 46–7
settler-colonialism *see* colonial
    perspective
shadow economy and migrant labour 97
slave trade/slavery 4–6, 57, 111, 114
social cooperation 20
social reproduction 32–3
  and capitalist reproduction 155–6
  and datafication 127
  and debt 38–43
  housewifization 16–17, 38
  impact of shift in 33–8
  and platform capitalism 42–3
  positioning 45–9
  as target of organized violence 43–5
  without privilege of family 49–51
solidarity, disrupting 20–4

South Africa: apartheid system 6
Soviet Union: demise and end of Cold
    War 13
Spaan, E. 91
spaces of sovereignty 90, 92, 93
spatial dynamics of capitalism 14
spatial fix 12, 14
Stankovic, A. 84, 93
Stumpf, J. 93
subjugation and inclusion 151–2
subordination of racialized groups 26
  debt 55, 59, 62–3
  labour market 69–73
  and racial pleasure 156–9
  and social reproduction 37–8, 39–40,
    50–1
surplus populations 27–9
surveillance
  disciplinary regimes 162
  of migrants 81–2, 99, 100
  of workers 26, 133
surveillance capitalism 137
'survival migrants' 92

Tang, C. S. 140
time and distribution issues 141–2
transnational migration *see* borders/
    cooperative bordering
travellers, categories of 97–8

Uber 74, 129, 132–4
United Nations (UN)
  IOM 95–6
  OHCHR 113
  UNHCR 95, 114
United States (US)
  border controls 93–4, 100
  prisons and carcerality 111–12
  urbanization/mega-cities 114–16, 144–5,
    145–6

vagabondage
  precarity and debt 63–6
  prisons and carcerality 114–16
value extraction
  disrupting solidarity 20
  modes of 7, 23, 34, 61, 137–8

see also debt/indebtedness; extractivism
value scraping 17, 34, 42–3, 61, 69
digital capitalism 125, 151, 154
van Doorn, N. 26, 131, 135
van Naerssen, T. 91
Veelenturf, L. P. 140
violence
of dispossession 12, 49–51
and pleasure 153–4, 157–8
social reproduction as target of 43–5
violent state structures *see* borders/cooperative bordering; prisons and carcerality

Wacquant, L. 59, 108, 109, 116
wage
fall in real value of 52
inequalities 85

wagedness/waged work
and debt 58, 62
displacement of 33–4, 60–1
subjugation and inclusion 151–2
transition in 40–2
Walia, H. 102
Wang, J. 53–4, 109, 113, 114
war/conflict, post-Cold War 13–14
Wark, M. 115, 138–9
Westenra, S. 93, 94
whodunnit approach 24–6
working conditions
and differential status 69–73
platform capitalism 73–5

xeno-racism 79–80, 81, 82, 84

Zuboff, S. 127, 137